BOLLYWOOD'S TOP 20

BOLLYWOOD'S TOP 20

SUPERSTARS OF
INDIAN CINEMA

EDITED BY

BHAICHAND PATEL

PENGUIN
VIKING

9030 0000 140 010

VIKING
Published by the Penguin Group
Penguin Books India Pvt. Ltd, 11 Community Centre, Panchsheel Park,
New Delhi 110 017, India
Penguin Group (USA) Inc., 375 Hudson Street, New York, New York
10014, USA
Penguin Group (Canada), 90 Eglinton Avenue East, Suite 700, Toronto,
Ontario, M4P 2Y3, Canada (a division of Pearson Penguin Canada Inc.)
Penguin Books Ltd, 80 Strand, London WC2R 0RL, England
Penguin Ireland, 25 St Stephen's Green, Dublin 2, Ireland (a division of
Penguin Books Ltd)
Penguin Group (Australia), 250 Camberwell Road, Camberwell,
Victoria 3124, Australia (a division of Pearson Australia Group Pty Ltd)
Penguin Group (NZ), 67 Apollo Drive, Rosedale, Auckland 0632,
New Zealand (a division of Pearson New Zealand Ltd)
Penguin Group (South Africa) (Pty) Ltd, 24 Sturdee Avenue, Rosebank,
Johannesburg 2196, South Africa

Penguin Books Ltd, Registered Offices: 80 Strand, London WC2R 0RL, England

First published in Viking by Penguin Books India 2012

Anthology copyright © Penguin Books India 2012
Introduction copyright © Bhaichand Patel 2012

The copyright for individual pieces vests with the authors or their estates

All rights reserved

10 9 8 7 6 5 4 3 2 1

The views and opinions expressed in this book are the authors' own and the facts
are as reported by him/her, which have been verified to the extent possible, and
the publishers are not in any way liable for the same.

ISBN 9780670085729

Typeset in AGaramond by Guru Typograph Technology, New Delhi
Printed at Thomson Press India Ltd, New Delhi

*In memory of Lilac Theatre in Suva, Fiji Islands,
and all single-screen cinema halls of the past everywhere.
Many of them were flea pits with uncomfortable
seats and bad projections
but there was a time when they gave us so much joy,
two to three hours at a time.*

CONTENTS

Introduction

The first film I saw was Wadia Movietone's *Bambaiwali* (1941) starring Fearless Nadia. At least that's how I remember it. It was a long time ago, ten years after 'talkies' came to India in 1931. I saw the film, sitting on my mother's lap, in a large tin shed masquerading as a cinema hall. It was a time when it was not wise to invest much money in such places. They tended to burn down since the films that went through projectors were highly inflammable in the early days of cinema.

I come from a family of film buffs. My father was a fan of Zubaida who had the lead in the first talkie, *Alam Ara* (1931). She was pretty but my father's fascination may have something to do with the fact that she was the daughter, unacknowledged, of the Nawab of Sachin. Our ancestral village in Gujarat was close to Sachin. My mother's taste ran towards mythologicals, preferably something from Prakash Pictures starring Prem Adib playing Ram and Shobhana Samarth playing Sita. I met Shobhanaji many years later; she was the mother of a close friend. By that time my mother had gone to the big multiplex in the sky but she must have been pleased.

My first English film was Michael Powell's *The Thief of Baghdad* (1940) when it finally reached our theatre. It had a scene of Sabu in a violent storm at sea. That scene scared the shit out of me. My parents should have known better than take a kid my age to such a film but it developed a taste in me for Hollywood before I could understand English.

As a child, I saw an average of three films a week. I had all the time in the world after school. There was little else by way of entertainment in that small faraway country, Fiji Islands. I was not yet into serious reading and, of course, there was no television. The films arrived late by ship. The Hindi films were mostly from Bombay, some from Lahore, Calcutta and Poona. The first film from Madras was *Chandralekha* (1948), a hugely successful remake of a Tamil extravaganza. As for English films, most of them were from Hollywood with an occasional production from the two British studios, J. Arthur Rank and London Films. They came to us after they were shown all over New Zealand.

We lived a stone's throw from a theatre named Lilac. The other theatre in town, Regal, was more posh. It was European-owned and catered largely to a white clientele but we were allowed in. Regal showed films produced by MGM, Twentieth Century Fox, RKO and Paramount studios.

When I came to study in Delhi, I went to the cinema halls on the periphery of the old city since they were closer to the campus. I saw *Mother India* (1957) and *Pyaasa* (1957) at the Moti in Chandni Chowk. I went further out to Connaught Place, also by bus, if I wished to see an English film. *The Ten Commandments* (1956) and *Ben Hur* (1959) ran at the Odeon. Later in Bombay, I took the local train from Churchgate to the seedy screens on Grant Road and Lamington Road. Some of these halls surely must have become victims of the multiplexes by now.

I have to confess there is a gap in my enjoyment of Hindi films. For five years from early 1961 I was in London. This was before Indians, Pakistanis and Uganda Asians invaded Britain in large numbers. There was only one theatre, a disused opera house off Tottenham Court Road, where Hindi films were occasionally screened on Sundays. I saw only four films from India in those years—a revival of *Baiju Bawra* (1952, one of my all-time favourites), *Dharmaputra* (1961, an awful Yash Chopra film), *Prem Patra* (1962, Bimal Roy's worst film) and Guru Dutt's classic *Sahib Bibi Aur Ghulam* (1962, which was some consolation).

Be that as it may, I hope I have somewhat established my credentials for editing a book that encompasses eighty years of Indian cinema. So let's get down to the nitty-gritty. This book is a celebration of Hindi films or, if you prefer, Hindustani films, from the introduction of sound in 1931 to the present day. We are covering these eight decades through twenty stars, the brightest, and often the best, men and women who gave us so much pleasure over the years.

Choosing the title of this book was not easy. There was considerable debate on the wisdom of using the word 'Bollywood'. The moniker was coined sometime in the early 1980s and no one knows for sure who the culprit was. But it has stuck. We are aware that there are some in the film business who dislike the use of the word. They have a point: it is derivative, a nod to the word 'Hollywood'. But there are others who are quite comfortable with the word. We were wavering until Shekhar Kapur and Rakeysh Mehra made a documentary titled *In Search of Bollywood*. It was screened at the Cannes Film Festival in May 2011 where it received some acclaim. We figured that if the word 'Bollywood' was good enough for these established film-makers, it was good enough for us! Frankly, there really is no other single word that describes the film industry that operates out of Mumbai.

The twenty stars we have chosen to honour are not necessarily the most talented, though heaven knows they are all talented enough, but they were—and some of them still are—the most popular of their time. They could—and some still do—fill up the cinema halls across the country on the opening weekend and often for much longer. Some of them have also acted in spectacular flops, the biggest duds of all time, but that comes with the territory.

Any such listing of stars would be absurd, if not downright eccentric, if it did not include Dilip Kumar, Nargis, Raj Kapoor, Madhubala, Dev Anand, Meena Kumari, Amitabh Bachchan and Shahrukh Khan. Selecting them was the easy part. Picking others, especially from the '50s and the '60s—the so-called Golden

Age of Hindi cinema—was more problematic. There was an abundance of terrific actors at that time. Look at the names of the actors, in no particular order, whom we could not accommodate among our top twenty: Geeta Bali, Nalini Jaywant, Vyjayanthimala, Balraj Sahni, Nutan, Sunil Dutt, Nimmi, Rajendra Kumar, Sharmila Tagore, Kishore Kumar, Kamini Kaushal, Guru Dutt, Suchitra Sen, Manoj Kumar, Dharmendra, Sadhana and Asha Parekh. We could have extended the list to twenty-five, even thirty. But that would have been too easy. We were determined to keep it down to just twenty. It gave more glory to the ones that made the list.

The reader may well ask why Kareena Kapoor found her way among the twenty and not, say, Nutan or Vyjayanthimala. Let me explain. Kareena's competition was neither Nutan nor Vyjayanthimala. Her competition was Katrina Kaif, Priyanka Chopra and Imran Khan. She is the most successful of the current crop. Nutan and Vyjayanthimala's competitors were elsewhere, several decades ago. Once you understand that, the selection process will, hopefully, make sense.

The absence of Salman Khan from the top twenty also needs explaining. As I write this, the actor has come up with three huge hits in a row with one film, *Dabangg* (2010), ending up as one of the biggest grossers of all time. Since we were determined to keep the list restricted to twenty, one of the three Khans—Aamir, Shahrukh or Salman—had to go. The axe fell on Salman. The decision was not that difficult. This is a personal opinion but I would say that, in talent and popularity, Aamir is today's Dilip Kumar while Shahrukh is this generation's Amitabh Bachchan. Perhaps I am being unfair but Salman is the equivalent of Rajendra Kumar who was hugely popular in the late '50s and early '60s. That actor came up with hit after hit. But does anyone today remember any of the Rajendra Kumar films? None of them left a lasting impression with the exception of *Sangam* (1964) in which he played second fiddle to Raj Kapoor. Unlike Salman, Aamir and Shahrukh are here for the long run.

My personal regret is that Fearless Nadia, a star from an earlier era, missed the cut by a whisker. She was the twenty-first on the list. I was smitten by her as a child. Nadia was a blue-eyed, blonde Australian, and her real name was Mary Evans. In her films she carried a whip, wore a mask and went about in high leather boots. She could carry a man on her shoulder and run on top of a moving train. She leapt on a horse from a rooftop and swung on chandeliers. Her horse was named 'Punjab Ka Beta' and she rode in a car with the name 'Rolls Royce Ki Beti'.

My favourite story concerns Nadia's difficulty in speaking Hindi. During the shooting of one scene the villain was trying to take liberties with her. Nadia's lines were just two words, '*Mujhe chhodo!*' (Let me go). Despite several takes she kept pronouncing them badly. Poor Nadia could not understand why everyone on the set was laughing hysterically.

The '70s and '80s were terrible decades for Hindi cinema. The muses were in retreat and the films were almost uniformly bad. Cinema halls, built fifty or so years earlier, had decayed with rats taking over. You had to be very brave, or in very dire need, to use the toilets. Amitabh Bachchan played the Angry Young Man time and again while Dharmendra's favourite phrase seemed to be '*kutte kaminey*'. There were lots of fisticuffs, very little by way of plots. Bappi Lahiri was a successful music director. Need I say more? As a result the middle class gave up going to theatres and watched pirated videos of foreign films at home.

Bollywood has been up and running again for a few years now. The multiplexes that have come up have comfortable seats, edible popcorn and clean toilets. They have changed things dramatically. There is no shortage of screens. Small-budget movies that once failed to find distributors or were previously confined to morning shows now get a chance to be seen in the afternoons and evenings. As a result, we are now entering a second Golden Age of Hindi cinema. I will not name names but there is no shortage of talent in front as well as behind the camera. While the front benches are still taken care of, there are films that are targeted to a more sophisticated, educated audience.

Most of the writers who have contributed to this volume are familiar names, eminent writers on cinema through books, magazines and newspapers. A number of them happen to be my friends; we share a passion for movies. Some contributors are new even to me. Let me introduce them. Cary Sawhney works with the British Film Institute in London. I had the good fortune of being directed towards him by Shyam Benegal when I needed someone to write on Devika Rani. The name Urmila Lanba may also not ring a bell. I reviewed her fine book on Dilip Kumar some years ago. I tracked her down in Noida, across the river from Delhi, and requested her to write on Madhubala.

Niranjan Iyengar has put his journalism days behind him and now wins awards for scripts and dialogue he writes for Karan Johar and others. He knows Kajol well and it was not too difficult to persuade him to write a piece on that wonderful actor. I have seen Kajol grow up, doing homework as a child, but that is another story.

As for Vikram Sampath, I heard him speak at India International Centre in Delhi one afternoon on Gauhar Jaan, one of the first artistes to be heard on a gramophone record. I was struck by this young man's expertise on the music of that era and I decided right there and then that I wanted him to write on K.L. Saigal. I like to thank them all, the eminent ones as well as the not so eminent, for taking time off from their pressing duties and coming up with the wonderful profiles that follow.

Udayan Mitra, who commissioned this book on behalf of Penguin, has been a huge help. He is much younger than I am and certainly more knowledgeable when it comes to more recent films and their music. I have sought his expertise whenever I wavered or had doubts on some of the selections. This book is as much his as it is mine.

I am also fortunate to have had Ambar Sahil Chatterjee as my editor. He has been good at curbing the enthusiasm of some of the contributors, including mine! I cannot speak for others but his editing of my profile of Ashok Kumar has made me look a better writer than I actually am.

When the publishers showed me the cover they had in mind for this book, I was floored. It is an amazing piece of work that evokes memories of the enormous hoardings that were once put up outside cinema halls like the Majestic in Chandni Chowk and Maratha Mandir in Byculla. They were all hand-painted. These days it is all done with computers and, frankly, they lack the panache that an artist can put into them. Hand-painted posters is art form that is slowly disappearing. The late M.F. Husain started his career painting such hoardings. Our cover is the work of a Delhi-based painter, Vijay Kumar, who was guided and encouraged by a diligent design team at Penguin consisting of Gavin Morris, Saurav Das and Ajanta Guhathakurta.

There is a free disc of songs that comes with the book. These songs were filmed on the twenty stars who have been profiled. You will find songs from films that did not do well at the box office and have been forgotten. But their music lives on and continues to enchant us. I hope they give you as much pleasure as they have given me.

Let me leave you with a thought. I loved the 'item' numbers in three recent films, *Omkara* (2006), *Dabangg* (2010) and *Tees Maar Khan* (2010). They featured three absolutely stunning women—Bipasha Basu, Malaika Arora and Katrina Kaif—and the choreography was amazing. You can watch them again and again on YouTube. But I suggest to the younger readers that they watch something else also. Click on the dance number 'Piya tose naina laage re' from *Guide* (1965). The film was made almost fifty years ago. The song was composed by S.D. Burman with words provided by Shailendra. The director was that genius, Vijay Anand, and the song has been picturized on Waheeda Rehman who, covered from neck to toe, mesmerizes us with her effortless sensuality. Now tell me, which of the four dance numbers is the most erotic? There is no contest!

BHAICHAND PATEL

K.L. SAIGAL

MUSIC MAESTRO AND MOVIE LEGEND

VIKRAM SAMPATH

The owner of the little paan shop on Calcutta's (now Kolkata) bustling Chowringhee Road, opposite the Metro Cinema, eagerly awaited his most valued customer who stopped by his shop to buy paan and cigarettes. It was a ritual that the flamboyant producer of the Indian Broadcasting Company (the precursor of All India Radio), Roy Chand Boral, followed every evening on his way back home after a long, tiring day at the radio station. That winter evening of 1931, as Boral stood there lighting his cigarette, the lilting tunes of a melodious song reached his ears suddenly from nowhere. He had never heard something like this before and involuntarily turned his head in the direction of the voice. He barely caught sight of a slightly tallish young man who was humming this tune. Strangely enough, the voice stopped as suddenly as it had begun. Thoroughly intrigued, Boral drove back home captivated by the little he had heard serendipitously that evening.

His house on P.C. Boral Street in Calcutta—marbled, spacious, opulent and dotted with palm fronds—was a veritable confluence of the who's who in Indian music and theatre in Calcutta those days. Harish Chandra Bali, a classical singer from Jalandhar, was

1

his guest then. The next morning Bali introduced Boral to a young man who stood in front of him obediently with folded hands. Tall by contemporary standards at about 6'1", large-boned, lanky and unimpressive to look at, the young man seemed like a thoroughly confused adolescent. He was nervous and edgy and was tucking at the ends of his spotless white kurta, trying hard to remain composed. Bali informed him that this was Kundan from Jalandhar, who might be good 'raw material' for Boral, though he hastened to add that Kundan had no formal training in classical music whatsoever. Boral immediately recognized him to be the same young man he had heard in passing at the paan shop the previous evening. Though hugely sceptic of the lad's ability to sing, with no classical moorings, he implored him to present anything that he wished. Unsure and diffident, Kundan began a bhajan in a morning raga, most probably Bhairavi or Asavari. Boral was stunned to hear the clear, precise and perfectly timbred voice of this impassive young man singing with his lips barely moving. It seemed as though an invisible sarangi was following his plaintive voice and nudging him to make delightful meanders across the notes. The song and the demeanour of the singer left a deep impression on Boral and he made up his mind to help the lad.

He took him to Birendra Nath Sircar, the owner of the recently founded New Theatres, to help him find some role in the films that the latter was producing. One look at the young man and Sircar flatly refused to have anything to do with him. After much persuasion, an audition of sorts was arranged where Kundan's melodious renditions in Yaman and Bageshri, to the accompaniment of the harmonium that he played himself, drew everyone in the studios to him, including musician K.C. Dey. Dey waited for him to complete and showered him with the choicest blessings. Sircar was impressed too and signed a five-year contract with him on a monthly salary of Rs 200.

Thus did Kundan Lal Saigal, the most unlikely of entrants into the showbiz of Indian cinema, romp into its portals in his characteristically quiet and understated—yet impactful—way!

Born on 11 April 1904 in Nawa Shehar in Jammu, Kundan Lal was the third of four sons of Amar Chand Saigal and Kesar Kaur. Amar Chand was a tehsildar in the Jammu State and Kesar a devoted housewife who had great passion for music. Kundan was deeply attached to his mother who was his first musical inspiration. He accompanied her in his tuneful, childish voice as she sang melodious bhajans and folk songs at home. Right from the age of ten, young Saigal played the role of Sita in the local Ramlilas, screaming and singing so shrilly when being kidnapped by Ravan that the audience feared that the actor playing the demon king might just drop him on stage and run away in fright!

But unlike his other 'normal' siblings, Kundan was always lost in a world of his own. His total disinterest in studies, his inability to pass most examinations, his complete lack of ambition coupled with his dreamy and entranced state of mind, his unkempt appearance and, of course, his intense love for music were enough to draw the ire of his father. He would often run away from school to listen to the songs of some wandering minstrels, folk singers or the dancing girls of Jammu. He seemed to be in some eternal search of the true 'note', something that his materialistic father could neither fathom nor empathize with. Often he would get beaten and punished, with Kesar making frantic attempts to save her wayward son. On one occasion Amar Chand made him cook the meals for the entire household and wait upon his brothers like their orderly. But none of it had any impact on the boy.

Astrologers and priests were consulted to rectify him. Eleven-year-old Kundan was then brought to Pir Sheikh Salman Yousuf, a mystic sufi of the Yesevi sect who had blessed the boy after his birth. Looking compassionately at the despondent child, the pir told Kesar that her son was born for great fame and universal adulation and that she must rest her fears. Knowing the child's interest in music, the pir blessed him with *zikr* and *riyaz*, elements of the sect's secret discipline—the training of the *swaras* and the act of spiritual inwardness which gave the voice unusual prowess. Strangely, this was the only musical 'training' that Saigal ever got as he never had the opportunity of formal training in classical music under any guru. No wonder that Saigal would narrate this incident to Ali Bukhari, his long-time friend and confidant at All India Radio, saying, 'I was born at the age of about eleven in a pir's hut one windy evening in Jammu.'

The advent of adolescence brought about a catastrophe in its wake for young Kundan. His voice cracked and left him completely unable to sing anything and his high soprano had dissipated into rough squeaks. The thirteen-year-old panicked and went into a bout of terrible depression, weeping himself to sleep every night. When all household remedies and medications failed, the mother and son decided to make another trip to Pir Salman Yousuf. With tears rolling down his cheeks the young boy fell at the saint's feet, sobbing inconsolably and wishing for death rather than the loss of his voice. The pir lifted up the boy, caressed him and swung him like a child. He advised the boy to take the crack in his voice as a blessing, an opportunity to find his true, natural voice, to stop singing for two years and practise the riyaz and zikr that he had initiated him into. Convinced and confident, the boy returned home and followed every word of the pir's advice, building back his voice, in a way, from scratch. The two years of musical silence that followed moulded the young Saigal and changed his very outlook to music.

By then his father had retired and the family moved to Jalandhar, near the Panj Pir gate. The stifling condition at home was suffocating Saigal, who, without informing anyone, finally decided around 1922–23 to leave home in search of his own destiny. But all the years that he was away, he dutifully kept his mother informed about his well-being, though without ever revealing his exact whereabouts. There were rumours that he wandered around aimlessly in several cities like Kanpur, Moradabad, Allahabad, Lucknow, Simla, Bareilly, Delhi, Bombay (now Mumbai), Bihar—presumably in the same search for the true 'note', and to prepare himself for life, all the while soaking in the music in these cities. He is said to have worked in various occupations: in the railways, with Remington Typewriter Company, with the Delhi Electricity Department, in a hotel in Simla, even as a sales agent of saris and other odd jobs.

Anecdotes abound of his eight long wanderlust years. Around 1923–24, Imitiaz Ahmed, a local sarangi player and hakim of Moradabad, was astonished to hear a young man render a beautiful thumri of Ustad Abdul Karim Khan in Jhinjoti on a deserted railway platform. The ustad had performed in the city the previous evening and Ahmed had accompanied him on this very thumri. The young boy, whom he remembered seeing in the audience, had seemingly picked up the song just by listening to it and was now trying to sing it in his own characteristic style. Imtiaz took him home and made him sing. Saigal presented a wonderful Ghalib ghazal in his soft, mellow voice, set to Raga Abhogi Kanada, 'Dayam pada hum tere dar par'. Imitiaz was enraptured.

Saigal stayed on at Moradabad for a few years and the wife of the English stationmaster there is said to have even taught him some English. The accomplished musician Pahari Sanyal recalls seeing Saigal first in 1927–28 as a shift attendant in New Delhi Cantonment. He met him again towards the end of 1929 in Moradabad at a private soirée where everyone was agog with excitement about this new singer who would be coming in to charm them with his melodious voice.

With *Alam Ara* in 1931, Indian cinema was emerging out of the silent era with the coming of sound in films. Madan Theatres had dominated the cinema scene in Calcutta since 1902 with several hits to their credit like *Shirin Farhad* and *Laila Majnu*, after the advent of sound in films. The New Theatres of B.N. Sircar was to give steady competition. The first to set up a modern recording studio, it attracted some of the best musical talents, be they singers or composers, and introduced a new style of film music based on classical ragas and folk tunes.

Saigal's first movie with the New Theatres was *Mohabbat ke Ansoo* in 1932, followed by *Subah ka Sitara* and *Zinda Laash* the same year. To hide his identity he used the name Saigal Kashmiri in all these films, where R.C. Boral served as the music director.

Director Nitin Bose recounts how, in his first film, he angered and irritated the director Premankur Atorthy with seven unsuccessful retakes and his nervous rendering of the dialogues. These films were no outstanding hits and did not establish Saigal in any major way, till the time of *Chandidas* in 1934, a remake of Debaki Bose's 1932 Bengali film. The songs of love and yearning—especially 'Prem nagar mein banaoongi ghar main', sung as a duet with Uma Shashi, and 'Tarapat beete din rain'—won Saigal nationwide fame. 1933 saw Saigal appearing in *Puran Bhakat*, directed again by Debaki Bose, where his songs 'Bhajun main to', 'Din neekey beetey jaat' and 'Radhey rani dey daro' were widely appreciated.

But greater fame awaited Saigal and this was to come about through the legendary role he was to play as Devdas, the forlorn and self-destructive lover of Saratchandra Chattopadhyay's novel. The flamboyant Promotesh Barua, with his distinctive charm and aristocratic elegance, was all set to recreate Chattopadhyay's Devdas on celluloid, enacting the lead role himself. Boral approached him with an offer of having Saigal sing a couple of songs in the Bengali film. This was turned down by Barua as he knew that, being a non-Bengali, Saigal's intonation and pronunciation of the language would be incorrect. Eminent music director Pankaj Mullick was called upon to train and help Saigal with his Bengali and he recounts how Saigal would insist on knowing the meaning of every word of the song to be able to emote with perfection. However, Barua was not greatly impressed. It was not until the novelist Chattopadhyay himself intervened and heard Saigal that he was permitted to sing his evergreen songs 'Kaharey je jodathey chai' and 'Golab hue uthuk phutey'. The film was a resounding success and both Barua and Saigal became household names in Bengal.

For an all-India exhibition New Theatres decided to recreate the magic of *Devdas* in its Hindi remake in 1935. Saigal became the natural choice to play the lead role, with Jamuna as Parbati and Rajkumari as Chandramukhi. Saigal—with his drooping lock of hair falling out carelessly from his protruding hat and wandering aimlessly, gun in hand, looking for birds to shoot—epitomized the tragic hero to perfection and became an overnight sensation all over the country. His 'Dukh ke din bitat nahin', 'Balam aye baso' and 'Piya bina nahin avat chain' wrenched the hearts of millions of cine-goers. The latter thumri had been popularized by Ustad Abdul Karim Khan who, incidentally, had wept uncontrollably like a child on hearing Saigal's rendition on his first ever visit to a cinema hall. Timar Baran, the film's music director recalls that Saigal was a born singer with a perfectly tuned voice and that his seemingly effortless talent was the result of a deep, meditative training style nurtured not by any gharana but by intense riyaz and mad passion for the 'inner world'.

Devdas was truly a turning point in Saigal's career. Those who had hitherto rejected him were rushing to sign him up for the roles of a romantic hero. Nitin Bose, who had once snapped at Boral when the latter asked him to cast Saigal as a hero, saying the lens of his camera would crack if he set it on the uncouth man, hurriedly signed him for several of his hits like *President* (1937), *Dharti Mata* (1938), *Dushman* (1939) and *Lagan* (1941) with some of the most glamorous heroines of the time—Uma Shashi, Kanan Devi, Leela Desai, Kamlesh Kumari and Chandrabati. Saigal's greatest musical hit was *Street Singer* (1938) where he immortalized Wajid Ali Shah's famous thumri in Bhairavi 'Babul mora naihar chhooto jay' in his characteristic dulcet voice.

The unknown, unkempt and confused youth from Jalandhar had finally arrived as the superstar of the Indian silver screen.

With the coming of professional success, Saigal decided to settle down in his personal life. In 1934 he married Asharani, a simple and uneducated girl of Hoshiarpur. It is said that she had once burst into tears on seeing her husband romancing a pretty heroine on screen, whom he married later in the film. Saigal had to take her to the studio to convince her that the whole thing was unreal. Asharani was a dutiful wife who supported her husband in all that he did, though she recalled later that he was impossible to fathom and the most complex creation of God. In 1935 the couple was blessed with their first son Madan Mohan. They had two daughters thereafter, Neena and Beena, born in 1937 and 1941 respectively, and adopted Durgesh Mehta, Saigal's niece. Saigal, being the perennially self-effacing man he was, spoke very little of his work at home and in fact made light of all his achievements. If someone praised his singing he would turn bashful and often exclaim, 'I haven't shot a tiger my friend, it's just a song. Forget it!'

Saigal was a darling on the sets. As Kanan Devi remembers in her autobiography, 'Even if the childlike, ignorant and careless Saigal committed any blunder, it was hard to get irritated with him. Often it happened that the set was ready . . . but he would not be seen anywhere. Weary and tired of waiting for him, everybody would prepare for "pack-up". Suddenly someone would inform us that he had been singing songs at the tune of a broken harmonium in a small room at the farthest end, forgetting the world around.' After coming so late he would try to make light of the situation by his innocent antics so that no one could ever get angry with him.

A striking feature of Saigal's personality, apart from his disarming humility and childlike innocence, was his boundless generosity. Even in childhood, his habit of giving away his things to the poor and needy without thinking twice would add to his father's anger. This trait remained with him all his life. Harish Chandra Bali recounts with amusement about how Saigal came in from the rain one day, dressed only in his shorts and vest as he had given away his clothing to an old beggar who was shivering in the rain. Once, without a second thought, he gave away his diamond ring to a widow in distress whom he met on the road in Pune. Asharani would, in fact, insist that his driver collect Saigal's salary from the studio so that the money didn't get distributed among needy people he would meet on the way back home! Class differences, successes and failures, rich and poor—these disparities were unknown to this man who had a heart as golden as his voice.

Though the trend of including songs in films had begun with

the advent of the talkie era, the Gramophone Company did
not bother to release film songs on discs regularly. The playback
singing technique was first adopted in 1935 in a film titled *Dhoop
Chhaon*. Soon Hindustan Records of Calcutta and its owner,
Chandi Charan Saha, made a lifetime agreement with Saigal to
release all his non-film songs on seventy-eight rpm discs, while his
film songs started appearing on the HMV label much later. The
first two non-film songs released on the disc were 'Jhoolna Jhulao
re' in Asavari-gandhari and 'Hori ho brajraj dulare' in Hori Ragini
in the complex Jhap taal. Saigal then made a contract with them
to sing on a royalty basis, something new in the music industry
at the time. His gramophone records sold widely and were often
played in restaurants and shops to attract customers. Some
cinema halls would have live dance performances of nautch girls
or else gramophone records were played in the middle of the
film screening—and in all of these, Saigal's records, whether film
songs, ghazals or bhajans, were the most sought after.

Few know that Saigal was also an expert singer of ghazals which
he sang only at private gatherings and functions. Being a poet
himself who was well versed in Urdu, Saigal managed to make the
lofty ghazal accessible to the common man by highlighting its
poetry and the meaning therein through his emotional renditions.
He created a unique style of rendering ghazals in a variety of
classical ragas and sang to the least accompaniment. There was no
heavy orchestra and arrangements, but just a tanpura, harmonium,
tabla and sometimes a sarangi. He is said to have recorded about
thirty ghazals for the Hindustan Records Company. The poetry
of Ghalib and its metaphysical nature deeply impacted him and,
in a way, shaped his musical personality. He was the first artiste to
sing Ghalib in a way that appealed to the masses. The first ghazal
of Ghalib that he sang, 'Nukta chin hai gham-e-dil usko sunaye na
bane' for the film *Yahudi ki Ladki* (1933), became an evergreen
favourite of the masses. Saigal would recite his own verses too
in private gatherings, though he never got his poems recorded,
barring one devotional 'Main baithi thi phulwari mein'. Asharani

recalls that he wrote this song lying on her lap, asking for pen and ink to write its words down. 'Suno suno hai Krishna kala', another all-time hit of his, was also apparently his own composition.

What was it that made Saigal the voice of an entire nation? His voice had a predominant nasal resonance and the pitch was extraordinarily high for a male singer by the prevalent standards. The remarkable tonal variations that Saigal used deeply moved listeners. The manner in which he caressed the words while singing almost brought them to life. Pankaj Mullick recounts that Saigal became the hero with the golden voice 'mainly due to his peerless tenor with a wonderful command over the three octaves and a special capacity for maintaining unvarying pitch without the least effort.'[1] It soon began to be hailed as 'The Saigal Voice'.

The music of a man, who had absolutely no classical training, ironically inspired many classical musicians. Pahari Sanyal recalls Ustad Faiyaz Khan sitting mesmerized and motionless for hours as he listened to Saigal perform live. Complimenting Saigal as he departed, he said that even *gharanedar* ustads who had musical legacies of many generations could never dream of singing so effortlessly. It is even said that Faiyaz Khan offered to take him as a student and the ritual *gandabandhan* ceremony was performed. Not much is known though of the training thereafter or even if it happened at all.

Asharani Saigal recounts with great pride that at the height of his stardom in 1938 Saigal was invited to a big musical conference in Allahabad where several luminaries of classical music like Pt Omkarnath Thakur, Ustad Faiyaz Khan, Narayan Rao Vyas, Vinayak Rao Patwardhan and others were present. Saigal had come to the conference with his frail, old mother. He sang ghazals and songs from his films and had the audience eating out of his hand. His name resounded everywhere in the hall that day as the enthusiastic crowd clamoured for more. Getting down from the

[1] See interview with Pankaj Mullick in *Filmfare*, 20 January 1967.

stage, Saigal hastened to his old mother, lifted her in his arms and swung her around in joy, saying, 'Listen, Mother! They are shouting for me to sing more. They think I am a musician!' His mother shed tears of joy as she saw the consummation of her dreams—her little wayward son who would get mercilessly beaten by his father was today a public hero.

The true nature of Saigal's musical personality comes forth in the few interviews that he gave to Kirit Ghosh, editor of the film magazine *Jayathi* where he says, 'I am not a singer . . . I can only be called a phraser. I have had no true classical training except what I have heard and remembered . . . I have no clear understanding of the grammar of music, I manage to sing because of a strong feeling about how certain sounds should feel in a given raga . . . People who learn to sing with the help of their ears alone cannot explain how they do it. All I can say about my own singing is that I do not use ten notes if I can manage to do the same with one . . . I hear very little when I sing except the meaning of the song, as I feel it and the way it moves about.' In the same interview he revealed that Bhairavi was his favourite raga because 'to know Bhairavi is to know all the ragas . . . If I had Bhairavi I would not pine for any other raga very much.'

The golden era of New Theatres was soon coming to an end as it struggled to sustain its employees. Stars were now migrating to Bombay, the emerging *mecca* of Indian cinema which was booming with new producers, superior processing laboratories and better technical facilities. The resignation of Nitin Bose from New Theatres in 1941 sounded its death knell. Saigal too bid farewell to Calcutta and his mentors there and relocated to Bombay the same year, renting a flat in Matunga. Chandulal Shah of Ranjit Movietone signed him for an attractive offer of over Rs 1,00,000 for a three-movie contract. *Bhakta Surdas* was his first film there in 1942 and the mellifluous bhajans that he rendered for it cast a magical spell on the audience. *Tansen* (1943) was his next major success story in Bombay, with him in the lead role as Emperor Akbar's legendary court musician and the beautiful and talented Khurshid as his heroine. He went back to Calcutta in 1944 to complete *My Sister* with New Theatres.

Though Saigal acted in quite a few films in Bombay like *Bhanwara* (1944), *Tadbir* (1945), *Shah Jehan* (1946) and *Omar Khayyam* (1946), the old magic of the New Theatres era was gone and none could match up to his earlier films. As Baburao Patel rues, 'The Bombay producers seemed to throttle the great artiste and squeeze the soul out of his throat. They fed the body but murdered the spirit . . . Gold had taken the golden out of his voice in the city where the smoke coming out of the mill-chimneys smells of human souls.' Saigal missed the ambience of New Theatres and Calcutta, and felt totally out of place in the pretentious world of Bombay cinema. He had very few friends in Bombay other than Jaddanbai, Nargis's mother, and the actor K.N. Singh, whose homes he frequented.

His health was failing by then and he would often stumble and faint on the sets. He was heavily addicted to alcohol and developed diabetes and acute liver cirrhosis. He left for Jalandhar with his family for a change of scene in December 1946. However, he committed to his directors about completing all pending assignments—as he did to J.K. Nanda whose *Parwana* (1947) had Saigal and Suraiya in the lead, saying, 'I shall tell even death to wait for a while and cause no interruption to the work . . . I will die only after completing this film.'

Saigal perhaps had some premonition of the inevitable. Son Madan Mohan recalls how he had turned deeply introspective and spiritual during this time. He would sit in his balcony in the early morning with a harmonium and sing bhajans, his favourite being 'Hari bina koi kaam na aayo'. All through his life Saigal had one constant worry—while his horoscope clearly indicated universal fame, it also portended an early death. All along he had this morbid preoccupation with his own death, a sense of needing to hurry in order to accomplish tasks before it was too late. Finally, his planetary positions proved right. The immortal singer shed his mortal coils in the early hours of the

morning of 18 January 1947. For a week the papers flashed
the news of his death. Riots, politics, Pakistan had all gone out
of the headlines as the entire nation was submerged in mourning
the greatest singer that the Indian screen had ever produced in
its long history of misadventure.

In a short career spanning about fifteen years, Saigal's contribution
through close to thirty-nine films in which he was connected,
directly or indirectly, and the 185 known songs rendered for Hindi
films, regional films (like Tamil, Bengali, Punjabi, Urdu, Persian)
and non-film songs like ghazals and bhajans are an unparalleled
contribution to the world of Indian cinema and its music. For
today's generation, which feeds on reality shows on television to
make a career in film singing, the character and musical personality
of this man might seem unreal and difficult to relate to. But the
honesty of that voice which held an entire nation in thrall—be
it in his soulful renditions of 'Jab dil hi toot gaya' and 'Babul
mora', or the jubilant optimism of 'Ek Bangla bane nyaara' or
even the heartbreaking pathos of 'Bina pankh panchi hoon main'
and 'So ja rajkumari'—speaks for itself.

MY FIVE FAVOURITE K.L. SAIGAL FILMS

1. *Devdas* (1935). Directed by P.C. Barua. Co-stars: Jamuna,
   Rajkumari, P.C. Barua, K.C. Dey, Pahari Sanyal, Kidar
   Sharma. Music by Timir Baran. The evergreen love story of a
   tragic hero who wilfully destroys himself. The film inspired
   many remakes, even until recently, and established Saigal's
   place in the film firmament.
2. *Street Singer* (1938). Directed by Phani Mazumdar. Co-stars:
   Kanan Devi, Bikram Kapoor, Jagdish. Music directed by
   R.C. Boral. Saigal played the memorable role of Bhulwa in this
   film, which also features the famous thumri 'Babul mora
   naihar chhooto jay', considered one of Saigal's all-time hits. The
   singing duo of Saigal and Kanan Devi created a sensation
   all over the country.

3. *President* (1937). Directed by Nitin Bose. Co-stars: Kamlesh Kumari, Leela Desai, Jagdish Sethi, Prithviraj Kapoor. Music by R.C. Boral and Pankaj Mullick. A wonderful film with a social message highlighting the plight of the workers of the Prabhavati Cotton Mills Ltd, headed by a woman president who falls in love with the same man as her sister— a worker in the mill. Features the evergreen song 'Ek Bangla bane nyaara'.

4. *Tansen* (1943). Directed by Jayant Desai. Co-stars: Khurshid, Mubarak, Kesari. Music by Khemchand Prakash. One of Saigal's most memorable performances as the court singer of Akbar. The film also has a commentary in the beginning about Tansen in the voice of Saigal where a balding and bespectacled Saigal speaks to the audience about the maestro.

5. *Zindagi* (1940). Directed by P.C. Barua. Co-stars: Pahari Sanyal, Ashalata, Jamuna, Nemo. Music directed by Pankaj Mullick. The film had an unconventional and bold theme for its times—a rich married woman deserts her wicked husband and falls in love with an educated but unemployed young man. This was also Saigal's last film for the New Theatres before moving to Bombay. Features Saigal's famous song 'So ja rajkumari so ja.'

DEVIKA RANI

QUEEN OF TWO WORLDS

CARY RAJINDER SAWHNEY

As a young film student, I first came across an image of Devika Rani in the British Film Institute Library in London. I remember being amazed by this immaculate beauty gazing out at me from a very old book. Adorned with white flowers in her hair, her features seemed to cross worlds, both Indian and Western. She was a far cry from the Bolly-dollies who were dangling off the biceps of heroes of the '80s. Her alluring eyes and posture suggested dignity and intelligence. Years later, with the help of noted film historian Amrit Gangar and archival collections in UK and India, I began to dig deeper into the story of this actress who has haunted me over the decades.

Certainly one of the most influential and controversial women of early Indian cinema, Devika Rani's spectacular story is veiled in the mists of legend. Educated in swinging 1920s' London, she became the teenage wife of the Svengali actor-producer Himanshu Rai. She was adored by millions of fans in her time and was even courted by Hollywood. She was admired by both the British rulers and Jawaharlal Nehru, although the Mahatma criticized her for wearing far too expensive clothes. The subject of constant rumours about extra-marital affairs, she was blamed by some for her husband's death, but still went on to successfully run the magnificent Bombay Talkies studio, producing some of its greatest hits. She then walked away from cinema forever, to start a new life as the sober wife of an acclaimed Russian painter.

Devika Rani's incredible life was set against a tumultuous period in both Indian and world history, and this would prove to strongly impact her successes and failures. The independence movement of India was finally gaining ground while the might of the British Raj was waning. Western Europe, in which Devika lived as a girl, was poised between the World Wars but also brimming with great technical and artistic innovation, and with the coming of the talkie films the modern age of communication had arrived.

Devika was descended from Bengali artistic aristocracy, the grandniece of the great writer and Nobel Prize–winner Rabindranath Tagore. Her parents were wealthy and Westernized, and her successful father, Col M.N. Chaudhury, was the first Surgeon General of Madras (now Chennai). Devika described her mother, Leela Chaudhury, as an artistic and enthusiastic woman 'full of beans and young in spirit'. Devika was born on 30 March 1908 in Waltair (Visakhapatnam). As was more common with the Westernised upper classes of the day, Devika travelled to England at an early age to be educated as a young lady, the necessary preparation for marriage. In a meeting with cineaste Rosie Thomas, Devika reminisced that she went to South Hampstead High School and then at sixteen she won a scholarship to study at the Royal Academy of Dramatic Art. She also studied architecture, design and décor courses at the Slade School of Fine Art. There was also some talk of Cambridge University, but Devika was undecided. The young Devika spent much of the 1920s in London, where she lodged with other Indian students; many such students of this time were fuelled with nationalist, Free-India politics, including one-time fellow lodger Subhash Bose who insisted that Devika learn to speak Bengali, her mother tongue.

Devika quoted her liberal-minded father as saying, 'A woman must learn to take care of herself.' She supplemented her studies by working in textile design for clients, including Liberty, and as an apprentice beautician at the newly opened American-owned store Elizabeth Arden, where she would have learnt the latest make-up and beauty skills. Little is known of her personality at those times, except from an autobiography of pioneering playwright and screenwriter Niranjan Pal, in whose house she lodged with his Yorkshire wife Lily and son. Pal described Devika as 'a sweet little kid' who mostly wore simple frocks. Although she studied and worked hard Devika, it is said, lacked a focus in her life, but this was all about to change and although she didn't know it at the time, she had learnt in London many skills that would be invaluable to her future career.

Devika was introduced at a party to Himanshu Rai, an ex-barrister turned actor and producer, who was already well known for his role as the Buddha in the successful silent film *The Light of Asia* (1925). He was a good friend and business partner of Niranjan Pal and they had already made two epic silent feature films together. Pal had scripted *The Light of Asia* while the subsequent hit *Shiraz* (1928) was based on his stage play. These movies were funded by German and, later, British money; the crew was partly German, led by director Franz Osten, Rai's partner in Munich. Both these lavish films pandered to the European fascination for 'exotic' India and were shot in grand locations such as the palaces of Rajasthan.

Himanshu Rai had a reputation as a wheeler-dealer and ladies' man, and must have been bowled over by Pal's stunningly beautiful and talented young house guest Devika Chaudhury. Devika described Rai in an interview with journalist Siddharth Kak as 'a great nationalist. For him the stage and cinema were means to project and build the culture of the country.' Rai soon encouraged Devika to work for him in the film industry; and the enthusiastic Devika quickly sent her mother a telegram, informing her about her decision. She began her film career as an assistant set designer under Himanshu's cousin Promode Rai, working on their next venture, the silent film *Prapancha Pash* (1929), also titled *A Throw of Dice*, starring Himanshu Rai and Seeta Devi, and directed by Franz Osten. The movie was bankrolled by British Instructional Films Ltd and the world-famous UFA Studios in Berlin. So began a partnership that would mould Devika's future. Himanshu Rai was much older than Devika and became her mentor in the film industry; she mentioned that he was more like a father figure to her. On a personal note Devika stated that Rai was a strict disciplinarian and often stopped her from pursuing her other passion for eating cakes and sweets—he was even known to have said, 'Indian girls are not meant to make a pig of themselves.'

In the next couple of year's Devika's father had passed away. She had also come of age and was now a free agent. When Pal met her again at a party at UFA Studios, Berlin, he was shocked to see the eighteen-year-old 'transformed into a glamour girl . . . complete with cigarette-holder in her mouth and clothed in an exquisite sari'. Even worse for the times was that she was drinking alcohol freely and clearly flaunting her newly found sex appeal. Rai could apparently see the attention that Devika was getting from his German financiers, which was a useful asset in the film industry. Devika, however, mentioned at this time that she was keen to learn about the industry and said, 'I knew we were doing something totally new. Something engrossingly exciting. I took my work very seriously. All of us did.'

Himanshu Rai's and Devika's relationship grew closer, and after a quiet romance they married in London before she set off with Promode Rai for Calcutta (now Kolkata) to prepare for *A Throw of Dice*. It is quite possible that Devika didn't know that Rai had already secretly married a German actress, Mary Hainlin, some years earlier. Niranjan Pal stated that Rai had told him about the German marriage, but swore him to secrecy. Devika did meet Mary; and perhaps as a testimony to the generosity of spirit of both women, they became friends. To all the world, however, Devika was Mrs Himanshu Rai and his earlier wife and child were left to struggle in obscurity. Rai's descendents from his first marriage now live in Australia.

Himanshu and Devika returned to Weimar Berlin and UFA for
editing the film. Rai was keen for them both to learn all elements
of modern studio production, and Devika's tough apprenticeship
began. In Weimar Berlin young Devika came into contact with
the German Expressionist directors. She trained under Erich
Pommer's film unit, and even called G.W. Pabst her 'guru'—he had
a talent for developing strong roles for actresses, including legends
like Greta Garbo and Louise Brooks. Talkie films, after the 1927
US hit *The Jazz Singer*, were now taking the world by storm and
Himanshu learnt about the latest studio and sound production,
while Devika also became a student in the legendary stage director
Max Reinhardt's highly sought-after production unit. She could
speak German and assisted on make-up, lighting tests and costumes
when on film sets. Devika mixed with leading actors such as Emil
Jannings and the young star Marlene Dietrich, and learnt the new,
less exaggerated styles of acting and performance required for the
sound age. Devika said the young Dietrich called her 'Liebling'.
Marlene taught her a lot and was always 'full of fun'. In an interview
with Amita Malik, Devika stated, 'I underwent training, not to
be a specialist, but because Rai wished me to have all-round
knowledge to help me as an artiste.' On completing her training
she was offered a part in a 20th Century Fox production to be shot
in Bali and also a role in a German film *The Snake Charmer's
Daughter*, but Rai was not keen and wanted to focus the couple's
interests on their homeland. *A Throw of Dice* was released in 1929
and became a success across Europe. Devika accompanied Rai on
the film's tour of Switzerland and Scandinavia and performed a
play of the story with Rai, before the picture was screened at each
location; the acting couple were very popular.

Ever ambitious, Rai was determined to make 'India's first talking
picture in English and Hindustani'. He raised finances from British
company IBP and the film *Karma* was shot in India and completed
at Stoll Studios, London. It was a fabulous tale of ancient India,
about a troubled love affair between a prince (played by Rai)
and the maharani of a neighbouring kingdom (played by Devika).

This was Devika's debut role and her natural acting talent, cut-glass English accent and unabashed sexuality—kissing her hero back to life at the finale—immediately attracted attention when it was premiered in London in May 1933, leaving her husband's performance in the shadows. Critics across the UK raved about the new talkie actress. *The Star* newspaper reported: 'You'll never hear a lovelier voice or diction, or see a lovelier face.' Devika had become a star.

Devika's fame grew as the BBC asked her to inaugurate its short-wave radio transmission to India, and it is said she performed, in Bengali, Tagore's 'Gram Chhara'. *Karma* was released at the Capitol Cinema in Bombay (now Mumbai) in 1934. The great female poet and socialite Sarojini Naidu was asked to write the foreword of the programme booklet. She was ebullient about Devika, describing her as 'a magical flower of romance'. Although the Hindustani version was not a success with Indian mass audiences the couple had made their mark on Bombay society.

With the rise of the Nazis, Weimar Germany came to an end and Europe was changing. The couple now turned their full attention to India and their dream of using all they had learnt to open India's best-equipped sound studio. Rai was also keen to give a new morality to the Indian movies which had, in the past, often been a playground for rich businessmen to 'recruit' young women. High-born and educated Devika was, of course, an essential ingredient in this new image of respectability.

They enlisted the support of an Englishman, Sir Richard Temple, who was the son of a former Governor of Bombay and therefore highly influential. Temple adored Devika and showed great generosity to the couple. Temple, in turn, enlisted the help of Lord Brabourne, the Governor of Bombay at the time, who also became a devotee of Devika. With Himanshu's skill, Devika's charm and the support offered by Temple, Brabourne and important Indian industrialists—notably Chimanlal Setalvad, Sir Pheroze Sethna and others—Rai was rapidly able to secure the finances for the new company, 'Himanshu Rai Indo-International Talkies Ltd', managing agents of Bombay Talkies. The studio was built in Malad, north Bombay, in 1934. It was based on a European model, with a rigorous schedule, strict work ethic and the latest imported equipment. Rai brought German technicians to work in the studio, and these included his old friends like Franz Osten, production designer Carl von Spreti and cinematographer Josef Wirsching. Niranjan Pal took charge of the story department.

Rai, Devika, Temple, the German families—all lived in the large studio complex. Devika said that they aimed to 'select a number of first-rate students from all over India' and they set about recruiting 300 graduate students each year. 'It was our aim to attract the best element in Indian society, with an educated and cultured background, to produce the highest type of art.' Groundbreaking at the time was the education for young Indian technicians provided by the studio, with Indian and foreign musicians, writers and scholars invited to speak at Bombay Talkies. The studio had a huge range of facilities including its own sound stage, processing laboratory, editing department, preview theatre, library, subsidized canteen and cricket ground. Devika was actively involved in many aspects of the production process including recruiting musicians, singers and actors for their films as well as taking decisions on costume design and the studio's publicity.

Film production began in earnest in 1935. Devika was the bankable name for these mostly heroine-focused productions, and she acted as lead actress in a string of early films including *Jawani Ki Hawa* (1935), *Jeevan Naya* (1936), *Janmabhoomi* (1936), *Savitri* (1937), *Jeevan Prabhat* (1937), *Izzat* (1937), and *Durga* (1939). These films enabled her to build a huge fan base, but her best-loved role came with the highly successful *Achhut Kanya* in 1936.

To the world, Bombay Talkies—with its great scripts, talented actors and high technical quality—seemed one of the most successful studios in India. This image of success, however, covered the personal cost of running such an intensive film factory; strains and cracks were beginning to take place within. Rai had become a workaholic, desperately trying to balance finances and productions, some of which flopped in the market. There was also gossip that his young wife Devika was having affairs. True or false, Niranjan Pal alleged that Devika became close to her co-star while shooting the film *Jawani Ki Hawa*. The handsome young actor, Najmul Hussain, was descended from Lucknow nobility and he was signed for a string of films. Devika and Hussain ran away together. Rai was distraught at the loss of his wife and leading lady. It was alleged by Bombay Talkies staff that he became quite unbalanced at the time. He was then tipped off that Devika and Hussain were in Calcutta and trying to get into the New Theatres film studios. According to Pal's account, Rai found Devika at the Grand Hotel in Calcutta and requested her to return with him. Devika had a change of heart and agreed.

Rai re-installed Devika to the Bombay Talkies set. Najmul Hussain's career in Bombay Talkies ended. There were no freelancers at the time so Rai had to find a new actor in the studio; he pulled the handsome young Ashok Kumar Ganguly (Ashok Kumar) out from the processing laboratory, and reluctantly at first—as he wasn't keen to become an actor—Ashok Kumar became Devika's new leading man in *Achhut Kanya*.

It was scripted by Niranjan Pal and seemed to capture the spirit of the age, highlighting the need for social reform with its portrayal of an ill-fated romance beset by Hindu inter-caste prejudice. The movie had its premiere at the Roxy Cinema in Bombay, and the audience included Congress leader Jawaharlal Nehru who heaped it with praise and became a lifelong friend of Devika. In spite of her Western-style plucked eyebrows Devika gave a credible and riveting performance as an untouchable girl, Kasturi, the daughter of a railway level-crossing guard, who falls in love with a Brahmin boy. There was real, on-screen chemistry between her and new-to-the-screen hero Ashok Kumar. The film was also legendary for its hit songs, especially Devika's and Ashok's joyous arboreal duet 'Mein ban ki chidiya', with music by Saraswati Devi.

The studio's parade of hits continued. As an actress Devika

was versatile, equally at home in a wide range of roles. What was notable of Bombay Talkies' films, as stated by critic Parvathi Nair, was a 'clever camouflaging of a social purpose in entertainment, not forgetting Devika Rani's own magnetism to draw crowds with her superb portrayal of the character—whether it was that of an untouchable girl (*Achhut Kanya*), a wronged wife (*Jeevan Prabhat*), a Rajput princess (*Vachan*), a tribal (*Izzat*), a barren woman (*Nirmala*)'. On my meetings with Bombay Talkies studio veterans, one thing they all had in common was when I asked them about the actress—each, to a man, smiled and went quiet for a moment, as if holding a magic memory of someone quite special who was adored and put on a pedestal.

Disaster struck Bombay Talkies just five years after it had opened. Himanshu Rai suddenly suffered a heart attack and, after a brief time in hospital where he continued working on film scripts, died at the age of just forty-eight in May 1940. Some blamed Devika's alleged affair for his untimely death, but the pressure of running a film studio, and the sudden loss of close friends and allies—the arrest and internment of his lead director Franz Osten, cameraman Joseph Wirsching and other Germans by the British authorities at the advent of World War II, as well as his major fallout with trusted screenwriter Niranjan Pal—all may have taken its toll.

Devika kept her views on Rai's death private, but she was suddenly alone, without her husband and mentor. Rival companies quickly began bidding for the studio's artistes and to make matters worse British India was also now at War and this affected supplies coming to the studios. Dressed in a white widow's sari, Devika mentioned she knew she was the heart of Bombay Talkies and that if she had left the studio it would have folded straight away. She took over as Controller of Productions. Few women had achieved this level in the film industry before, or since. Devika's strength of personality, intelligence and knowledge of all aspects of production carried her through. Producers Sasadhar Mukherjee and Amiya Chakrabarty were appointed and they brought new story formulas into the studio. In spite of many challenges she led the company to make hits like *Basant* (1942), the record-breaking hit *Kismet* (1943), with its powerful anti-British Raj sentiments, directed by Gyan Mukherjee, and her last on-screen role in *Hamari Baat* (1943) alongside P. Jairaj and a young Raj Kapoor. Under Devika Bombay Talkies went on creating opportunities and training for nascent talents including bringing to the Indian screen an ambitious Yusuf Khan, who Devika had talent-spotted, renamed as Dilip Kumar and cast in *Jwar Bhata* (1944), and there was also the screen goddess Madhubala who began her career at Bombay Talkies.

Devika's one-time private secretary Guruswamy, who joined her in 1941, mentioned in *Screen* that she was a strict disciplinarian, and that included actors, but always cared for the workers. He mentioned that during the War she set up a vegetable garden, a dispensary and ration shop for the workers. 'I found the work too much and wanted to get out. When I told her, all she did as a consolation was to offer me a glass of milk in the morning and a pudding in the afternoon which was an incentive for me to stay on. With such a kind-hearted person I decided to stay on.'

Devika had a vision of making a colour studio and began negotiations with US companies, but her international outlook was not supported by Bombay Talkies' financiers, or producer S. Mukherjee. The hard realities of post-War India, with the changing political atmosphere and growth of the black-market economy, and the advent of freelance actors meant that the film industry had changed and there was now cut-throat competition. In-fighting within the company eventually led to a split, and S. Mukherjee with Ashok Kumar, Rai Bahadur Chunilal and others formed another company—Filmistan, near Bombay Talkies. Devika Rani was ultimately out of step with the changing times. Frustrated with the changing audience tastes, lack of support in the company for her vision and changing values, Devika finally sold her assets and turned her back on the film industry. She mentioned to journalist Raju Bharatan about refusing to compromise artistic values, 'The moment I discerned it wasn't possible to uphold those values, I chose to call it a day.' The brief moment in early cinema, when everyone was participating in the building of a new Indian film industry, had drawn to a close.

Devika had met a handsome painter Svetoslav Roerich, son of the acclaimed Russian artist Nicholas Roerich, who had visited Bombay Talkies some years earlier. She married Roerich and they moved to Kulu Manali in Himachal Pradesh, where they set up home and became close friends of the Nehru family, including Indira Gandhi; here Devika attested that she had not given up filmmaking and was making documentaries on local wildlife. They then acquired a large estate near Bangalore, where Devika managed a perfumery-base export company. The couple shared a passion for arts and culture and became patrons in the art world. They remained closely married for over 40 years. Devika stated about children she had no regrets and that although she loved children, she had no time and was always too busy working.

In recognition of her pioneering services to cinema Devika Rani, commonly called the 'First Lady of Indian cinema', was awarded the title Padma Shri by the President of India in January 1958. This was followed by the first ever Dada Saheb Phalke Award for her distinct services to the Indian film industry in 1969. Devika Rani passed away a year after her husband on 9 March 1994, aged 86.

Today the marble pillars marking the entrance to Bombay Talkies still stand like a half-broken-down film set, marooned in a cheek by jowl maze of poor industrial shacks. Devika Rani and Himanshu Rai's contribution to world cinema is mostly forgotten, even the work of the jolly Josef Wirsching, who stayed behind after World War II and filmed many great Indian films, including *Pakeezah* (1972), is remembered by very few, but when the silver images of these past movies like *Achhut Kanya* have a rare showing, the images of gorgeous Devika

Rani, serene, sweet and intelligent, come to life again and fill one with wonderment of another age.

MY FIVE FAVOURITE DEVIKA RANI FILMS

1. *Karma* (1933). Directed by J.L. Freer-Hunt. Co-stars: Himanshu Rai, Abraham Sofaer. One of India's first talkies, *Karma* was shot in India and completed at Stoll Studios, London. This fabulous tale of ancient India looks rigid and outdated today, but has some timeless images—a gorgeous Devika Rani shimmering in a silver pool of light as she pines for her prince, locked in her palace, as well as the film's intense finale where she vigorously kisses her hero back to life!

2. *Achhut Kanya* (1936). Directed by Franz Osten. Co-star: Ashok Kumar. A great classic of Indian cinema that was to influence many later films in portraying Indian village life. What is probably Devika Rani's greatest role is played with intensity and a joyous energy that compliments perfectly her romantic lead, the young Ashok Kumar as a lovestruck village boy. Their innocence and love is finally destroyed in a heartrending inter-caste feud.

3. *Jawani Ki Hawa* (1935). Directed by Franz Osten. Co-stars: Najmul Hussain, Chandraprabha. The notorious film that launched and nearly broke Bombay Talkies Studio. Life imitated art in this romantic crime thriller. A heroine elopes with a childhood sweetheart on her wedding day, leading to mysterious and dramatic circumstances. The palpable on-screen chemistry between Devika and the dashing Najmul Hussain supposedly carried on after the shoot as the actors allegedly ran off together on a train in real life.

4. *Jeevan Prabhat* (1937). Directed by Franz Osten. Co-stars: Kishore Sahu, Mumtaz Ali. Following in *Achhut Kanya*'s footsteps, this rural-based story with a theme of social concern explores Hindu caste divisions. Devika Rani plays Uma, a Brahmin girl whose husband takes a second wife when she

is thought to be infertile. However, when Uma suddenly becomes pregnant her husband accuses her of infidelity.

5. *Anjaan* (1941). Directed by Amiya Chakrabarty. Co-stars: Ashok Kumar, V.H. Desai, David Abraham. A late coupling of romantic duo Devika Rani and Ashok Kumar, with a charming musical score by the legendary Pannalal Ghosh. A virtuous doctor Ajit (Ashok Kumar) and a devious country estate manager are rivals for the hand of a beautiful ayah Indra (Devika Rani). Falsely accused of murder Ajit must clear his name and win his lady.

ASHOK KUMAR

THE ACCIDENTAL HERO

BHAICHAND PATEL

I saw *Kangan* (1939) when I was four years old. The only scene in the film that has stayed with me all these years is the climax where a woman, played by Leela Chitnis, tries to commit suicide by walking into the ocean. She is rescued by the hero, Ashok Kumar, at the last minute and the film ends on a happy note.

Kangan was made in 1939 and arrived in our small town a few years later, after the film's print, by now quite scratched, had entertained crowds in more important centres. Even at that age, I was aware that I was watching a sophisticated bioscope—that's what we called movies in those days—unlike those that came out of studios like Prakash Pictures, which specialized in cheaply produced mythologicals, and Wadia Movietone, which prolifically rolled out stunt films that mostly featured their in-house heroine, Fearless Nadia.

Kangan was produced by Bombay Talkies, at that time India's most high-tech film studio with technicians and directors recruited from Britain, France and Germany. The production house was in Malad, then a distant suburb of Bombay (now Mumbai). The studio, previously a weekend retreat of a wealthy

Parsi family, had sound-proof stages, swank laboratories and editing rooms as well as its own preview theatre.

A Bombay Talkies film was easily recognizable: it had the Hollywood look, something that its two main competitors, New Theatres in Calcutta (now Kolkata) and Prabhat in Poona (now Pune), could not quite match. Himanshu Rai, who owned the studio together with his wife, Devika Rani, had been trained in London where he produced two well-received silent films, *Light of Asia* (1925) and *Shiraz* (1928).

Ashok Kumar was certainly an unlikely hero, and he came into acting quite by accident. But we will come to that later.

Born on 13 October 1911 in Bhagalpur, Bihar, Ashok Kumar grew up in Khandwa, a town in present-day Madhya Pradesh. His parents named him Kumudlal and he was oldest of four children—three sons and a daughter. His two brothers were to follow him into the acting profession. The career of the middle brother, Anoop Kumar, never took off though he displayed a flair for comedy in *Chalti Ka Naam Gaadi* (1958). The youngest sibling, however, flourished as a very competent comic actor and was cast opposite some of the most popular leading ladies of that time, including Meena Kumari, Nutan, Vyjayanthimala and, last but not least, with Madhubala whom he married. He was also a hugely successful singer. Kishore Kumar was the voice of choice for Dev Anand and Rajesh Khanna. He was the last of the great male playback singers that included Rafi, Mukesh, Talat and Hemant.

Their father was a lawyer and he wanted his eldest son to follow in his profession. He had that in mind when he sent Ashok Kumar to study in Presidency College in Calcutta. The young man, however, had other ideas. He wanted to direct films and sought help from Sasadhar Mukherjee who was married to his sister, Sati Devi. Fortuitously, the brother-in-law was already working at Bombay Talkies, recording the soundtrack of the various films being made there.

Ashok Kumar landed in Bombay in January 1934 without

telling his parents. The train ticket was bought with the money they had sent him for the examination fee. Mukherjee got him employed as a camera assistant so that he could learn the tricks of the trade. He started on a monthly salary of Rs 150, enough in those days for a young man to live modestly. He found a place to stay near the studio. When the news reached his father the man was distraught; he had hoped his son would one day become the chief justice of India. His mother, for her part, was worried that no girl from a respectable family would marry her son now that he was involved in such a disreputable line of business.

Eight months after he arrived in Bombay, Ashok Kumar's life changed. The studio was shooting *Jeevan Naya* (1936) with Devika Rani in the lead when she ran off to Calcutta with the hero, Najmul Hussain, in the middle of the shoot. In other circumstances this might have created a minor scandal and some production hiccups but here the implications were greater: not only was Devika Rani married but her husband was the man who owned Bombay Talkies! Understandably, Himanshu Rai was hugely upset. Sasadhar Mukherjee, his right-hand man at that time, took pity on him and went off to Calcutta and somehow persuaded Devika Rani to return to her husband and the film. There is no record of what words were exchanged between the husband and the wayward wife on her return though it seems that Himanshu forgave her. But there was no question of taking back Najmul Hussain. He wisely decided to stay put in Calcutta and found work at New Theatres.

The situation left Himanshu Rai and the German director, Franz Osten, without a hero for *Jeevan Naya*. Rai remembered that Ashok Kumar had auditioned for acting when he first arrived in Bombay. The young man had done it reluctantly at Rai's insistence with Osten directing him. It had not gone well and Osten had suggested to Ashok Kumar to return to Calcutta and continue his law studies.

Ashok Kumar had ignored the gratuitous advice and continued working at the studio as assistant to the cameraman. By the time

Najmul Hussain was fired he had been shifted to the post of an assistant in the studio's laboratory and his salary had risen to Rs 250 a month. Without consulting Franz Osten, Himanshu Rai decided to make Ashok Kumar the hero of *Jeevan Naya*.

The film tells the story of a dancer handing over her child to a social worker for adoption so that she could be brought up in a decent home. The child, Lata—now grown up and played by Devika Rani—gets engaged to Ranjit, played by Ashok Kumar. Before the wedding, the social worker takes her to meet her ailing mother and she learns about her parentage. Someone threatens to expose her and, to buy his silence, Lata parts with the necklace that Ranjit had gifted her. Ranjit finds out and walks out on his bride. He loses his eyesight and Lata, now a nurse, tends to him without being found out. Ranjit gets his sight back and the film ends the way all films of this genre end.

The first scene that the director decided to shoot was of Ashok Kumar putting the necklace on Devika Rani. He was very nervous, running to the toilet every few minutes. It took many shots and lots of encouragement from the more experienced heroine before Ashok Kumar got it right.

The name 'Kumudlal' was found unsuitable for a hero. He started as Ashok Kumar Ganguly but by the time the shooting was completed, 'Ganguly' was dropped. Himanshu Rai decided that the plot of the film needed a casteless hero. He was our first 'Kumar' and many have followed over the years, dropping caste and regional names—Goswami, Jariwala, Tuli—in favour of the more neutral 'Kumar'.

Jeevan Naya did not set the box office on fire but it was his next film that made Ashok Kumar a star. The story of *Achhut Kanya* (1936) was written by Himanshu Rai himself, and the director and the two leads were repeated from the earlier film. The love between Kasturi, the daughter of a low-caste railway employee, and Pratap, the son of a Brahmin village grocer, is doomed from the start. She is married off to someone of her caste but Pratap cannot get her out of his mind. Kasturi is a dutiful wife but suspicions arise and her husband is incited to kill Pratap. The two clash on railway tracks and, to save them both, Kasturi tries to stop an oncoming train and dies in the process, saving the life of her husband and the man she loves.

The film was a huge hit. Himanshu Rai tried, unsuccessfully, to get Mahatma Gandhi to see it. Nehru saw it at a special screening in Bombay in the company of Sarojini Naidu who, the story goes, slept through most of it. There is no record of what Nehru made of *Achhut Kanya*. The film started a trend of making socially committed films.

Ashok Kumar was now permanently ensconced at Bombay Talkies. The Devika Rani–Ashok Kumar pair became very popular and they did six more films together, *Janmabhoomi* (1936), *Izzat* (1937), *Savitri* (1937), *Nirmala* (1938), *Vachan* (1938) and *Anjaan* (1941). In these films Ashok Kumar was always in the shadow of Devika Rani, the bigger star. Her name appeared before his in the credits and in larger letters on the films' posters.

Ashok Kumar came into his own opposite Leela Chitnis. After *Kangan* he co-starred with her in *Azad* (1940), *Bandhan* (1940), *Jhoola* (1941) and *Kiran* (1943). In her biography, written in Marathi years later, Leela Chitnis recalled Ashok Kumar: 'He had a very attractive face, beautiful eyes, a nice nose, six feet tall and a habit of talking while laughing . . . However, he seemed to have a weak build and, as an actor, his personality seemed unimpressive.'

In 1940 Himanshu Rai died following a nervous breakdown. Soon there were two camps at Bombay Talkies, one led by Sasadhar Mukherjee and the other by Amiya Chakrabarty who had directed Ashok Kumar and Devika Rani in their last film together, *Anjaan*. In the beginning Sasadhar and Ashok took charge under Devika Rani's leadership but soon she started siding with Amiya whenever disputes arose. The situation became intolerable and in 1944 the two left Bombay Talkies with some of the other senior employees and set up their own studio, Filmistan.

This happened soon after Ashok Kumar delivered the studio its biggest hit, *Kismet* (1943). To call the film a hit is an understatement. Its success was unequalled, before or after, in Indian cinema until *Sholay* came along thirty-two years later. It ran for over two years in Bombay and Calcutta. Ashok Kumar played a debonair cigarette-smoking anti-hero, a pickpocket who had run away from a wealthy home when he was a child. Reformed by a dancer who had been disabled and was on hard times, he reunites with his parents at the end. The songs, written by Pradeep and set to music by Anil Biswas, were part of the film's magic.

It was his last of fourteen films at Bombay Talkies. By now he was already freelancing. *Angoothi* (1943) was his first film outside the studio. The same year he acted in *Najma*, under the direction of Mehboob Khan. The director took him on again two years later in *Humayun* (1945) with a very young Nargis cast opposite him.

His first film at Filmistan, *Chal Chal Re Naujawan* (1944), took its title from a song in *Bandhan*. It did not do well. Now that he was a partner in a studio, he tried his hand at directing, the ambition that had brought him to Bombay in the first place. When *Eight Days* (1946) was completed Ashok Kumar realized that this line of work was not for him. He gave credit for it to Dattaram Pai, the editor, and did not direct another film.

Meanwhile at Bombay Talkies, Devika Rani showed little inclination towards running a studio with its endless hassles and headaches. She remarried a renowned Russian painter and left Bombay. The studio was in dire straits, having incurred huge debts due to mismanagement and corruption. Ashok Kumar decided to return to his alma mater, this time to take charge as producer. But it was not a complete break from his Filmistan partners; he returned to the studio later to give them another hit, *Samadhi* (1950).

His co-producer now was Savak Vacha whom he had brought along from Filmistan. He did not act in their first film, *Majboor* (1948), and it did not make waves except for the fact that it got Lata Mangeshkar noticed. The music director, the renowned

Ghulam Haider, spread the word that an amazing voice had arrived in the film industry. Naushad Ali and Khemchand Prakash were listening.

Their next, *Ziddi* (1948), was Dev Anand's break-out film. The story had been written by Ismat Chughtai with Ashok Kumar in mind for the lead opposite Kamini Kaushal, but he insisted on casting the young, handsome man who had been hanging around in the studio's compound hoping for a role. *Ziddi's* other claim to fame was that it introduced Kishore Kumar as a playback singer. His break as an actor was to come in one of the studio's subsequent films, *Tamasha* (1952).

The most successful film under the new management was *Mahal* (1949). Ashok Kumar cast himself opposite Madhubala who had earlier been a child star at the studio. *Mahal* is a beloved classic. Shankar, played by Ashok Kumar, moves into an abandoned mansion with a sad history. The person who had built it was murdered on his wedding night and the spirit of his bride was haunting the place. Shankar comes across the portrait of the previous owner who looks exactly like him and he is irresistibly attracted to the 'ghost' when he sees her walking around at midnight. It was Kamal Amrohi's debut and despite his brilliant script and artful direction, it was music director Khemchand Prakash who walked away with the honours. Every song is memorable but it was the unforgettable 'Ayega, ayega, ayega aanewala' that made Lata Mangeshkar a household name. It is still played over and over again on radio stations.

Gyan Mukherjee, who had directed Ashok Kumar in *Kismet*, was invited to take charge of *Sangram* (1950). Once again, he played a negative role, this time as Kunwar, the son of a police officer who turns into a gangster. In the end Kunwar is shot down by his own father. This was the first of many films in which Nalini Jaywant was cast opposite Ashok Kumar as his lady love. *Sangram* was running in its sixteenth week in Bombay, doing nicely, when the police establishment complained that it portrayed them in a bad light and the chief minister of the state, Morarji Desai, stopped further screening.

The studio barely survived for another few years with Ashok Kumar pumping his own money into it. Bimal Roy was invited from Calcutta to direct his first Bombay film, *Maa* (1952), with an old studio favourite, Leela Chitnis, playing the title role. *Baadbaan* (1954) was the last film at that grandest of studios. Appropriately, it had an all-star cast: Ashok Kumar, Meena Kumari, Dev Anand, Usha Kiran, Jairaj, Sheikh Mukhtar, Leela Chitnis and Mehmood. At least some of them must have returned to bid farewell to the institution that had once nurtured them. Years earlier, Mehmood had played young Ashok Kumar in *Kismet* and his father, Mumtaz Ali, was once an actor there and choreographer of some of the studio's biggest hits.

While he was involved in resurrecting Bombay Talkies, Ashok Kumar did not act in many films with other studios. He soon realized that three younger, handsome and talented actors—Dilip Kumar, Dev Anand and Raj Kapoor—were rushing past him in popularity while he had been neglecting his acting career. Incidentally, he was destined to co-star with all three of them, always receiving top billing: with Dilip in *Deedar* (1951), Dev in both *Tamasha* and *Baadbaan*, and Raj in *Bewafa* (1952).

In 1949 he had acted in only one film, *Mahal.* Three years later he was in as many as nine films, unfortunately almost all of them mediocre. Only *Tamasha,* a comedy co-starring Meena Kumari, Dev Anand and his brother, Kishore, was any good.

The following year, however, he was back in the fray under the direction of Bimal Roy. *Parineeta* (1953), based on a story by Saratchandra, was a love story between an orphan living with her impoverished uncle and the son of a rich family next door. The girl is always in and out of the landlord's house and the son takes her for granted until another man appears on the scene. He realizes he is in love with her. Both Ashok Kumar and Meena Kumari are superb and it is one of Bimal Roy's most admired films.

This is perhaps as good a place as any to acknowledge my debt for much of the information in this essay—especially dates and data—to the definitive biography, *Ashok Kumar:*

His Life and Times, by Nabendu Ghosh, published during the actor's lifetime. Mr Ghosh, a noted Bengali author, has written some of our cinema's best screenplays, most of them for Bimal Roy. These include *Parineeta, Devdas, Sujata, Bandini* and *Teesri Kasam.*

It was in the 1950s that Ashok Kumar also acted in three notable films in rapid succession for B.R. Chopra, a new talent who had arrived in Bombay from Punjab: *Afsana* (1951), *Shole* (1953) and *Ek Hi Rasta* (1955). His last film for Chopra was *Gumrah* (1963) and towards the end he played the lead in Chopra's television serial, *Bahadur Shah Zafar* (1988).

Ashok Kumar's glory days were over. His last significant film in the lead role was again under Bimal Roy's direction. There was a gap of ten years between *Bandini* (1963) and the earlier *Parineeta* due to a misunderstanding between the actor and the director. Ashok Kumar was the producer of *Parineeta* which was being made simultaneously with Roy's own production, *Do Bigha Zameen* (1953). Roy had gone to Calcutta without Ashok Kumar to take some outdoor shots for *Parineeta.* Ashok Kumar, rightly or wrongly, suspected that Roy, while he was in Calcutta, had diverted funds from his film for shooting scenes for *Do Bigha Zameen.*

In *Bandini,* Kalyani (Nutan) is imprisoned for murder and her past is told in flashback. She had been involved with Bikash (played by Ashok Kumar), a revolutionary in British times, and to save his life she claims to be his wife. Bikash disappears and when she finds out that Bikash has married another woman Kalyani poisons her and accepts responsibility. It really is Nutan's film but Ashok Kumar also gives a wonderful, subdued performance. Despite an age gap of twenty-five years between the two actors, one is easily convinced of their on-screen relationship.

By the 1960s Ashok Kumar started taking character roles and matched his wits, quite successfully, with young heroes like Sunil Dutt, Rajendra Kumar, Dharmendra, Sanjeev Kumar, Rajesh Khanna and Amitabh Bachchan.

He has acted in films by all prominent film-makers of his

era—Mehboob Khan, Kishore Sahu (*Saajan,* 1947), Kamal Amrohi
and B.R. Chopra—but he seemed most at ease under the guidance
of Bengali directors who had turned up in Bombay after the rapid
decline of the Calcutta studios following the creation of East
Pakistan, now Bangladesh. Chief among this crop of film-makers
were Nitin Bose (*Mashaal,* 1950), Bimal Roy (*Parineeta*), Arvind
Sen (*Kafila,* 1952), Hrishikesh Mukherjee (*Satyakam,* 1969), Basu
Chatterjee (*Khatta Meetha,* 1978), Phani Mazumdar (*Baadbaan*
and *Akashdeep,* 1965), Satyen Bose (*Bandish,* 1955, and *Chalti
Ka Naam Gaadi*) and Ashit Sen (*Sharafat,* 1970). These film-makers
made the kind of low-key films he excelled in.

Ashok Kumar was among a handful of stars who looked good
in a dhoti. At his prime, his hairstyle was enthusiastically emulated
by young men who also imitated the way he talked and smoked.
It seemed as if he always had a cigarette in hand in his films.
He introduced to films a natural style of acting. In the early years,
when silent films gave way to sound in 1931, acting was very
theatrical, taking its cue from nautanki and the Parsi theatre. This
verbose style was best personified by actors like Sohrab Modi,
Prithviraj Kapoor and Chandramohan. Ashok Kumar, on the
other hand, rarely made gestures and seldom raised his voice even
when he was angry. He made acting look easy! 'I dislike being
melodramatic,' he said years later. 'I behave on screen the way
I would at home.'

On the rare occasions when he was called do an action role—
Jalpari (1952), for instance—he seemed uncomfortable and
the audience was disappointed. Otherwise he was versatile and his
range encompassed comedy (*Khatta Meetha*), tragedy (*Mashaal*)
as well as period dramas (*Humayun*).

He seems to have acted opposite every leading lady of his
time, including Kanan Devi, Mumtaz Shanti, Nargis, Naseem,
Madhubala, Suraiya, Rehana, Geeta Bali, Meena Kumari, Nalini
Jaywant, Kamini Kaushal, Nirupa Roy, Nutan and Vyjayanthimala.
In perhaps a candid moment, he once said that of all his co-stars,
he admired the talents of Madhubala and Geeta Bali the most.

By the 1980s he was seen in fewer films and would occasionally appear on television, most famously as the anchor of the soap opera, *Hum Log*. He continued acting till 1997, a remarkable sixty-one-year innings. His last film was *Ankhon Mein Tum Ho* (1997), distinguished only by the presence of Rakhee Gulzar in the lead.

The government recognized his contribution to Indian cinema by awarding him its highest honour, the Dadasaheb Phalke Award, in 1988. He was also a recipient of a Padma Bhushan.

Dadamoni—or the elder brother, as everyone in the industry came to know him—died on 10 December 2001 at the age of ninety. He remained loved and respected in the film community till the end. According to one count, he had acted in 304 films.

At the height of his career, he lived with his family in a sprawling flat on Ramparts Row in south Bombay, over a shop that sold pianos and other musical instruments. In his sunset years, with mounting financial problems, he moved to Chembur, not far from the bungalow occupied by the reclusive Nalini Jaywant. He had acted opposite her in a maximum number of films, ten altogether, within an astonishingly short span of six years, beginning 1950. Ashok Kumar was known to be a ladies' man but a discreet one. His affair with Nalini Jaywant was the only one that he admitted to. They had parted company acrimoniously. I like to think that the two, by now both widowed, might have bumped into each other on their evening walks in Union Park.

MY FIVE FAVOURITE ASHOK KUMAR FILMS

1. *Kismet* (1943). Directed by Gyan Mukherjee. Co-star: Mumtaz Shanti. He played a negative role to great effect. It was his most successful film and it is still eminently watchable seven decades after it was made.
2. *Mahal* (1949). Directed by Kamal Amrohi. Co-star: Madhubala. The best 'ghost' story ever with great songs composed by Khemchand Prakash.

3. *Parineeta* (1953). Directed by Bimal Roy. Co-star: Meena Kumari. Great performances all round, even in smaller roles. My favourite Bimal Roy film.

4. *Deedar* (1951). Directed by Nitin Bose. Co-stars: Dilip Kumar, Nargis, Nimmi. One of the most popular films of the golden era. Ashok Kumar and Dilip Kumar come head to head for acting honours. The result? A draw!

5. *Bandini* (1963). Directed by Bimal Roy. Co-stars: Nutan, Dharmendra. It was his last major film as hero. He was fifty-two, the leading lady twenty-seven!

NARGIS

PEERLESS QUEEN OF THE SILVER SCREEN

S. THEODORE BASKARAN

You manufacture toys. You don't manufacture stars.

—Joan Crawford

When she died at the age of fifty-two, Nargis was already a legend, a celebrity in the modern sense, associated with the early decades of Indian cinema. As she had dominated the scene for nearly two decades her screen characters endeared her to the millions of fans, bringing in mass adulation.

Born into an affluent family, her mother a film producer, she grew up in Marine Drive, a prosperous Bombay (now Mumbai) locality, and studied in a convent. With these privileges, Nargis came to embody the elegance and dignity of a city girl. In her cinematic career spanning nearly two decades she shone as an unparalleled star, playing a variety of roles, from Hamida in *Humayun* (1945) to a woman suffering from multiple personality disorder in her last film, *Raat Aur Din* (1967). She acted in sixty-one films, including her stint as a child artiste, and had evolved into a top-billed actor. Some of her films, like *Awara* (1951) and *Shree 420* (1955) have frozen in the collective memory of Indians all over the world. Her movie career stretched back to the early years of Indian talkie films and lasted well into the 1960s when Indian cinema had gained a place on the world map. She had grown along with Indian cinema.

When Fatima Rashid, later to be Nargis, entered the world in Calcutta (now Kolkata) on 1 June 1929, she was destined to be one of the brightest stars of Indian filmdom that cast a spell over a whole generation. Her mother, Jaddanbai, was a well-known courtesan-singer whose parents hailed from the village Chilbilla in Uttar Pradesh. Her mother was a Brahmin child-widow who had fallen in love with a Muslim sarangi player and married him. Jaddanbai moved to Calcutta along with a group of dancers and began performing there. It was here that Uttamchand Mohanchand—also known as Mohanbabu—who was in the city with dreams of a career in medicine, met her. He, with his passion for music, fell in love with her and was keen on marrying her. His parents were opposed to this idea as Jaddanbai had been married before and had two sons. Mohanchand ignored his parents' wishes and married her in 1928 after converting to Islam and assuming a new name, Abdul Rashid. Even though he was not a practising Muslim, he would be buried according to Islamic tradition. He had ambitions to become a medical doctor but gave up his studies halfway and immersed himself in promoting Jaddanbai's career.

THE CHILD ARTISTE

One of the persons Jaddanbai got to know in Calcutta was the legendary K.L. Saigal who spotted her as a musical talent suited for films. On his advice, she moved to Lahore which was emerging as a film-producing centre. Sound had arrived on the cinema scene with *Alam Ara* (1931) and the industry needed singing stars. Jaddanbai fitted the bill. In 1933 she featured in two films made in Lahore: *Insaan Ya Shaitan*, directed by Moti Gidwani and *Raja Gopichand*, directed by B.M. Shukla. She soon made a name in the film industry with her third film *Seva Sadan* (1934).

She observed that things were happening in a big way in the realm of cinema in Bombay and decided to relocate. She arrived in Bombay with her family in 1934 and decided to set up a film company. She called her outfit Sangeet Movietone and in her second film, *Talash-e-Haque* (1935), in which she was the heroine, six-year-old Fatima featured as a child artiste and was credited as Baby Rani, a name that stuck to her for many years. In Bombay filmdom, both to studio workers and co-stars, she was often known as Babyji.

At this point of time, Jaddanbai moved into a flat in Marine Drive, on the ground floor in an apartment complex called Chateau Marine. The family of five—herself, her husband Mohanbabu, her sons Akhtar Hussain and Anwar Hussain, and the young Fatima—soon became a well-known family in the neighbourood. Jaddanbai had established considerable influence in Hindi cinema and her house became a meeting point for all people who mattered in the industry in Bombay. Fatima joined Queen Mary School and did not evince much interest in cinema. Keen on her studies, and much influenced by her father, she had dreams of becoming a doctor.

THE DEBUT

One day, while visiting Jaddanbai's home, Mehboob Khan, one of the successful directors of the period and a good friend of Jaddanbai—he had acted with her in one film—asked if she would let her daughter join films. He wanted to sign her up for a lead role in the film *Taqdeer* which he was planning. The hero of the film was Motilal, a well-known actor. Fatima was then only fourteen years old. Jaddanbai agreed and Mehboob Khan christened the teenager with the screen name 'Nargis'—an Urdu word meaning daffodil, with its roots in the Persian expression 'Narges'—as he had a fascination for names beginning with the letter 'N', perhaps because his first film, *Najma*, had done well. In a story inspired by Bernard Shaw's *Pygmalion* and set against the colourful backdrop of the Kumbh Mela celebrations, *Taqdeer* was released in 1943 with Nargis in the role of a glitzy dancer. Though not a great success, it went well with the audience. That year, *Filmindia* magazine commented, 'In Nargis the picture introduces a new girl to the Indian screen. Her success is the triumph of Mehboob, who has in addition photographed her very carefully and thus helped a lot to glamorize her.' Critics did not fail to notice Nargis's schoolgirl innocence and her unstylized acting. Since she had not come from the commercial stage, as many actors did in those days, she had a refreshing on-screen presence. However, her next film *Ismat* (1944), made by S. Fazli, did not do well either at the box office or with the critics.

By the early 1940s the Hindi film audience had developed their own favourites. Quite a few female stars had appeared on the scene in Bombay such as Noorjehan, Vanamala and Suraiya. Young Nargis had to compete with them to win and retain her position. These actors were singing stars but the distinct advantage they had was neutralized by a technological innovation that came to be instrinsic to Hindi cinema: playback singing. Singing star Suraiya was one of Nargis's few peers who was equally popular at that time, but her rivalry with Nargis came to an end when the phenomenon of playback singing brought singing talents like Lata Mangeshkar to the fore. Nargis had a few years to consolidate her position before formidable rivals like Madhubala and Geeta Bali came on the scene. Film historian Ashish Rajadhyaksha observes about her career in this period:

> From the beginning, Nargis's performances were authentic to a degree unprecedented in Indian cinema, giving Imperial and Sagar Studios' Arabian night's fantasies new layers of meaning. Mehboob used her as the pivotal figure in his attempts to merge the symbologies of feudal patriarchy into those of capitalism (*Andaz*, 1949) while Raj Kapoor injected oedipal impulses into his encounters with 'tradition'.[1]

[1] See Ashish Rajadhyaksha and Paul Willemen, *Encylopaedia of Indian Cinema* (British Film Institute, 1994).

Mehboob Khan, who was happy with the reception that both *Taqdeer* and Nargis received, decided to cast her in *Humayun*, the next production he was planning. In this film, Nargis teamed with Ashok Kumar, a major star at the time. It was a period in India when the film industry rested on stars and their charisma rather than the ability of individual directors. Nargis had refined her style that had grown unique in the three films and this came in handy as she played a glamorous role in *Humayun*. Her flawless Urdu diction was an added advantage in that film set in the early Mughal period. It was a grand production and it can be marked as the beginnings of a star image for Nargis.

Encouraged by the success of his sister, Akhtar Hussain launched a production company, Nargis Art Concern, through which he produced and directed films. One film made was *Bhishma Pratigya* (1950), directed by Vasant Rao Painter, which has gone down in film history as the only mythological in which Nargis acted. She did not get good reviews for her performance and she seems to have realized that mythological or historical films were not for her.

THE RAJ KAPOOR YEARS

Sometime in 1947, when he was preparing the ground work for the film *Aag* (1948), Raj Kapoor came knocking at the door of their apartment in Chateau Marine to meet Jaddanbai. He wished to rent her studio. Nargis, who was busy in the kitchen, hurriedly came and opened the door, patches of dough still sticking to her face and fingers. The meeting made such an impact on Raj Kapoor that he would later recall this encounter in a crucial scene in the film *Bobby* (1973) which he directed and produced.

Even while working on their first film, romance began to blossom between the two. It was later memorialized in the R.K. Films logo, which was inspired by an intimate scene between Nargis and Raj Kapoor from the film *Barsaat* (1949). Her family did not approve of this relationship, particularly her mother. One biographer notes that Nargis used to be beaten up by her brother Akhtar Hussain in an attempt to break the relationship. But the bond grew inexorably.

Beginning with *Aag*, Nargis paired with Raj Kapoor in seventeen films between 1948 and 1956, the years of their romantic partnership. *Shree 420*, a characteristic Nargis–Raj film—with the story by K.A. Abbas, songs by Shailendra and music by Shankar–Jaikishan—was a commercial hit. Nargis stood out by her spontaneity while Raj Kapoor carried on mimicking Charlie Chaplin, in body language and facial expressions. Noticing the popularity of their films, a number of producers signed them as romantic leads for their films. Raj Kapoor's association with Nargis was one of the factors in his rise to fame.

Later, after *Awara* (1951) opened the Russian market to Indian films, the names of Nargis and Raj Kapoor went together in the Bombay film world. They were members of a film delegation to Russia. They went again two years later and by that time they had become very popular in that country. At airports they were received to the music of 'Awara hun', a hit song from that film. While in Russia, they were once entertained to a puppet show by a famous Russian puppeteer, and the lead puppets represented Raj Kapoor and Nargis. Soon *Shree 420* was also distributed in Russia.

All along Nargis had hoped that he would marry her. At the time, Raj Kapoor was already married to Krishna Kapoor. One biographer of Nargis records that Raj Kapoor at one stage had even drawn the divorce papers, so that he could marry Nargis, but his family won him over at the last minute.

While they were teaming together, he insisted that she should not act in film companies other than R.K. Films and began controlling her shooting schedule. This created problems for producers like Mehboob who was planning to feature Nargis in his *Aan* (1952). Similarly, when K. Asif was planning *Mughal-e-Azam* (1960) he tried to sign up Nargis for the role of Anarkali, but Raj Kapoor thwarted it. During the shooting of *Chori Chori*

(1956) in Madras (now Chennai), their relationship came under some strain, particularly when Raj Kapoor began developing an interest in a south Indian actress. Nargis soon took a decision to end the relationship. *Jagte Raho* (1956) in which she had a cameo role at the end, a climactic image of a nameless woman in a white sari giving the fugitive (Raj Kapoor) a drink of water, was the last film in which she appeared with him. Though in many of her memorable films she had teamed with Raj Kapoor, some of her best films, such as *Mother India* (1957) and *Andaz* (1949) were not made in R.K. Films and he was not the lead man in them.

THE IMAGE-DEFINING FILMS

Two films made in the 1950s can be pointed out as crucial to the screen image of Nargis: first *Awara*, and then *Mother India*.

In *Awara* Nargis plays the role of Rita, a lawyer who defends Raj (Raj Kapoor), her childhood friend, in a case filed against him for killing a criminal and for attacking a judge. In the opening sequence itself she pits her talents against the formidable Prithviraj Kapoor and as the film progresses continues to give a richly nuanced performance. Set in Bombay, the story revolves around a mother and her son who live in a slum and whose lives are in counterpoint to a judge and his daughter living in luxury. In many ways *Awara* was radical: it dealt with the slum-dwelling subaltern and a prison bird. It pointedly asks whether it is environment or heredity that shapes the character of a person. Based on a story by K.A. Abbas and V.P. Sathe, it proved to be a milestone film for Hindi cinema and was dubbed into many languages. By the time this film was made, R.K. Films had been built and a regular team had been formed by Raj Kapoor—K.A. Abbas for the story, Shankar–Jaikishan for music and Radhu Karmarkar for the camera.

The film proved to be a big hit at the box office, both in India and abroad. It was distributed in Russia and dubbed

into a number of languages. A number of girls in Russia were
even named after Nargis. In the Middle East the film played to
packed houses. T.J.S. George, Nargis's biographer, points out
that the duet in the boat scene was one of the best love scenes of
her career.[2] Her appearance in a bathing costume was pointed
out as one of the highlights of the film. Apart from Prithviraj
Kapoor, other cast members include Leela Chitnis and Shashi
Kapoor. Helen, then an unknown junior artiste, made an
uncredited appearance in the film.

For a long while, Nargis's films bore the stamp of her romantic
relationship with Raj Kapoor. However, it was with *Mother India*
that she established her identity individually and this marked a
major break in her career as well, catapulting Nargis to her
shining moment. It was a performance of a career that made
the film synonymous with the name of Nargis. A remake of a
successful film *Aurat* (1940), also made by Mehboob Khan, this
film was given an English title, a translation of the traditional
phrase 'Bharat Mata'. It tells the story of Radha, played by Nargis,
who lives with her husband, his mother and their three children
in a village that is virtually in the hands of a lecherous money
lender. Her travails and her indomitable spirit form the crux of
the story. It was a wrenching sentimental drama that kept the
moviegoers weeping and had come at a period when melodrama
was ruling the film scene.

Nargis won the Best Actress award at the Karlovy Vary
International Film Festival at Czechoslovakia, becoming the only
Indian artiste ever to win this award. It was her career's best
performance with her portrayal beginning as a young bride and
ending as an old woman. Film critic Subhash Jha wrote in 1988,
'More than the film it is the central character that has left an
indelible imprint on the face of cinema. *Mother India* is to Nargis
what *The Godfather* is to Marlon Brando and *The Sound of*

[2] See T.J.S. George, *The Life and Times of Nargis* (New Delhi:
HarperCollins, 1994).

Music to Julie Andrews.' Nargis did not shy away from essaying the role of an old woman, despite her perceived image of being a young star. One journalist compared this to Bette Davis getting her head shaven for her role as Queen Elizabeth in *The Virgin Queen* (1955). After *Mother India*, Nargis's image transformed from a romantic heroine to that of a long-suffering Indian mother. This did not diminish her star status in any way. In fact, it enhanced it, particularly after her entry into politics.

Ashish Rajadhyaksha points out that the plot and characters of this film became the models for some later films such as *Gunga Jumna* (1961) and *Deewar* (1975). It also set the pattern of removing the father from the scene quite early in the film itself so that there is undivided attention on the mother figure. Critic Raghavendra says that in this film, through visual echoes of the movie *Pather Panchali* (1955), tribute is paid to Satyajit Ray, against whom Nargis would launch a tirade in the Parliament years later. Shamu's mother returns from a sojourn to find her son having lost both his hands. This recalls Ray's film in which Harihar returns after a long absence to find that his daughter Durga is dead. The old woman's death is reminiscent of the scene of the death of old Indir in *Pather Panchali*.

Described as the subcontinental equivalent of *Gone With The Wind* (1939) and considered a national epic, *Mother India* did well commercially, but did not receive much critical acclaim. Mehboob Khan promoted this film by writing to various chief ministers. He managed to get a waiver on entertainment tax in Maharashtra but not in other states. Although *Mother India* did not win the top prize at the national level, it was nominated—though, at the time, this did not mean much—for an Academy Award in the Best Foreign Language Film.

Close on the heels of the success of *Mother India*, Nargis acted as Champa, a strong-willed village girl in *Pardesi* (1957), an Indo-Soviet co-production in Hindi and Russian, jointly directed by K.A. Abbas and V.M. Pronin. A period film, it was based on an authentic story about a Russian, Afanasi Nikitin, who in the

fifteenth century travelled down to India. In the film he meets
Champa through whose eyes he learns about India. The film
was symbolic of the growing ties between the two countries
during the Nehru era.

These two films marked the peak of her career and it was at
this point that she got married on 11 March 1958 to Sunil Dutt,
her co-star in *Mother India*. They had fallen in love with each
other during the shooting of the film in Gujarat. She recorded
in her diary, 'I can only pray to God to give me the strength
to bear everything smilingly and may my life be devoted in
looking after my husband's happiness. Always loving him more
and more. From today, I start a new chapter of life—may
God help me in this new road of life.' Subsequently, she lost
herself in domestic bliss and they had a son and two daughters,
Sanjay, Namrata and Priya.

Though she married a Hindu, she did not persuade him to
convert to Islam, as her mother had done when she got married
to Mohanbabu. In fact, Nargis had a very Catholic attitude to
religion. Temples and dargahs were equally important in her scheme
of things and she often visited both. Her visits to the nine-week
novena at Mahim Church in Bombay were well known. She was
devoted to Swami Muktananda and she, along with her family,
used to visit him in his ashram at Vajreshwari.

After a long break of nearly nine years since *Lajwanti* (1958),
Nargis acted in *Raat Aur Din*, produced by her brother Akhtar
Hussain and that was her last film. In the years that followed
very rarely did she participate in functions of the film world. In
1975 the Soviet Consulate in Bombay organized a function to
mark the thirtieth anniversary of Russian victory over Nazism
and Nargis was invited to speak. In 1976, in one of her unusual
public appearances, she spoke as the chief guest at the jubilee
function of the film *Jai Santoshi Maa* (1975) in Mumbai. In this
public appearance, which was made after a lapse of quite a
few years, she came with a tilak on her forehead which the
paparazzi did not fail to notice.

THE STARDOM

In the 1940s and 1950s, film producers heavily relied on star images and signed up prominent stars as insurance against commercial failure. The director came only after the stars. In the 1930s and 1940s, studios often had stars on their payrolls.

Nargis shone as a star in the 1950s, acting altogether in sixty-one films when the big studios were dominating the scene. It was a period before the cinema of Satyajit Ray and Mrinal Sen became widely known and appreciated. And it was before any trained actor from the film institutes came into the field to introduce new styles of acting. Nargis had developed her own distinct style.

As a child artiste she appeared in five films produced by Sangeet Movietones. Even in the first film she featured in the poster. In *Taqdeer*, her first film as an adult, she worked with an established senior actor like Motilal. Her subtle eroticism was different from any other actor of that period. It was clear that a new type of star had emerged. As Alexander Walker writes in *Stardom: The Hollywood Phenomenon*, 'It is always the first impact that should be examined in seeking the reasons for someone's rise to stardom.' Soon she was signed up for a film with the famous Ashok Kumar, before going full throttle on the highway to movie fame. Though she was only sixteen at this time, her rise to stardom was assured partly by her association with these stars. When she started acting with Raj Kapoor she was already an established stellar figure. In fact, film historian Neepa Majumdar points out that it is only after his association with Nargis and the films he teamed with her that he himself became a major player in Indian cinema.[3]

Nargis stood out from the actors of her times. She was convent-educated and represented the sophisticated, Westernized Indian woman. She read widely, from her favourite detective novels to plays like Eugene O'Neill's *Mourning becomes Electra*. Her screen

[3] See Neepa Majumdar, *Wanted Cultured Ladies Only!: Female Stardom and Cinema in India, 1930s–1950s* (New Delhi: Oxford University Press, 2010).

presence was pleasingly credible and her acting unstylized. She exuded a refreshing innocence. Few actors could express the delight of falling in love and being in love as she did with minimal effort, for instance, in *Shree 420*.

Through her, the star of Hindi cinema acquired a different screen image. She appeared in public with minimal make-up. While many stars entertained on the stage, during events like a 100th day of a film or anniversaries, Nargis never danced or sang on the stage. In fact she could barely dance and rarely danced on screen.

At the height of her fame Nargis dressed in white saris and was referred to as 'the woman in white'. But she would occasionally break the rule and draw attention. At the premiere of the film *Aan*, she came bejewelled and draped in a Benaresi sari, and stole the show.

There was always, day and night, a small crowd waiting in front of her house in Marine Drive to catch a glimpse of her as she set out for work. When she drove out in her car, some fans followed her in taxis. Even at the entrance to R.K. Films, a crowd waited to see her. In the 1950s, she bought an expensive low-seat sports car, a British made Riley, and had it painted black and white to make it even more distinct.

In 1949 during the premiere show of the film *Andaz*, there was an unprecedented number of stars and other luminaries from the Bombay film world and there was a big multitude in front of the cinema house. Nargis make a sneak entry through the back door. The disappointed crowd in front started chanting 'We want Nargis!' Mehboob Khan and Dilip Kumar appeared on the balcony and tried to quieten the fans. But they wouldn't give up and grew restive. Eventually, Nargis had to make an appearance and wave to the fans, like a monarch materializing before her citizens.

Her name featured with more prominence than Ashok Kumar's in the poster of the film *Deedar* (1951). Similarly, on the posters and in advertisements for the films *Mother India* and *Raat Aur Din*, her name appeared above the film title.

A number of writers have written the biography of Nargis.

Among these star memoirs the one by T.J.S. George is the most authentic and insightful.

THE LEGACY

By extending her area of functioning beyond films, Nargis gained for film actresses a new respectability. In a number of delegations to foreign countries she represented the film industry. In 1952 Nargis and Raj Kapoor formed part of a delegation of film personalities that visited the United States. They met with President Harry Truman at the White House. Later, she and Raj Kapoor also formed part of the delegation to the USSR in 1954 which included K.A. Abbas and Bimal Roy.

While she was on a visit to London, there was a screening of the film *Jagte Raho* and Peter Ustinov came for the show and met her. She also met Charlie Chaplin in Lausanne and spent two hours with him having tea. He had been her idol since childhood.

She retired from films at the peak of her stardom. She could have hung on to films, playing the role of mothers and aunts. That was how many actors managed to stay on. But she was sure of what she was doing. Talking about the years that followed her retirement, a journalist wrote in *Filmfare*, 'Mrs Dutt now spends her time fondly watching her husband rake in accolades.'

Nargis was awarded the Padma Shri in 1958, the first film artiste to receive that honour. She received the Best Actress Award—then known as the Urvashi Award—from the Government of India for her brilliant portrayal of a woman with multiple personality disorder in *Raat Aur Din*, her very last film. When her husband Sunil Dutt founded the Ajanta Arts and Cultural Group she worked with him. The group travelled to the Pakistan–India border and performed for the troops. For a short while she occupied the post of president of the Indian Motion Picture Producers' Association. But, finding it difficult to manage the affairs of the outfit, she resigned after a few months.

In 1972 she founded the Society and School for the Spastics which now has branches in numerous cities in the country.

When the Department of Posts issued a commemorative stamp for Nargis in 1993, in one rupee denomination, it had the emblem of the Spastic Society in one corner along with her profile.

Nargis's friendship with the Nehru family, right from the 1950s, was an important factor in her career and personal life. In 1948 she had met Jawaharlal Nehru at a reception at the Raj Bhavan and Nehru made it a point to meet her whenever he visited Bombay. This friendship continued with Indira Gandhi also. When she lost the elections in 1975, Nargis motored nearly 200 km from her shooting spot to be with Mrs Gandhi. Their loyalty to the Congress was so strong that the Dutts supported the Emergency. Her proximity to those in power came in handy on many occasions. In an ugly incident in London in 1976, she was charged with shoplifting at a Marks & Spencer store. Natwar Singh, then in charge of the British High Commission, intervened and she was let off with a light fine in the court. And because those were the Emergency years, he was able to ensure that the story did not spread in India.

In April 1980, when Indira Gandhi was PM, she was nominated as a member of Rajya Sabha. Earlier in 1959 she had been offered this position by Jawaharlal Nehru but she had declined it at the time as she had just given birth and preferred to devote herself to the routine of motherhood. But when the offer came again, she accepted it and took her role as a member of the Parliament seriously, representing the interests of the industry.

However, in one of her speeches in the Parliament she attacked the work of Satyajit Ray as a film-maker. She said that he was a peddler of Indian poverty. There was surprised reaction both from the press and fellow members of the Parliament at this unprovoked salvo. Reinforcing her views in an interview to the *Probe* magazine (October 1980), she said that Ray's 'films are not commercially successful. They only win awards.' This was in stark contrast to the earlier comments she had made while in London in 1958 on *Pather Panchali*. At the time she said, 'There had been several shows arranged by the Asian Film Society in London. Most of the people who had come there took a very depressive view of Indian films until they saw *Pather Panchali* and now *Jagte Raho.*'

In 1972 Nargis and Sunil Dutt had attended the Berlin Film Festival along with Satyajit Ray. The three were even on a cruise together during the festival. But things had changed in the 1980s. It was a period when the Bombay film industry was getting worried about what was described by some journalists as parallel cinema. Independent film-makers were making small-budget movies winning critical acclaim in and out of India and the trend was started by Satyajit Ray with *Pather Panchali.* This embarrassed many established film-makers from the industry. So the tirade of Nargis on the floor of the Parliament was very much in the interest of the film industry. Satyajit Ray never responded to this strike. Instead, he would say when she passed away, 'I have always greatly admired her.'

Before she could actively become an MP she fell ill when she was just fifty, afflicted with pancreatic cancer. She battled for months in a New York hospital. It was at this time that her son Sanjay's drug addiction became widely publicized, and so she had to struggle on two fronts. She was brought back to Bombay in March 1981. Her condition worsened here and the end came on 3 May 1981. Though she had not left any instructions about her funeral, Sunil Dutt decided to give her a Muslim burial and she was interred at Sonapur cemetery, along with her parents. The *Statesman* recorded in its editorial tribute: 'It is not easy to explain the importance of Nargis. Her most memorable quality was a rare combination of hard professionalism and quiet dignity. She represented a cinema which, though wholly commercial, had little trace of crassness.'

MY FIVE FAVOURITE NARGIS FILMS

1. *Deedar* (1951). Directed by Nitin Bose. Co-stars: Dilip Kumar, Ashok Kumar and Nimmi. A love triangle forms the basis of this story about childhood sweethearts. The film boasts of

a scintillating musical score by Naushad and contains some of Mohammad Rafi's best songs. But most memorable are the engaging performances by Nargis and Dilip Kumar. Incidentally, Bimal Roy edited the film.

2. *Awara* (1951). Directed by Raj Kapoor. Co-stars: Raj Kapoor, Prithviraj Kapoor and Leela Chitnis. Raj Kapoor's most famous film, this was based on a story by K.A. Abbas about a man on the wrong side of the law. Universal themes like love and loyalty, as well as the brilliant performances and some well-known songs make this an enduring classic.

3. *Shree 420* (1955). Directed by Raj Kapoor. Co-stars: Raj Kapoor, Nadira, Nana Palsikar and Lalita Pawar. Raj Kapoor's Chaplinesque character is further developed in this film, which centres around a man—and a nation—caught between tradition and modernity. It also contains the most popular song of the Nargis–Raj pair, sung in the rain, 'Pyar hua ikrar hua'.

4. *Jagte Raho* (1956). Directed by Sombhu Mitra. Co-stars: Raj Kapoor, Pahadi Sanyal and Motilal. A tale of a peasant who is mistaken for a thief, this story takes place over the course of a single night in Calcutta. Nargis makes a brief but stunning appearance in a white sari towards the end of the film in a song sequence.

5. *Mother India* (1957). Directed by Mehboob Khan. Co-stars: Raaj Kumar, Rajendra Kumar and Sunil Dutt. Nargis's career-defining role, and the one for which she will forever be remembered. The story revolves around Radha, a long-suffering farmer's wife and her two sons. The film takes the genre of melodrama to a whole new level, and remains one of the most popular films in the history of Hindi cinema.

SURAIYA

THE LAST SINGER-ACTOR

PRAN NEVILE

Suraiya, whose very name includes the word 'sur', was Hindi cinema's last illustrious singer-actor. Subsequently, this dual role—extolled by many talented performers who could both act and sing—was separated in the film industry with the emergence of playback singers. Starting out as a child artiste in 1942, Suraiya's career reached its peak by 1950. Her sweet, soul-stirring songs have dazzled audiences and continue to haunt music lovers even six decades later. Her voice and looks reflected the innocence and grace of a bygone era. In her heyday (1947–50) she became a rage and the highest paid artiste of her time. The 1950s are often referred to as the Golden Age of Hindi cinema when films were judged on the strength of their songs and music composers. Back then, the common formula recommended to producers who wanted to make a musical hit was to cast Suraiya and sign up Naushad or Husanlal Bhagatram who, using the fewest musical instruments, were able to bring out the melody of Suraiya's voice. Suraiya's career spanned a period of twenty years and she played the leading role with almost every famous star of her time—Prithviraj Kapoor, K.L. Saigal, Ashok

Kumar, Bharat Bhushan, Dev Anand, Mukesh and Talat. With a fascinating blend of dialogues and gestures as well as her mellifluous voice, she was able to enthral audiences of the time with her lively performances. Although she is no longer with us, the unforgettable Suraiya's voice and her vast repertoire of songs have become legendary and continue to delight millions of her fans everywhere.

Born in Lahore on 15 June 1929, Suraiya Jamal Sheikh was the only child of her parents. She was barely four years old when her family moved to Bombay (now Mumbai) to live with her maternal uncle M. Zahoor of Bhati Gate Group of Lahore, associated with theatre and cinema. He was then working in the Bombay film industry and later joined Prakash Pictures, Bombay. Suraiya attended school in the Fort area and received religious teaching in Persian at home. She never had any formal training in music but was fond of singing popular songs.

This was the time when the advent of sound had ushered in the talkies era of the film industry. The release of the first talkie, *Alam Ara*, in March 1931 had brought a revolution in the entertainment scene. From its inception, song and dance became the essential ingredients of Indian films. The songs for the first talkies were usually taken from the stage dramas based on classical music. This offered fresh opportunities to the singers and musicians of the time. With the phenomenal box office success of *Alam Ara*, a number of producers rushed to make their 'all talking, singing and dancing' films. They had to look for new actors and actresses with good voices and diction in Hindi and Urdu. The Anglo-Indian actresses who dominated the silent era were replaced with artistes from theatrical companies and also by professional singing girls accomplished in their art and used to singing in mehfils. Madan Theatres of Calcutta (now Kolkata), virtual leaders in the Indian cinema world (they owned a chain of cinema halls all over the country), surpassed *Alam Ara* within a couple of months with their two great hits *Shirin Farhad* and *Laila Majnu*. Their leading stars, Master Nissar and Miss Kajjan, both notable singers, soon became famous in the country. In Bombay, the singing actors included W.M. Khan, Master Bhagwan Dass, Ashraf Khan, Gauhar and Zubaida.

Most of the first-generation actors—Sulochana, Madhuri, Devika Rani, Durga Khote, Bilimoria Motilal and Ashok Kumar—though not particularly good singers, were made to sing as well as act in films. The mid-1930s ushered in the era of the singing stars led by the legendary musical genius K.L. Saigal, followed by Pahari Sanyal, K.C. Dey, Pankaj Mullick Surendra Nath, Kananbala, Uma Shashi, Shanta Apte and Khurshid. An important qualification for a singer-actor was a melodious voice, adequate training in classical music and proper diction in Urdu and Hindi. Early films, inspired by theatrical dramas, were loaded with songs. One film, *Inder Sabha*, had as many as sixty-nine songs. But the number dropped over the years and by 1940s the average number of songs came to around twelve only.

Suraiya made her debut as a child artiste in *Usne Kya Socha* (1937) with the help of her uncle Zahoor who was playing some minor roles in films. We come across his name in the cast of Prakash Pictures' films of 1939, namely, *Hukkum Ka Ekka*, *Bijli* and *Farzand-e-Vatan*. In 1941 during her school holidays, Zahoor—who had made up his mind to force Suraiya to work in the film industry—took her to the shooting of the film *Taj Mahal*, directed by Nanubhai Vakil. Noticing the innocence and charm of young Suraiya, Vakil selected her to play the role of young Mumtaz Mahal in the film. Around the same time, the upcoming music director Naushad happened to hear her singing in the children's programme at the All India Radio, Bombay, and was so impressed by her singing talent that he made her sing her first song 'Boot karun main paalish' for *Nayi Duniya* (1942). He gave her another chance the same year to sing as a twelve-year-old to playback for heroine Mehtab in Kardar's film *Sharda* (1942). This was that all-time popular number 'Panchhi ja peechhe raha hai bachpan mera', penned by the eminent lyricist of that time, D.N. Madhok, who wrote songs that were simple and yet had universal appeal. It was in this song that Naushad introduced for the first time the 'matka' rhythm, which made it very popular. Suraiya was so short then that she was made to stand on a stool in order to reach the microphone. Again in 1942 she sang for Naushad in Prakash Pictures' *Station Master*. Mehtab, who at first was hesitant about having the baby-voiced Suraiya as a playback singer, was so much impressed by her that she managed to have Suraiya again for her next two films, *Kanoon* (1960) and *Sanjog* (1961), both with Naushad's music. No one at that time could imagine that the dark, simple girl teasingly called 'Kalu' by Raj Kapoor, and without any training in music, would one day emerge as the Indian film world's leading singer-superstar.

As time passed, in addition to honing her singing talent, Suraiya slowly picked up the art of acting and also learned dance from the Bombay Talkies legendry entertainer Mumtaz Ali (father of actor Mehmood). She got her first chance as a singing star in the Bombay Talkies' Devika Rani–Jairaj starrer *Hamari Baat* (1943). Later in the same year there was J.K. Nanda's *Ishara* where she played the lead opposite Prithviraj Kapoor who was over thirty years senior to her and was somewhat embarrassed with this casting. With music by Khurshid Anwar the film was a big success for its hit songs, including the one sung by Suraiya—'Panghat pe muraliya baaje', memorable for its picturization of Prithviraj playing a sitar. After that there was no looking back; she was signed up for many singing and acting assignments. She had her first hit in K. Asif's *Phool* (1944). With an enchanting musical score by Ghulam Haider, this film signalled her true arrival on the scene.

Suraiya had the distinction and unique honour of co-starring in *Tadbir* (1945) with K.L. Saigal, the legendary singer-superstar who had created a sensation in Bombay with classics like *Bhakta Surdas* (1942) and *Tansen* (1943). Suraiya was a staunch Saigal fan and always dreamt of acting with him. In one of her interviews, Suraiya revealed that K.L. Saigal was surprised to see her in the studio and he told the director Jayant Desai that there was no role for a daughter in *Tadbir*. When told about Suraiya's singing talent he became fond of her and treated her as a daughter. Suraiya was lucky enough to sing a duet with Saigal in *Tadbir*. Saigal liked her voice and even recommended her to co-star with him in *Omar Khayyam* (1946) and *Parwana* (1947). According to Suraiya, she was scheduled to act with him in *Meri Surat Teri Ankhen* but when Saigal learned that the producers had changed the heroine he also left the studio. This shows that the legendary singer not only had great affection for her but also admired Suraiya's musical and acting talents. No wonder she is the only star having the proud distinction of playing the lead with K.L. Saigal in three films. Of these the most famous and admired was *Parwana*, released after Saigal's demise. In this film, Khurshid Anwar, the then leading music composer, turned every song into a hit. But he could not persuade Suraiya to record any duet with Saigal and he had to record only solos for each of them. No Suraiya fan can forget those sweet, melodious and emotionally charged popular hits: 'Jab tum hi nahin apne, duniya hi begani hai', 'Mere mundere na bol', 'Ja kaga ja' and 'Paapi papiha re pipi na bol'. Khurshid Anwar was full of praise for Suraiya for her perfect renditions of his compositions. Also it was a matter of pride and prestige for Suraiya to be known as the last heroine of legendary singer-actor K.L. Saigal.

During this period, Noorjehan had emerged as another superstar singer-actor in the film world. She had created a sensation with her impressive acting, soulful singing and glamorous personality. With the collapse of New Theatres, the retirement of melody queen Kananbala in Calcutta and decline of Khurshid in Bombay, there was no one to rival Noorjehan. Even Suraiya acknowledged Noorjehan's supremacy and is reported to have remarked that Noorjehan was born to sing while she herself was just lucky that her voice earned her some fame. Suraiya and Noorjehan shared a common Lahore background and were also gifted with voices to match their charming and lovely faces. Suraiya was overjoyed when they starred together in Mehboob Khan's musical *Anmol Ghadi* (1946), of which every song was a hit. Though overshadowed by the enchantress Noorjehan, it goes to her credit that Suraiya, albeit in a supportive role, was able to hold her own and make her presence felt with her superb performance and evergreen melodies scored by Naushad like 'Socha tha kya ho gaya', 'Man leta hai angdahi' and 'Main dil mein dard basa layi'. Noorjehan no doubt reached the zenith of her fame with her signature song 'Awaz de kahan hai', but Suraiya also won the audience's applause for her alluring portrayal of an innocent and diffident character. Again playing second lead, this time with Munawar Sultana in Kardar's great hit *Dard* (1947), Suraiya deeply impressed Naushad with her soulful rendition of his 'Beech bhanwar mein aan fhase hai'. In fact *Dard* was dominated by Suraiya and her every song was a hit, be it 'Dil dhadke ankh meri phadke, chale dil ki duniya ko barbad karke' or 'Hum thai tumare, tum thai hamare'.

The dawn of Independence in 1947 and the havoc of Partition led to the relocation of film-industry talent from Bombay to Lahore and vice versa. Suraiya was the only singing star who decided to stay back in India while Noorjehan and Khurshid left for Pakistan. As an actress Suraiya had an edge over her contemporaries like Nargis, Kamini Kaushal, Madhubala and Geeta Bali because she could sing her own songs. Though the system of playback singing had entered the scene, Suraiya—with her distinct individual style, her sweet, seasoned voice and clear diction—succeeded in captivating listeners. Her popularity knew no bounds. She surpassed all the heroines of the time. Suraiya's rise to fame between 1947–50 was indeed meteoric. Her biggest box office hits in quick succession were *Pyar Ki Jeet* (1948), *Badi Behan* (1949) and *Dillagi* (1949). The music for the first two was scored by the duo Husnlal–Bhagatram. They set a new milestone in film music by infusing their compositions with Punjabi folk roots, and their songs became superhits. We can still hear fans of old music humming some of those all-time great numbers from those films—'Wo pas rahen ya door rahen', 'Tum mujh ko bhool jao', 'Oh door jane wale', 'Tere nainon ne chori kiya' and 'Bigdi bananewale bigdi bana de'. Suraiya competed with Lata in *Badi*

Behan with equal success and, in fact, even more since her singing was integrated along with her superb acting and the alluring charm of her playful eyes. The famous Naushad also embellished Kardar's superhit *Dillagi* with her biggest hit 'Tu mera chand, main teri chandni' and also other all-time favourites penned by Shakil Badayuni like 'Nirala mohabat ka dastur dekha' and 'Tera khayal dil se bhulaya na jayega'. These songs were such great hits that the cinema stages would be showered with coins by crazy Suraiya fans as a mark of their appreciation. Besides, crowds of Suraiya fans would gather on Marine Drive in front of the Krishna Mahal building where she lived in order to catch a glimpse of her. This often led to traffic jams and police constables were even posted there to control the crowd.

These successive hits of Suraiya during 1948–49 placed her at the top of the ladder in the film world and she became a national rage. Suraiya's glamour was hailed by film scribes as comparable to the leading lights of Hollywood of the time such as Rita Hayworth, Lana Turner and Ava Gardner. Her fantastic popularity was not due to her singing alone but also her unique personality, her lifestyle, her femininity and her refined and courteous manners. Professionally, there was dignity and grace in her performance and she sang with her heart and soul. Lata was still plodding her way up in the playback business while Zohrabai Ambalewali, Amirbai Karnataki and some others, barring Shamshad, had faded away. Suraiya had therefore no challenge from any quarter and thus emerged as the highest paid star of that time.

During this period Suraiya appeared in some other films with music by Anil Biswas who was famous for his inventive musical scores. He gave some popular numbers in *Gajre* (1948) where Suraiya co-starred with the then famous hero Motilal. We still remember that haunting song 'Door papiha bola raat adhi rah gayi'. Biswas also composed music for Mohan Sinha's acclaimed film *Jeet* (1949) starring Suraiya and Dev Anand, in which Suraiya sang the popular number 'Tum meet mere tum pran mere'. Their other film *Do Sitare* (1951) was also handled by

Biswas. Here he made the best use of the jaltarang to lend special flavour to his compositions. Suraiya's two hits, 'Mere dil ki dhadkan mein ye kaun sama gaya' and 'Mujhe tumse mohabat hai', captivated the audience.

Suraiya blazed a new trail in *Dastan* (1950) where Naushad introduced Western musical instruments. Playing the lead with Raj Kapoor, Suraiya, by now a mature singer, gave the memorable hit 'Tariri yarari', a duet with Rafi. This was followed the same year by Navketan's *Afsar*, in which the music was scored by S.D. Burman. Suraiya co-starred with Dev Anand and the film was quite a success with two all-time favourite Suraiya songs—'Man mor hua matwala' and 'Nain diwane ik nahin mane'.

From 1952 onwards there was a downward slide in Suraiya's career. With the rising popularity of Lata Mangeshkar, who entranced one and all with her stunningly sweet voice, the glorious era of playback singing was now well established, and Geeta Roy and Shamshad also joined the bandwagon. This trend devalued a singing star like Suraiya whose hold on the audience dwindled on the music scene. Suraiya herself realized the superior competence of Lata while singing a duet with her in the film *Balam* (1949).

Suraiya continued acting and singing during the 1950s but the films did not do well. She played the lead with the singer-actor Surendra Nath in the film *1857* (1946), with music by Sajad Husain, which flopped even though Suraiya's songs, 'Teri nazar mein main rahun, meri nazar mein tu' and 'Game aashian satayega kab taq' were memorable gems. Suraiya did make a short-lived comeback in *Mirza Ghalib* (1954), produced by Sohrab Modi. Its success at the box office brought fresh laurels to Suraiya especially since she had bagged this role when other top stars of the time like Madhubala and Nargis could not. She played a Domni professional singing girl who became Ghalib's lover. It was not only her superb acting but also her lively and enchanting rendering of the poet's famous verses and the feeling she put into them that won her countrywide fame and also praise from no less a personality than the then prime minister Jawaharlal Nehru. It was the first feature film to be awarded the President's medal and the prime minister had graced the function with his presence and is said to have told Suraiya, sitting next to him, 'Tumne Mirza Ghalib ki rooh ko zinda kar diya.' ('You have brought Mirza Ghalib to life.') No doubt Suraiya showed her mastery in marrying music to poetry and immortalizing Ghalib's ghazals, namely 'Ye na thee hamari kismat', 'Aah ko chahiye ik umar asar hone taq' and 'Dil-e-nadan tujhe hua kya hai'. Musically, her performance was incomparable. No other singer has been able to surpass the greatness of what she had achieved in *Mirza Ghalib*. Suraiya just stunned the listeners and music lovers the way she sang the lines 'Humko unse wafa ki hai umeed jo nahin jante wafa kya hai'. The music director, Ghulam Mohammed, equally deserves credit for his amazing compositions in *Mirza Ghalib* which Suraiya enlivened with her golden voice. He had earlier composed for the Suraiya starrer *Kajal* (1948) without making much impact on listeners. But with *Mirza Ghalib*, Ghulam Mohammed came to be counted among the foremost music directors of the film world. His major contribution was the fusion of classical traditional ghazal gayaki with film geet. Unfortunately he achieved real fame only posthumously with his memorable music in that Kamal Amrohi's great classic *Pakeezah* (1972).

In 1954, Suraiya co-starred with the handsome singer Talat Mehmood in Waris. Barring one duet—'Rahi matwale'—which became popular for a while, the film had failed at the box office. By this time a whole new generation of actresses like Asha Parekh, Sadhana and Saira Banu had appeared on the scene and the era of films in colour was also ushered in. Bollywood films beagn to exhibit an increasingly Western influence. The heroines would appear in colourful modern outfits and dance around trees while traditional melodious music was losing ground. In this new environment, Suraiya was a misfit and so producers also distanced themselves from her. Besides, the playback singers now ruled the world of film music. Suraiya did appear in some films and sang appealing songs which, however, never became popular because the films flopped. There were haunting melodies like 'Mera dildar na milaya' in *Shama Parwana* (1954), 'Dhadakte dil ki tamana' and 'Aap se pyar hua jata hai' in *Shama* (1961). Finally, Suraiya sang her swan song 'Ye kaisi ajab dastan ho gayi hai' in her last film *Rustam Sohrab* (1963) with music by Sajjad Hussain. The film sank at the box office but Suraiya, breathing life and feeling into every word and note with her mellifluous voice, captivated listeners and this song figures among her all-time greatest hits. Ironically, her co-star in the film was Prithviraj Kapoor who, twenty years earlier, had been her hero in *Ishara*. Still in the prime of her life, Suraiya called it a day and retired from the film world forever.

For a critical appreciation of Suraiya as a singing artiste I would like to refer to Professor Ashok D. Ranade, an eminent authority on Indian music, and his definitive book, *Hindi Film Song: Music Beyond Boundaries* (Bibliophile South Asia, 2006). According to him, after Suraiya gained a firm foothold as an actress she sang only for herself, i.e., for her own roles in films. Ranade writes: 'Suraiya's voice is neither thin nor broad and its strength is clearly felt in the pronunciation of individual words, projection of line endings, and the facility with which she moves in the given tonal framework. Her voice does not enjoy remarkable range, but is adequate for a kind of singing which maintains a relationship of continuity with speech tone.' He points out that Suraiya was able to move quickly in between notes from higher to lower unerringly and quite smoothly. As a genuinely consummate actress and singer her voice impressed the listeners as a voice of a singer at ease. She also succeeded in doing vocal enactment effectively as expected from singer-actors as well as playback singers. Thus, Suraiya stands high in the first generation of singer-actors. And yet her renderings strike us as song-recitations and not as songs 'really sung'. Some responsibility in this respect lies with her composers. He concludes that 'Suraiya was instrumental in evolving the actress-singer category to a high standard'.

It should be interesting to note the remarks of late Naushad who groomed Suraiya into a superstar of her time. In one of his rare interviews published in the *Sunday Observer* (9 November 1986), he said that 'Suraiya, unlike other playback singers like Lata, Asha, Geeta and Rajkumari, was never basically a singer. She had never taken any lessons in music, but till date you will never be able to find a voice like hers. It has that "next-door appeal", a voice that bears a natural tonal quality. Of course, unlike other established singers her voice had a very narrow range and she needed a number of rehearsals but if you kept the defects in mind, she was unbeatable.' Naushad mentions that he had asked her around 1984 to stage a comeback but she politely turned down his request, saying, 'I gave up singing a long time ago. Today if I begin again, and if my voice is not up to the mark, the people who hear my bad voice will lose whatever respect they have for me. So please don't force me to stage a comeback.'

No story of Suraiya's life and career would be complete without mentioning the most noteworthy and much-publicized episode of her love affair with the then upcoming young actor Dev Anand in the early 1950s. It was then the talk of the town, the very stuff legends are made of. She was Dev Anand's heroine in seven films which had a moderate success but none of them was a box-office hit like her earlier triumphs of 1948–49—films like *Pyar Ki Jeet*, *Badi Behan* and *Dillagi* which zoomed her to the pinnacle of fame and popularity. Both Suraiya and Dev have spoken or written about their love affair. Coming from Dev's generation with a common Punjabi background, I would like to make an objective study of the whole affair in the context of the prevailing social and cultural milieu of the time.

There is a graphic first-hand account of the Suraiya–Dev romance and love affair carried by the *Star & Style* in its February 1987 issue. The author, Sheila Vesuna, who interviewed both of them, claimed that it was for the first time the two of them went down memory lane and recollected with nostalgia the tender romantic moments they shared. It was an attempt of the *Star & Style* 'to recreate the romance that had the whole-hearted involvement of all movie buffs of the time. Reportedly, Suraiya spoke reluctantly and that too after much persuasion. But when she did, her memories of those passionate days were crystal clear while Dev recollected his first love with a nostalgia that betrayed his outward indifference. The account contains fascinating details of their first encounter on the sets of *Vidya* (1948) when Suraiya was already an established star and he was a newcomer. Dev was smitten by her charm and she was also attracted by his youthful looks and slight resemblance to her matinee idol Gregory Peck. While shooting in a boat which capsized Dev managed to save Suraiya from drowning. This supposedly stimulated their mutual attraction which soon graduated into full-blown romance. Both were young and not mature enough—they labelled their romance an undying love—especially Dev, who expressed that he could not live without her. Suraiya hailed from a family akin to those of professional artistes in Lahore where young presentable girls were given intensive training in music and dance and groomed to entertain the elite. Their goal was to become gramophone and radio singers and seek a foothold in theatres and the upcoming film industry. Her uncle Zahoor and grandmother Badshah Begum had firmly decided to put her into the film industry and strive to make her a singer-actor after learning about her potential as a child artiste and a singer. For them there was no role or scope for marriage in this profession of climbing the ladder of fame and fortune. To them Suraiya was a treasure to be protected and distanced from all suitors. Rightly so, since in those times, marriage for an actress meant the end of a lucrative career.

It would be relevant here to cite the case of Malka Pukhraj, the legendary singer from Jammu and Lahore. After her exit from the J&K maharaja's court, her family set up an establishment in Lahore where the already famous singer became a rage and was invited to sing in mehfils for sumptuous payments and gifts. In her own words, 'There was no one at Lahore who danced or used dance gestures while singing like I did.' Her family too rejected all marriage proposals from a number of wealthy suitors. Finally, Pukhraj was courageous and bold enough to leave her wealthy family and chose to elope with Shabir Shah, a modest government official, whom she married. They were both mature and loved each other.

Suraiya was too young to decide for herself, nor did she have the courage to defy her grandmother and uncle who had nurtured her. Suraiya kept meeting Dev secretly and exchanging letters with the help of some film colleagues including Om Parkash, S.D. Burman and others. Dev was, however, restless and in his autobiography, *Romancing with Life* (Penguin Viking, 2007), he gives us an absorbing account of his memorable meeting with Suraiya on the terrace of her house since he was virtually threatened not to enter their house any more. Dev writes: 'We held each other in a long hot embrace. After a long silence that said everything we looked at each other. I wanted to protect her from all the evil that ever befell her. "Will you marry me?" I asked. She hugged me again and nodded, mumbling, 'I love you! I love you! I love you.'"

This tête-à-tête emboldened Dev to rush to Zaveri Bazar and buy one of the costliest diamond rings and send it to her through his cinematographer friend Divecha who was able to gain access to Suraiya's house. Suraiya was charmed by the ring and conveyed how much she loved Dev. Dev was full of joy, imagining that he was now engaged to her. For a long period, there was no more response from Suraiya's side. Even Divecha was denied entry to her house.

An objective study of Dev's marriage proposal shows that he was impetuous and not mature enough to understand the complexities of man–woman relationships. He was seemingly burdened with a small-town outlook and ideas imbibed in the Punjab mofussil. His two-year stay in the vibrant city of Lahore was too short a period for a small-town lad to learn the intricacies of growing up from boyhood to youth. He was not familiar with the customs and manners of the professional artistes, i.e., singers and dancers who strove to get a foothold in theatre and the film industry. Incidentally, Lahore was then the recruiting ground for the film industry which picked up artistes like Noorjehan, Munnawar Sultana, Khursheed and others.

Dev's very idea of a marriage proposal to Suraiya, the leading superstar of her time, appears naïve. Perhaps it was their strong physical attraction, mutual infatuation or even his common, misplaced Punjabi overconfidence that impelled Dev to propose to Suraiya. He was seemingly ignorant about the strong family bonds of professional artistes. The legendary Noorjehan continued singing despite her advancing years and poor health for the sake of her large family. Suraiya was under tremendous family pressure and was also acutely aware that she was the family's sole breadwinner. It is no wonder that, after considering the implications of such a matrimonial bond, its obvious repercussions on her growing career and her emotional ties and duties towards her family, Suraiya made the heartbreaking decision to reject Dev's proposal. According to Dev, Suraiya herself threw the ring far into the sea 'to sing songs about our romance to the rising and falling tides'. The end of this sad love story, however, proved to be a blessing in disguise for both of them. Suraiya was able to carry on with her profession, her fame skyrocketed and she eventually immortalized herself with her superb performance in *Mirza Ghalib*. Dev Anand, on the other hand, successfully climbed up the ladder of fame and dazzled audiences as the evergreen hero.

After her retirement, she led a lonely life and kept away from the film media as well as other major social functions. She neither accepted any offer to sing playback nor did she sing at private parties. She passed away on 31 January 2004, a lonely woman— her mother and grandmother having died several years ago and the rest of her family having migrated to Pakistan. It's a pity that after her demise, the media carried so many stories of her wealth and estate, her controversial heirs and not enough about her remarkable career as the last singer-actor of India.

My Five Favourite Suraiya Films

1. *Parwana* (1947). Directed by J.K. Nanda. Co-star: K.L. Saigal. Suraiya was fortunate to play the lead role in legendary superstar K.L. Saigal's last film. She gave a remarkable performance as a young girl of seventeen in love with a married man. This unusual and tragic story was enlivened with some haunting melodies scored by the eminent composer Khurshid Anwar. It featured some of Suraiya's greatest hits—'Jab tum hi nahin apne, duniya hi begani hai' and 'Papi papiha re pi pi na bol'.

2. *Badi Behan* (1949). Directed by D.D. Kashyap. Co-stars: Rehman, Geeta Bali and Ulhas. This was the greatest musical hit of its time. Suraiya, just twenty and already the most popular singer-actor, was even mobbed at the premiere of the film in Bombay. The film is most memorable for Husanlal–Bhagatram's beautiful music score, and features some brilliant songs of Suraiya's, namely 'O door jane wale' 'Vada na bhool jana', 'Tere nainon ne chori kiya' and 'Likhnewale ne likh di meri taqdeer'—most are still played in various All India Radio programmes—which amply display how Suraiya's mellifluous voice could at times even surpass that of Lata Mangeshkar who also sang some songs in this film.

3. *Dillagi* (1949). Directed by Abdul Rashid Kardar. Co-star: Shyam. A retelling of the legend of Heer–Ranjha, this film revolved around Suraiya and her dance and music. Naushad, Suraiya's mentor, made this film a great musical hit and Suraiya's every song came to be hummed even by beggars and hawkers, especially the evergreen numbers like 'Char din ki chandni', 'Nirala muhabat ka dastur dekha' and her all-time famous duet with Shyam, 'Tu mera chand, main teri chandni'.

4. *Dastan* (1950). Directed by Abdul Rashid Kardar. Co-star: Raj Kapoor. One of the biggest commercial hits of its time in which Suraiya played an orphan in an age-old tale of two brothers in love with the same woman. Her marvellous

performance overshadowed Raj Kapoor's not-so-impressive overacting. Besides, Suraiya by now was a mature singer and dazzled the audience with her 'Aa ra ri aa ra ri' which had a Western flavour. Other impressive songs include 'Ye mausam aur ye tanhai', 'Ai shama tu bata' and 'Nam tera hai zuban par'.

5. *Mirza Ghalib* (1954). Directed by Sohrab Modi. Co-star: Bharat Bhushan. Suraiya's comeback film in the mid-1950s, after a string of insignificant films, was noted for her most accomplished performance as both an actress and singer. It was even observed that the doomed love story in *Mirza Ghalib* was so close to her own devastating affair with Dev Anand that it stimulated her to put her heart and soul into her stirring performance.

DILIP KUMAR

AN EMPEROR AMONG ACTORS

RAUF AHMED

'He is the marker,' said Martin Scorsese of Marlon Brando. 'There's "before Brando" and "after Brando".' I think it's fair to say that about Dilip Kumar, the actor who initiated a significant paradigm shift in the art of acting in Hindi cinema in the late 1940s and dominated the scene through the '50s and the early '60s. The history of acting in Hindi cinema can be categorized into two distinct phases, 'before' and 'after' Dilip Kumar.

Dilip Kumar had happened to Hindi films by a quirk of destiny. He had never fancied being a film actor. He knew nothing about the art of film acting. He had just about seen a film or two when he was suddenly thrust before a movie camera. All he was looking for was a decent job to alleviate the financial mess his large family had gotten into, when the first lady of Indian cinema, Devika Rani, flung an out-of-the-blue offer at him. 'I didn't imagine that a chance meeting with Devika Rani would change the course of my life,' he reflected years later. It did much more. It changed the course of film acting in India, and redefined the way people looked at it.

The early talkies had been characterized by loud, melodramatic rhetoric and animated gesticulations peculiar to the popular

Parsi theatre of the time. Legends like Sohrab Modi and Prithviraj Kapoor had epitomized the best in 'acting' with their booming voices, exaggerated expressions and gesticulations. Actors like Motilal and later Ashok Kumar and Balraj Sahni did infuse a semblance of subtlety with their brand of 'natural' acting, but it was left to Dilip Kumar to give acting a new dimension. Through intelligent voice modulation and consistent underplay, he introduced a minimalist style, which, as a critic put it, 'lent a meditative resonance to film acting'. Maithili Rao, one of our best-known film critics, once wrote, 'Dilip Kumar created his own laboratory in the interiority of his being . . . and devised a new, subtle rhetoric of screen acting . . .'

Elaborating, Rao said: 'He towered like a mountain in the middle of Hindi film history, obscuring his predecessors and dwarfing his contemporaries.[1] Dilip Kumar bequeathed a readymade school for heirs who tried to appropriate his mannerisms without striving for the interiority that was integral to the man hailed as the emperor of acting.'

Mohammed Yusuf Sarwar Khan, known to the world as Dilip Kumar, was born on 11 December 1922, in Peshawar (now in Pakistan) to Ghulam Sarwar Khan and Ayesha Begum. He was the fourth of twelve children—six boys and six girls. They were Pathans who spoke Hindko, an amalgam of the Persian and Punjabi languages.

Yusuf was very attached to his family from whom he 'always drew sustenance'. He was the closest to his mother, 'a true companion' whom he adored as 'a fountainhead of love and understanding'. He was also attached to his brother Ayub Khan, older to him by two years, whom he looked up to for inspiration.

---

[1] Raj Kapoor laboured over his one-dimensional Raju, the would-be Chaplinesque tramp with an unvaryingly glazed expression to denote natural goodness. After the early straight dramatic roles, Dev Anand's debonair narcissism degenerated into the Noddy land of toothy smiles with body balanced at a gravity-defying angle.

Ayub had been bedridden for a long spell following a freak fall while riding horseback during a visit to Kashmir.

Ayub's insatiable quest for knowledge seemed to rub off on young Yusuf. He was into the best of English literature early in life, from Charles Dickens, Bernard Shaw and Shakespeare to Jane Austin, Emily Bronte and Guy De Maupassant. He was even known to be greatly interested in Karl Marx. Yusuf was particularly fascinated by the character of Heathcliff in Bronte's *Wuthering Heights*, whose inspiration could be felt in some of the early characters he played in films like *Arzoo* (1950) and *Hulchul* (1951) and much later *Dil Diya Dard Liya* (1966). He easily related to the melancholy of Maupassant as well.

Unlike most of his generation, Yusuf had absolutely no interest in histrionics. In fact, he was never drawn to dramatics at the school or college levels. He was more fascinated by outdoor activity, especially sports. He was an outstanding football player and was keenly interested in cricket. He recalls having dreamt of playing cricket for India and scoring centuries! Football, though, was his first love. In an interview to the annual edition of *Cinema in India* (1992) he had said, 'Soccer has been my first love, my passion. It inspires a spirit of healthy combat, to lead, to work your way through odds. I played football till I was 57. It helped me tremendously as an actor . . . gave me a strong, flexible body . . .'

He was equally brilliant at studies, passing his matriculation in the first division. With his fascination for the English language, he was keen to major in English literature at college, but his father insisted on him studying science. Disappointed, he decided to concentrate more on his football. However, there was a stumbling block. A strong Anglo-Indian lobby at Wilson College, Bombay, kept him out of the football team. Upset, he moved to Khalsa College, where he excelled as a football player. College life, however, was cut short in the third year when his father's fruit business ran into losses and the family's financial situation took a sudden dip. Recalling those 'difficult days' he once remarked, tongue-in-cheek, 'During the war, all businessmen made money but my father, honest and upright as he was, accumulated losses.'

Ghulam Sarwar Khan had relocated to India from Pakistan in the late 1920s in quest of greener pastures. It was the done thing in the Khan family for youngsters to venture out in search of fortune. A wholesale fruit merchant, Khan had left Peshawar and moved first to Calcutta (now Kolkata), then to Bombay (now Mumbai) in the late '20s. He bought a shop in Crawford Market in south Bombay for his business, and the family lived in two flats on the fourth floor of a building in the nearby Nagdevi Road. Much later they built a house in Bandra.

Yusuf found a job in the army canteen at Poona (now Pune) with the help of a family friend on a monthly salary of Rs 36. As assistant manager, his job was to run the store, keep accounts and interact with customers. His ability to speak fluent English endeared him to the Englishmen who frequented the canteen. To augment his meagre remuneration he set up a fruit stall next to the swimming pool frequented by the British soldiers. Yusuf had seen them bring fruits while coming to swim. On day one, he recalled having made a profit of Rs 22 in just four hours on an investment of Rs 40! Yusuf was delighted, but the joy was short-lived. With the advent of the Field Rationing Scheme, the canteen was shut down.

Even as he kept wondering 'what next?', something imponderable happened! On a trip to Nainital to buy fruits for his father's business, he ran into Devika Rani, who had just taken over the reins of Bombay Talkies following the sudden death of her husband Himanshu Rai. She was there with Amiya Chakrabarty, the director of her company's next film, *Jwar Bhata* (1944), looking for locations. Yusuf had no clue who she was, but she saw a potential star in the bright-eyed youngster. Would he like to work in films? she asked. He nodded and she asked him to see her in her office at Bombay Talkies in Malad, a suburb of Bombay.

As Yusuf recalled, his first encounter with Devika Rani in Bombay didn't raise any great hopes in him. So he got busy with what he'd been contemplating for a while: 'of setting up classy mobile tea-stalls all over Bombay.' Then came the crucial call from Devika Rani's office. 'In a matter of two hours I had signed a contract. Bombay Talkies had hired me as an actor on a monthly salary of Rs 500 with a raise of Rs 200 every year!' The first impulse was to rush home and share the good news with his brother, Ayub. 'I took him to a nearby restaurant. After a spell of uncomfortable silence, I broke the news to him. Ayub continued to sip his tea in silence, then looked away expressionlessly and said: "Good."' His brother's dispassionate response might not have matched Yusuf's excitement, but 'his approval was comforting'. Ayub's 'enviable poise and calm' had always had a 'soothing effect' on him.

'I idolized my brother, admired his cerebral and spiritual qualities,' he said. 'Prolonged illness and suffering had made him very calm.' The two would often go on long walks in total silence. 'He would intently watch the sun go down and express his joy in one word: 'Nice.'

A conservative Ghulam Sarwar Khan had a very poor opinion of nautankiwalas, which included film actors. He called them *kanjars*, implying pimps. He was never tired of taunting his close buddy Dewan Basheshwarnath Kapoor for letting his handsome son Prithviraj become a film actor. Shammi Kapoor once revealed, 'Yusuf's father would call my grandfather *kanjar da pyo*.' Yusuf knew his father would never let him become an actor. But Ayub took upon himself the task of bailing out his brother, at least for the time being. He told his father that Yusuf had found a good job with the Glaxo company! Ghulam Sarwar was pleased. 'Now you can get us Glaxo biscuits regularly,' he said with a smile. It was wartime and food products were in short supply, especially biscuits. Caught in a trap, Yusuf desperately looked for a way out, and found a close buddy who'd pick up packs of Glaxo biscuits from the black market almost every evening for Yusuf to take home!

It wasn't long before the bluff was called. Recalls Shammi, 'One day my grandfather saw a photograph of Yusuf's in a magazine and barged into Ghulam Sarwar's shop with it, demanding, "*Ab bol, kanjar da pyo koun hai?*" It took a long time for Ghulam Sarwar to get over the 'humiliation' his son had subjected him to.

Yusuf's first day on the set of *Jwar Bhata* was anything but memorable. For the first take, he was required to run and prevent the heroine from committing suicide. Midway through the shot, the director yelled for a 'cut'.

'You are running too fast,' he told him. 'The camera can't capture you.' Yusuf did get his run right in 4–5 takes, but there was a more daunting hurdle ahead. 'I had to hold the heroine in my arms and whisper tender words, which I found very embarrassing,' he reminisced. 'The heroine [Mridula] was a newcomer like me, but she looked calm and had a smile on her face, but I was in jitters! I continued to be ill at ease throughout the film. I kept feeling that a clever footballer had strayed into the wrong field. The ambience was totally unfamiliar, but there was no escape . . .'

His shy, timid demeanour had made him a reclusive of sorts during his early days in Bombay. 'When I came to Bombay to join college, I began feeling romantic. I was drawn to girls . . . and would strike silent attachments in my heart, but they would end there. I could not gather the courage to move towards them, to reach out and form a relationship . . . I was not the only lonely heart who was nervous to talk to girls . . . there were many. In frustration, we formed a league to run down the bolder types. We were jealous of them. We said they trailed the "chickens"—that's what we called them—because they lacked self-respect.'

Dilip Kumar's performance in *Jwar Bhata* evoked extreme reactions. Baburao Patel, the editor of *Filmindia*, a leading periodical of the time, and a feared critic, had blasted Devika Rani's new discovery as 'an anaemic edition to the roster of actors'. Continuing his vitriolic review, Patel wrote, 'He looks gaunt and famished and strikes as an ill-treated convict who has escaped from jail.' A review couldn't have been more devastating. However, *Cine Herald*, a film monthly published from Lahore, had a divergent view. Its editor-critic, Baldev Raj Chopra (who was to become one of India's most revered film-makers after Partition), was all praise for Dilip's performance. 'There is something unique about the way Dilip Kumar delivered his dialogues,' he wrote, 'which sets him apart from the other actors . . .' Motilal, one of the finest actors of his time, had found him very promising too.

Jwar Bhata didn't work at the box office, though. It was followed by another Bombay Talkies film, *Pratima* (1945), where Yusuf was cast opposite Swarnalata, who was fresh from a major blockbuster in *Rattan*, released the previous year. Pratima, in fact, was Yusuf's first film as a full-fledged hero. In *Jwar Bhata*, his role was parallel to that of Agha Jani, who was to later become famous as the comedian Agha. P. Jairaj, an established hero on the rolls of Bombay Talkies, had directed *Pratima*. 'I was surprised when Devika Rani asked me to direct the film,' recalled Jairaj. 'I had not directed a film before but she said, "Just follow the script."' Jairaj recalled his first encounter with Yusuf on the set of *Pratima*. 'His *tehzeeb* was endearing. He met me and his co-actors on the first day of the shooting and said politely, "Please bear with me, I am new to this profession."' *Pratima* didn't do well at the box office either. He had to wait until his third film, *Milan* (1946), for the tide to turn.

Directed by Nitin Bose and based on Rabindranath Tagore's story, 'Nauka Dubi', *Milan* made people sit up and take note of Dilip Kumar, the actor. He attributed his vastly improved performance to Nitin Bose, who ignited the creative fire in him. 'Nitinda understood me well,' he observed. 'By creating the right ambience, he helped me express myself freely.' Bose impressed upon Yusuf the virtues of understatement, which was to soon become the hallmark of the 'Dilip Kumar style'. He also talked about the power of silence in emoting. Dilip's association with Bose lasted over three decades. He directed Yusuf's home production, *Gunga Jumna* (1961), which saw him at his histrionic best, though it is common knowledge that Yusuf had called all the shots. A product of New Theatres, Calcutta, Nitin Bose had started out as a cameraman and shot the silent version of *Devdas* in 1928. As a director he had worked with the best of actors of the time, from Pahari Sanyal and Ashok Kumar to K.L. Saigal.

His fourth film, *Jugnu* (1947), where he was cast opposite the legendary singing-star Noorjehan, gave Dilip the first taste of big-time success. A runaway hit, *Jugnu* turned him into an overnight star! It was followed by four more blockbusters: *Nadiya Ke Paar* (1948), *Shaheed* (1948), *Shabnam* (1949) and *Andaz* (1949). For someone who had no grounding in histrionics, Dilip had hit a startling pinnacle in no time. Baburao Patel, who had savaged Dilip in his review of *Jwar Bhata*, was now effusive in his praise of him in *Shaheed*. 'Dilip Kumar,' he wrote, 'steals the picture with his perfectly natural delineation of the main role . . . Sensitivity and intelligent understatement are the outstanding characteristics of his acting . . .' Along with Raj Kapoor and Dev Anand, Dilip Kumar went on to dominate the marquee for the next two decades as the celebrated trinity!

Shaheed was special to Yusuf on an emotional plane as well. His father, who had shunned Yusuf for straying into the acting profession, finally forgave him and agreed to watch a film of his with the family four years after he had become an actor. He was very impressed by *Shaheed* and his son's brilliant performance. He had tears in his eyes when he watched the revolutionary played by Yusuf die at the end. He patted him on the back and made one suggestion: 'Avoid doing films where you have to die!' Yusuf could only chuckle under his breath. There was little he could do to change the destiny of the doomed characters that came in search of him! The runaway success of films like *Jugnu*, *Mela* (1948) and *Shaheed* had branded him the ultimate tragedian. Audiences loved to brood over his angst and despair. They came back to theatres in droves, again and again, to mourn his 'death'!

*

By the turn of the '50s, the shy, reticent Dilip Kumar, who had blushed at the thought of taking the heroine in his arms, had become the country's foremost romantic hero, who made female hearts flutter with his intense, eloquent glances and the sweet nothings he mumbled! As he candidly confessed, it had taken the 'lonely heart' a long time to break the shackles of self-doubt and free himself from the shell he had lived in. The first flush of love had done it for him!

'I am desperately in love,' he wrote. 'The vacuum I had been living in, without knowing the meaning of life, is now filled with warmth and exhilarating happiness . . . A friendly hand reaches out to me . . . leads me out of the jungle of doubt, fear and ignorance towards bright sunshine . . . and confidence . . . It is the richest episode in my troubled existence. Life had never been so beautiful.' He wouldn't identify the 'friendly hand'. But those in the know, like Sitara Devi, the legendary kathak queen who was once married to K. Asif, revealed years later that 'Uma [Kamini Kaushal] was the only woman Yusuf truly loved' and that he was 'completely shattered' when circumstances separated them.

Turning nostalgic about the 'fascinating early days' in Bombay, 'when life was leisurely and dream-like', he had once let out, in an unguarded moment, a fascinating nugget: 'The first-class compartments would be totally empty during off-peak hours, after 11a.m. . . . and we'd occasionally hop into a first-class compartment and travel blissfully from Malad to Churchgate and back, again and again, lost in ourselves . . .' He declined to decode the 'we' but from his oblique references it was easy to guess that his fellow traveller was Kamini Kaushal! They were the hot pair of the time. All the four films they had romanced in—*Nadiya Ke Paar*, *Shaheed*, *Shabnam* and *Arzoo*—had been hits, and the sizzling on-screen chemistry between the two had naturally spilled on to real life.

Uma Kashyap, a beauty pageant winner from Mussoorie, had made her debut as Kamini Kaushal in Chetan Anand's *Neecha Nagar* (1946), the first ever Indian film to win an international award (at the Cannes Film Festival). An emerging star, she had met Yusuf on the sets of *Nadiya Ke Paar* and the two had hit it off like a house on fire. The only hitch was that she had just married her brother-in-law, an officer in Bombay Port Trust, following the premature death of his first wife, who happened to be her elder sister, in the best interests of his two little kids by her sister! Kamini had to eventually turn away from Dilip under pressure from her family, especially a brother of hers, a hot-headed Army officer, who had threatened her with bloody consequences.

Dilip was smarting under the painful break-up when Madhubala literally barged into his life. The two had met on the set of *Tarana* (1951). With her impish exuberance she had charmed Dilip instantly. Legend has it that Madhubala had dramatically sent a red rose to Dilip through her hairdresser with a note in Urdu asking him to accept it only if he loved her! Though taken aback, Dilip had accepted the rose gracefully! Around the same time, Madhubala had been flirting with actor Prem Nath, her co-star of *Badal* (1951). When he came to know that she was playing for his friend Dilip, Prem Nath was said to have moved on.

The growing Dilip–Madhubala relationship, however, began giving sleepless nights to Madhubala's father Ataullah Khan, who began seeing disconcerting visions of the huge family's sole bread-winner deserting him. Madhubala had eleven siblings. With her hitting the purple patch early in her career, Ataullah didn't have to look for a job. Before relocating to Bombay, he had lost his job at Imperial Tobacco Company in Peshawar. To pre-empt any 'misdemeanour' on Madhubala's part, Khan began keeping a strict vigil on the lovebirds. His insecurity was said to have intensified when, for the first time, Dilip escorted Madhubala to a public event—the premiere of his film *Insaniyat* (1955). It was seen as an open proclamation of the relationship between the two. It was his insecurity that made Khan irrationally refuse to let Madhubala go with Dilip to Budni (near Bhopal) for an outdoor shoot of B.R. Chopra's *Naya Daur* (1957). The resulting wrangle led to her being replaced by Vyjayanthimala in the film and the matter being dragged to court.

Contrary to the sentimental expectations of Madhubala, Dilip stood by reason and testified for Chopra, all the while asserting from the witness box that he loved Madhubala and would continue to love her to the last day of his life. The imbroglio marked the end of one of the most talked-about love stories in Bollywood forever! It's a great tribute to the professionalism of the two actors that they shot some of the most memorable love scenes for *Mughal-e-Azam* (1960), including the now famous 'feather scene', when they were not on talking terms!

After the two traumatic experiences in love, Dilip Kumar, sometime in the mid-'60s, was said to have seriously contemplated settling with Waheeda Rehman, whose mature, cultured bearing had appealed to him. Waheeda had replaced Vyjayanthimala in *Ram Aur Shyam* (1967) after the latter chose to do Raj Kapoor's *Sangam* (1964). However, even before he could propose to her, the Saira Banu tsunami had hit him, turning his plans on their head. It's no secret that Saira's mother Naseem Banu had pulled off the Dilip–Saira marriage like a coup with great skill. As legend had it, she had been traumatized by the prospect of her daughter marrying a much-married actor with three kids!

After his whirlwind marriage to Saira, Dilip's life settled down a bit—until the sensational news of his second marriage to Asma caused a major upheaval. To be fair to the man, he had done no wrong. Hemmed in by too many family factors, he was looking for a breath of fresh air. It had come in the form of the beautiful Asma. Her eloquence and fascination for poetry and literature did the rest. But Dilip messed up a legitimate act by getting on the defensive and trying to fictionalize it when the media blew the lid off a dextrously guarded secret. Bizarre, verbose statements to the media (like 'it happened one night') drafted by a friendly journalist, whose thinking was stuck in a time warp, made a laughing stock of a complex but manageable situation!

*

Ghulam Sarwar Khan's advice to Dilip—to refrain from 'dying' in his films—might have been an emotional one, but the melancholic characters he kept playing in film after film did seem to affect his psyche. It had him reaching out to some of the best-known psychiatrists in business, including Dr W.D. Nichols, who had been a consultant to King George VI! The outcome: he was told to go slow on playing melancholic characters. Grim though it was, the situation had a positive spin. The hopelessness of the characters he was playing had begun to wear down an emerging generation of fans whose outlook on life was becoming optimistic. It gave Dilip an opportunity to extend his enormous histrionic range to the next level. The phenomenal success of *Azaad* (1955)—a Hindi remake of a Tamil blockbuster, *Malai Kallan*—which he had done reluctantly, was an eye-opener, just like Mehboob Khan's *Aan* (1952) before it, where he had played a swashbuckler with élan. Interestingly, released in the same year as *Devdas*—another iconic film of his—*Azaad* went on to out-gross almost all the films released in 1955! *Azaad* and *Kohinoor* (1960), which, ironically, had 'tragedy queen' Meena Kumari romancing him, brought out Dilip Kumar's incredible flair for comedy. Suddenly, he seemed to be relishing the range of roles he was now getting to play, like *Ram Aur Shyam, Naya Daur, Madhumati* (1958), *Leader* (1964) and *Gopi* (1970).

When Dilip's career ground to a halt in the mid-'70s in the wake of the failure of films like *Dastaan* (1972) and *Bairaag* (1976), the obvious assumption was that he was out of tune with a milieu dominated by a new breed of popular stars led by the likes of Rajesh Khanna and Amitabh Bachchan. But he came back with a vengeance in 1981 with producer-director-actor Manoj Kumar's *Kranti* to prove that talent, like the mind, never ages! In the post-*Kranti* phase Dilip reinvented himself to play the 'angry old man' to great effect in a series of films like *Vidhaata* (1982), *Karma* (1986), *Saudagar* (1991)—all with Subhash Ghai, the Showman of the '80s and '90s—as well as *Shakti* (1982), *Duniya* (1984), *Mashaal* (1984).

At the pinnacle of his career, the media had at times projected Dilip Kumar as the ogre who swipes the chair from under the director and takes over the film! He refused to discuss the 'insane' charge, nor was he apologetic about his 'participation' in the making of a film. 'They call it "interference" only when a film flops. I find it very amusing!' When Salim–Javed obliquely referred to it while narrating *Shakti* to him, his response was candid: 'I do have my say whenever I feel that incompetence is taking a toll on a film I am a part of.' He made no bones about his desire to work on his role in *Shakti* to make it more credible. A decade later, Salim Khan wrote in the annual edition of *Cinema in India* (1992), 'When we saw the rushes of *Shakti*, we were amazed by the new dimension he had given the character [of the police officer] we had conceived.' Khan acknowledged the 'positive' difference it had made to a screenplay which they had believed was 'complete'!

Ashok Kumar, who had worked with Dilip in *Deedar* (1951), had this tó say about his young co-star's passion for perfection: 'Yusuf thought of every film of his as something to be converted into a landmark . . . [During *Deedar*] he would sit with the director [Nitin Bose] and work out details of each scene.'

Few know that Dilip had turned down *Naya Daur* (1957) when it was first offered to him by B.R. Chopra. In an interview to *Screen Weekly* in 1997, Chopra had said,

I had gone to Yusuf with writer Akhtar Mirza [and] the script of *Naya Daur*. Barely had I said, 'I have come with a great script . . .' he countered, 'Is it the one about a *tongawala*?' and added abruptly, 'Sorry Chopra Saab, I won't do it.' He had obviously heard that the script had been rejected by the likes of Mehboob Khan, Raj Kapoor and S. Mukherji. He didn't give me a chance to reason with him. I was very disappointed and went to Dadamoni [Ashok Kumar] the next morning. He liked the script, but said 'I'm too sophisticated to play a *tongawala*, go to Yusuf, he is the only actor who can pull it off.' I told him frankly that Yusuf had already turned it down. He said, 'Don't worry, I'll talk to him.' When I called Yusuf again he said he would come over to my house to listen to the script. After listening to it carefully, he said, 'We need to work on it together for 15 days.' I agreed. Those days he used to have a shack in Juhu. We sat there every day from 10 in the morning to 6 in the evening and discussed every scene, every action threadbare.

On the day of the *muhurat*, however, he dropped a bombshell. He looked at the outfits we had designed for him and said, 'I won't wear them.' I explained to him that we had gotten them designed on the lines of the clothes I had seen *tongawalas* wear in Lahore.' He thought over and said, 'Give me two days, I'll let you know.' He called me back the next day to say that he was ready to start shooting. Apparently, he had worn the outfits and enacted his scenes in front of a mirror to convince himself that he looked the character he was playing. That's Yusuf. I could have easily thought of his attitude as high-handed, but I understood his intentions. I have never seen a more conscientious actor in my long career. I know for certain that Shapoorji Pallonji, who financed *Mughal-e-Azam*, stood by the project for over 12 years in spite of the film going enormously over-budget, only because he believed in Yusuf. He knew that as long as he was involved in the film, it had a future. Time proved him right!'

Hrishikesh Mukherjee once shared with me a story which reflects on the human side of Dilip Kumar:

Those days I was working at a feverish pitch, shooting for my film *Musafir* during the day and editing *Gotama the Buddha* [a film produced by Bimal Roy and directed by Raj Bans Khanna] through the night. The pressure got to me so badly that I had a nervous breakdown. That evening Yusuf parked his Plymouth outside my house and called out to me. I told him I would change and join him in five minutes. He said, 'Just come out, we'll sit in the car and talk.' As soon as I got into the car he drove off, ignoring my protests. 'I believe you had a nervous breakdown,' he said. 'We are not returning to Bombay until you are fully fit.' He drove me straight to Khandala. We stayed there for three days in the clothes we were wearing, played cricket with stones and sticks, discussed poetry, literature, cinema and everything under the sun, and had a great time. By the end of the third day, when I felt good and was ready to get back to work, he brought me back. I cannot imagine any star of today being so concerned about a colleague. That's why he is so special to those who are close to him.

For stars down the years, from Amitabh Bachchan to Shah Rukh Khan, Dilip Kumar has been a muse they can rely on. Rajendra Kumar was never apologetic about modelling himself after 'the best actor in business'. Manoj Kumar, another die-hard Dilip Kumar fan, had changed his name (from Harikishen Goswami) for the screen after being inspired by Dilip Kumar's name in *Shabnam*, the first ever film he had seen!

That Dilip Kumar has been a benchmark for acting in India is best illustrated by an interesting incident during the making of Raj Kapoor's *Prem Rog* (1982), starring his son Rishi Kapoor. Raj was trying hard to create a certain 'mood' in a scene, but Rishi, a brilliant actor at all times, wasn't getting it right. After a few takes, Raj told his son, 'Chintu, I want Yusuf in this scene.' It took a while for Rishi to grasp what his father was driving at, but once he did, he got the act right in one take!

'Yusuf was the poorest among stars even at the peak of his career,' Hrishikesh Mukherjee had said in an interview to *Screen Weekly* in 1997, 'because he never did more than two or three films a year. And his choice was always guided by a good script and a good director, not merely a good role for himself or big money. It explains why he has remained an emperor among actors.'

MY FIVE FAVOURITE DILIP KUMAR FILMS

1. *Andaz* (1949). Directed by Mehboob Khan. Co-stars: Nargis and Raj Kapoor. A love triangle which takes a sardonic dig at 'Western' morality and thrashes the possibility of legitimate platonic love, the film stood out for a virtuoso-like performance from Dilip Kumar besides its controversial theme. Dilip was just about six films old at the time. Even though both Raj Kapoor and Nargis were at their best as the couple in love, Dilip towers over them with a brilliantly calibrated range of expressions which gives his character with negative streaks a new dimension.
2. *Devdas* (1955). Directed by Bimal Roy. Co-stars: Suchitra

Sen and Vyjayanthimala. This film was in danger of paling before P.C. Barua's classic version (of 1935) starring the legendry K.L. Saigal. But if it didn't, it was essentially because of the compelling presence of Dilip Kumar in the title role. With his brilliantly nuanced delineation of the tragic, self-destructive protagonist who, weighed down by the compulsions of tradition, punishes the woman he loves intensely and himself, he ensures that the film didn't look out of tune with the '50s generation. Sharply etched in memory are two poignant scenes—one, where Devdas silently redirects mourners who come to him at the death of his father, and two, when he comes back from Calcutta and meets his childhood friend Parvati who has now grown up.

3. *Jogan* (1950). Directed by Kidar Sharma. Co-star: Nargis. As the title connotes, the film was a woman-oriented film dominated by Nargis, who plays a young woman who renounces the pleasures of living to attain a state of inner equanimity. Yet Dilip makes a lasting impression in the role of a young man who gatecrashes into the Jogan's life and ignites the natural impulses she had been trying to subdue, and sets off a storm within her. What set his performance apart was his immense capacity to convey the most complex of emotions with few words and spells of silence.

4. *Gunga Jumna* (1960). Directed by Nitin Bose. Co-stars: Vyjayanthimala and Nasir Khan. The theme of *Gunga Jumna* might have been rerun in varied versions over the years, yet the original stands apart for a flawless, brilliantly nuanced performance by Dilip Kumar in the role of the older brother Gunga, who is ranged against a cold-blooded self-serving system which makes a mockery of the law.

5. *Shakti* (1982). Directed by Ramesh Sippy. Co-stars: Amitabh Bachchan, Raakhee and Smita Patil. Dilip Kumar once again hit the histrionic pinnacle in the third phase of his career after a long hiatus. Ranged against the reigning megastar of the time, Amitabh Bachchan, he gave his role (of an upright

police officer) a new dimension with intelligently devised nuances, as admitted by Salim Khan of the Salim–Javed duo, who scripted the film. Legend has it that the night Raj Kapoor saw *Shakti* he woke up Dilip Kumar with a midnight call to say, 'There is just one Dilip Kumar!'

RAJ KAPOOR

AN ENDURING ICON

MEGHNAD DESAI

INTRODUCTION

Raj Kapoor (1924–88, born Ranbeer Raj Kapoor) was one of the three superstars of the 1950s along with Dilip Kumar and Dev Anand in what is agreed to be the golden decade of Hindustani cinema. He was the youngest and lived the shortest life of the three, dying at sixty-five due to asthma and cardiac complications soon after receiving the Dadasaheb Phalke award. The other two are pushing their way towards ninety. Along with Dilip Kumar and Dev Anand, Raj Kapoor defined the male ideal as far as the young of India of those days were concerned. When he rolled up his trousers in *Awara* (1951), that became a fashion norm as much as Dev Anand's quiff or Dilip Kumar's hair falling on his face in romantic sequences. Yet, unlike them, he became a director-producer early in his career and became a studio owner. R.K. Films was an achievement and a burden because it was financed out of Raj Kapoor's earnings. When a film flopped—*Aah* (1953), for example—it was Raj Kapoor who had to work double time, starring in films of dubious merit to make up the losses. Only this can account for some shockers such as *Kanhaiya* (1959), *Do Ustad* (1959), *Main Nashe Men Hoon* (1959) and *Chhaliya* (1960). Dilip Kumar, by contrast, could afford to be much choosier in what he acted in, and did no more than one film per year in the 1950s. Dev Anand had his brother's studio, Navketan, which he later made his own but at least the Navketan films he starred in did not place any burden on him by being flops.

It is this double burden—acting and being a producer and studio owner—which characterizes his output as an actor. There is a third factor no less important, at least till the mid-1950s, which marks his output. His partnership with Nargis was romantic in real life as much as reel life. For the sake of being together, they made some dreadful films together in the early 1950s— *Bewafa* (1952), *Aashiyana* (1952), *Amber*[1] (1952), *Paapi* (1953), *Dhoon* (1953), which are best forgotten, and *Anhonee* (1952) which was not bad. He made sixty-two films in all as an adult and three as a child actor.

RAJU AND RAJAN

Raj Kapoor is best known for his Chaplinesque Raju, a character he created who became a sort of everyman's orphan/tramp. From early beginnings in *Awara*, where the character is not yet fully defined, he explored the Indianization of Chaplin. By the time he made *Shree 420* (1955), Raju was fully fledged. He then made *Jis Desh Men Ganga Behti Hai* (*JDMGBH*) in 1960, in which Raju was a brand image, and *Mera Naam Joker* a decade later, which finally was the disastrous apotheosis of Raju. Somewhere in between was *Jagte Raho* (1956) where Sombhu Mitra built on the ingredients of Raju, but made him a lonely, almost tragic, figure.

There was a comic side to Raj Kapoor's acting before he invented Raju. This comes out in films such as *Sargam* (1950, with Rehana), *Dastan* (1950, with Suraiya) and also, of course, in *Andaz* (1949) where he has comic sequences with bagpipes which are also repeated in *Sangam* (1964). He kept up this clowning even

---

[1] A costume film—his only one, not counting the early mythological *Valmiki* (1946).

without the Raju mask in many films which he made later on such as *Chhaliya, Kanhaiya* and *Do Ustad.*

But he also had another image as a romantic hero—call it Rajan, the name of his character in *Andaz*—often in tragic roles. This aspect of his career became less well known and yet this is how he began. Kidar Sharma had hired him as an assistant director when Raj began his film career. It was Kidar Sharma who gave him (along with Madhubala) his first break in *Neel Kamal* (1947). Kidar Sharma had started in New Theatres in the 1930s with Devaki Bose and he wrote the dialogues and lyrics of P.C. Barua's great classic *Devdas* (1935). The highly stylized romantic characters that Kidar Sharma created for Raj Kapoor in *Neel Kamal, Bawre Nain* (1950)—as well as for Dilip Kumar in *Jogan* (1950)—belonged to his times at New Theatres. This romantic hero, much given to crying and losing, became obsolete once the audience began to prefer humorous and action-oriented heroes. Raj Kapoor adapted himself to that as well. But in his oeuvre, films such as *Aag* (1948), *Gopinath* (1948), *Barsaat* (1949), *Andaz, Bawre Nain, Aah, Sharda* (1957), *Nazrana* (1961) and even, to some extent, *Sangam* illustrate his acting ability as a tragic hero. A rare return to a sober and angry but tragic hero was in Ramesh Saigal's *Phir Subah Hogi* (1958), a film loosely based on *Crime and Punishment*, in which he acted with Mala Sinha. Raj Kapoor played Ram, a struggling young man with a kind heart who gets into trouble helping a sick boy and his alcoholic father while falling in love with the daughter. There are shades of *Awara* in this and he got a nomination as Best Actor for the Filmfare awards that year. In *Anari* (1959), Hrishikesh Mukherjee made him develop this Rajan character as someone who is a good person but gets hurt because of his honesty.

R.K. FILMS

As a producer-director and a showman, Raj Kapoor was outstanding. His earlier productions also featured himself as the hero. He was the star in *Aag, Barsaat, Awara, Aah, Shree 420, Jagte Raho, JDMGBH, Sangam* and *Mera Naam Joker.* His studio also made *Boot Polish* (1958) and *Ab Dilli Door Nahin* (1957) in the 1950s. After the flop of *Mera Naam Joker* he made *Kal Aaj Aur Kal* (1971) where he launched his son Randhir Raj Kapoor and *Bobby* (1973), in which he gave the lead to his other son, Rishi. *Bobby* was a hit which rescued R.K. Films. He then made *Satyam Shivam Sundaram* (1978), *Prem Rog* (1982) and *Ram Teri Ganga Maili* (1985). When he died his Indo-Pakistani production, *Henna,* was unfinished. Rishi Kapoor finished it and it became a great hit when it was released in 1991.

Raj Kapoor was also the first of the Indian film-makers whose films became a big hit in the USSR and other Eastern European countries. *Awara* was received with great enthusiasm and the title song became a sort of national anthem across many countries in the socialist camp. He also started the practice of shooting sequences abroad when, for *Sangam,* he went to Switzerland. In his films *Satyam Shivam Sundaram, Prem Rog* and *Ram Teri Ganga Maili,* he explored the limits to which the female form could be exposed in Indian films.

RAJ KAPOOR AS AN ACTOR

But it is as an actor that I wish to consider him in this essay. Raj Kapoor was trained as an actor in the theatre by his father, Prithviraj Kapoor, who ran Prithvi Theatres for many years out of the Royal Opera House in Bombay (now Mumbai).[2] Unlike Dilip Kumar, he never took to method acting, but was very theatrical in many of his films as, for example, during the long soliloquy in *Aag* on stage where he does not know he is being watched by the owner of the theatre, played by Prem Nath Barsaat. The film itself is also very verbose as he and Prem Nath discuss their rival philosophy of love. His outbursts in court in *Andaz* and *Awara* are theatrical bits of melodramatic acting.

[2] Raj Kapoor used this setting in his *Aag.*

His devastating good looks with a fair complexion and grey-green eyes made him a natural for romantic lead. Yet it is in slightly negative roles like the one he played in *Andaz*—of a husband who thinks he has been jilted—that he rose to fame. Mehboob Khan had the knack of getting the best out of his stars, as he showed again later in *Mother India* (1957) with Sunil Dutt. Rajan appears almost a quarter of the way through the film. But we see him in flashback as something of a comic man playing his bagpipes to annoy Nina, the heroine, played by Nargis. He plays the comic husband on honeymoon when confronted by a cobra that is attracted by his playing of the *been*. It is only later that the flash of anger is seen as he confronts Dileep (the character played by Dilip Kumar) and hits him with his tennis racket. This is a man who thinks he has been wronged.

Despite this role, Raj Kapoor refused to play a straight villain's role in Mehboob's next film, *Aan*; the role was eventually played by Prem Nath. Raj Kapoor also prevented Nargis from playing the lead in *Aan*. Mehboob could not repeat his trio of *Andaz* in his *Aan*. Raj Kapoor's own dream of a film with a love triangle was based on a story, 'Ghironda', by Inder Raj Anand. He too could not reproduce the magic trio of *Andaz* as by that time his possessiveness over Nargis would not allow him to let Dilip Kumar play a romantic lead opposite her. He eventually made it as *Sangam* with Vyjayanthimala and Rajendra Kumar.

But his heroes were also deviant. Dilip Kumar for his part refused to play negative roles even when he was playing a criminal as in *Gunga Jumna* (1961).[3] Dev Anand was like Raj in being willing to play the charming rogue, often on the wrong side of the law. Raj Kapoor's *Awara* became an iconic film. He portrayed a young man growing up in the slums of Bombay raised by a mother who is the abandoned wife of Judge Raghunath (played by his own father, Prithviraj Kapoor). Raj, as the character was named, is a small-time crook and gets into trouble but is not shy

---

[3] The two exceptions in his case are *Footpath* (1953) and *Amar* (1954).

to admit it—he even says so explicitly when he sings '*Main chor hoon kaam hai chori, duniya men hoon badnam*' in the duet 'Dambhar jo udhar mooh phere'. This crook character was followed in *Shree 420* by the naive young man arriving in Bombay who gets caught in the midst of a criminal gang. His one ability is to cheat at cards and this takes him to the sleazy top which he later regrets. It is in *Shree 420* that he imitates the Chaplin walk and dons the clothes of a tramp most explicitly.

Raju, as he evolved in these two films, became an orphan in his later avatars. Why a man who came from a closely knit family with a father and two brothers also in film-making should see himself as an orphan is a matter best left to psychiatrists. There is a rebellious anti-father streak in Rajan/Raju as we see in *Aag* and *Awara*, but by *Shree 420* he has jettisoned any family. In the song 'Mera naam Raju', the Raju of *JDMGBH* sings '*Mera naam Raju, gharana anaam*' ('My name is Raju, I belong to no home') and adds, about his singing,

> *Kaam naye neet geet banana,*
> *geet bana ke jahan ko soonana,*
> *koi na meele to akele me gana.*

(I make new songs which I sing to the world; if I find no one, I sing to myself)

The orphan is also a lonely man always seeking a family. The hero of *Jagte Raho* is nameless and indeed speechless till the very end. All he wants is a drink of water which he does not get till the very end.

Jagte Raho is probably his best acted film in the Raju genre. Under Sombhu Mitra's direction, Raj Kapoor was disciplined in avoiding the tomfoolery which he displayed in his other Raju characters. With no dialogue till the soliloquy at the end, he had to emote entirely by his expressions and he succeeds eminently in this. He is like a frightened rabbit throughout the film, slinking from one corner to another in the sprawling chawl, observing the absurdities of humankind yet unable to get a drink of water which is all he wants. The Raju of *JDMGBH* adopts the garb of the *Jagte Raho* character to a large extent, but is jollier. He is baffled by the dacoit families as much as he is in the urban chawl of *Jagte Raho*, but this time he resists and wins them over. The orphan acquires himself a family by persuading them to follow his ways, not theirs.

By the time *Mera Naam Joker* (*MNJ*) is made, the Raju character is overblown. The joker element which was a minor part of the character becomes major since he now plays a circus clown. The heavy make-up does not help and the character becomes maudlin rather than tragic. The theme of *MNJ* has parallels with his first film, *Aag*—a man's quest for his childhood idol/ sweetheart. In *Aag*, he is reunited with Nimmi of his childhood while in *MNJ* all his sweethearts come to his farewell performance. But the joker's jokes are as feeble as his finale—though others may contest this view.

It is Rajan who has a longer list of films to his credit than Raju in Raj Kapoor's oeuvre. This is partly because a Rajan-type character fits in with the usual tragic hero of Hindustani cinema. Raj Kapoor tried often to combine some humour with the tragic elements. Many films of the 1940s and in the initial years of the 1950s had a happy first half with the hero and heroine laughing and loving, and, after the interval, an angst-ridden second half with a good deal of crying and moaning. This pattern made for good songs which were more tragic than comic. Perhaps the last film in this mould was *Aah* which Raj Kapoor made after *Awara*, and by which time his fans were bewildered as to why the happy-go-lucky rogue of *Awara* had turned into a lachrymose lover. *Aah* was a throwback to his early Kidar Sharma days. It is well acted especially in the sadder parts, but the story did not appeal to the audience. His final journey to see his beloved (played by Nargis) getting married to his best friend (played by Pran) was an echo of the final journey of Devdas as he is trying to reach Parvati's village with the singing cart driver played by Prithviraj in *Devdas* (1935) and Mukesh in *Aah*.

The best film of this kind was the first film he directed and produced, *Aag*. His subsequent films have been much more popular and somehow *Aag* has not received its due recognition. But the sheer intensity of emotion he brings to the screen as an actor and as a director makes this film one of his best. *Aag* tells the story of a boy obsessed with theatre and his childhood girlfriend, Nimmi. She soon leaves town as her parents have to move. The boy grows up to be a youth still interested in dramatics and chasing another girl called Nimmi who, like his childhood friend, also leaves but to marry someone else. The young man fails his college exams and is thrown out by his father and drifts to Bombay. Here he meets the man who owns the theatre where he can realize his dreams. He casts a refugee woman who has had a searing past. She becomes his muse. He names her Nimmi but he discovers that she is the woman who is also the muse of his friend, the theatre owner, who is also a painter. He deliberately sets fire to himself and to the theatre. Despite his disfigured face he is married off, only to discover that his wife is his very first Nimmi, his childhood sweetheart.

To each of the two episodes of the grown-up man, Raj Kapoor brings great feeling. His passion for theatre and his love for Nimmi are constants. Kamini Kaushal (as the college sweetheart) and Nargis (as the woman who has just escaped the horrors of Partition) play the two Nimmis. Here it is Nargis who matches the intensity that Raj Kapoor brings to the role.

Barsaat continues the trajectory of the Rajan character—the sentimental, sensitive lover who refuses to follow his cynical friend played by Prem Nath in exploiting local Kashmiri women. The acting, however, lacks the intensity exhibited in *Aag*. It is Shankar Jaikishan's debut musical score which made the film a hit, not the acting. *Andaz* brings out the best of Raj Kapoor's acting talents in those early days. He is given his comic moments but it is his intensity as the suspicious husband which puts him up there with Dilip Kumar and Nargis in what is, for me, the best Hindi film ever made.

Few directors could actually instruct Raj Kapoor on how to deal
with his role, much to his own loss. The three directors who
did make him act against his grain and superbly are Mehboob
Khan (in *Andaz*), Sombhu Mitra (in *Jagte Raho*) and Basudev
Bhattacharya (in *Teesri Kasam*). The roles he played for Ramesh
Saigal (in *Phir Subah Hogi*) and Hrishikesh Mukherjee (in *Anari*)
are versions of Rajan and while both are superbly performed, they
don't extend the limits of his range. He either was his own director
even in *Aah*, which Raja Nawathe directed, or he ignored what the
director said in many of his later films with Nargis. The results
are mediocre, if not bad. The best of the 1950s' lot is *Anhonee*,
which K.A. Abbas directed, but even here it is Nargis who scores
with the double role. Raj Kapoor is just a prop for her acting. This
may be one reason why he soon stopped casting Nargis as the
sole heroine. After *Awara*, she had to share the female lead with
Nadira in *Shree 420*, with Vijayalakshmi in *Aah* and by the
time we get to *Jagte Raho* she is totally marginalized with a
cameo appearance at the end.

After Nargis, Raj Kapoor never found a muse to match
his own creativity. Padmini in *JDMGBH* and *MNJ* or even
Vyjayanthimala in *Sangam* and *Nazrana* do not bring out the
best in Raj Kapoor's acting. The films themselves do not match
his earlier films, especially *Aag* or *Awara*, in their quality.

It is Basu Bhattacharya's *Teesri Kasam* (1966) which is a real
blinder. Raj Kapoor had mostly played urban heroes. His rural
roles are few. *Jagte Raho* may count as one where a rural outsider
is trapped in the Big City. In *JDMGBH* Raju is rural and indeed
the whole film plays out in remote Chambal valley surroundings.
In K.A. Abbas's *Char Dil Char Rahen* (1959) he had a role in
a rural setting but this was a multi-starrer and his role was not
central to the film. But in *Teesri Kasam* we have a powerful story
of Phanishwar Nath Renu and Basu Bhattacharya from the Bimal
Roy stable as director with Shailendra as producer. Raj Kapoor
plays a bullock-cart driver who carries various loads from one
location to another. He is a country bumpkin with no Raju

characteristics. Indeed none of his previous films prepare us for this Raj Kapoor. One presumes he did it as a favour to Shailendra. With Waheeda Rahman playing a nautanki artiste, there is a powerful match for Raj Kapoor. As the reluctant lover dragged out of his rural macho male self, he manages to combine humour, bravado and finally a sense of hurt at the strange cards destiny has dealt him. Even as he reaffirms his *teesri kasam* (third oath) about not transporting women we know that he has been deeply moved by the experience of having the nautanki woman in his bullock cart.

CONCLUSION

Raj Kapoor was an immense powerful presence across the twenty years (1945–65) which were the golden years of Hindi cinema. He enriched it as much by his acting as by his film-making. He loved, perhaps, too much but not too well. Yet he became the first global icon of Hindi cinema; the clown could reach out to everyone precisely because his gharana indeed was *anaam*. The world became his home.

MY FIVE FAVOURITE RAJ KAPOOR FILMS

1. *Aag* (1948). Directed by Raj Kapoor. Co-stars: Nargis, Prem Nath. This was Raj's debut film as producer-director, lead actor. Full of intensity which only a newcomer can bring to cinema.
2. *Andaz* (1949). Directed by Mehboob Khan. Co-stars: Nargis, Dilip Kumar. Mehboob Khan brought out the steely character in Raj's acting and made him play a rare part as a villain.
3. *Awara* (1951). Directed by Raj Kapoor. Co-star: Nargis. The iconinc film which defined the character of Raju and kept him chained in that persona forever. It also made him a global star.
4. *Jagte Raho* (1956). Directed by Sombhu Mitra. Co-stars: Pradeep Kumar, Sumitra Devi. Sombhu Mitra's experimental film stretched Raj Kapoor's acting ability to the utmost.

5. *Anari* (1959). Directed by Hrishikesh Mukherjee. Co-star: Nutan. An understated but great performance in which Raj Kapoor manages to play opposite Nutan without overwhelming her or being outclassed by her.

DEV ANAND

THE DASHING AND DEBONAIR LADIES' MAN

MADHU JAIN

It is way past dinner time for octogenarians. Dev Anand shows no signs of calling it a day. Frail and somewhat shrunken, he is barely visible behind a huge pile of papers on the desk in his office. Spread out before him are huge posters of the freshly resurrected and coloured version of *Hum Dono*, his 1961 classic film with Nanda and Sadhana. For a moment he seems stuck in the quagmire of nostalgia, time-travelling to his younger self with the trademark puff, flirty, sparkling eyes and nonchalant air that you see on the glossy posters of the film. Snapping out of the reverie, he sprints up and begins to talk, in his rapid-fire way, about his latest film *Chargesheet* (2011), which he has directed and also acted in, along with Naseeruddin Shah and Jackie Shroff.

Perhaps, the enduring hero simultaneously exists in two time zones. Internally, in his mind's eye he is still the lanky, dashing hero romancing Geeta Bali, Madhubala, Kalpana Kartik, Mumtaz, Nutan, Vyjayanthimala, Hema Malini, Sharmila Tagore, Zeenat Aman and scores of younger actresses. Dev Anand was no dancing lover: he literally walks through, rather elegantly, the song-and-dance sequences set to some of the most romantic songs in Hindi cinema. On the sets, in real life and real time, he holds the director's baton and keeps his Navketan banner fluttering on after over six decades. There are no intervals in his working life. When one film is over, it's on to the next one right away. If you get out of the habit of making films you will, according to him, no longer be able to make them. Were he to stop making films he might not be able to exist. His elixir of life is his belief in his own stardom and the limitless possibilities of the future.

During this meeting in 2011, he said to me, 'A star should never show himself as old in a film. He should not use a stick or have white hair or be stooped. It is not fair to those who come to see him on screen. He should always remain a star.'

The stars were certainly in his eyes that hot summer day in 1943 when Dev Anand hopped on to a third-class compartment of the Frontier Mail in Lahore to go to Bombay (now Mumbai) to become a film star. All he had with him was a 'meagre' thirty rupees and big dreams. Prithviraj Kapoor had boarded the Frontier Mail at Peshawar for Bombay nearly two decades earlier: the founder of the Kapoor film dynasty was equally determined to act. The train that connected the North West Frontier Provinces and Punjab to Bombay took countless young star-struck Punjabi men (including Dharmendra) to this citadel of cinema.

Born in 1923 in Gurdaspur, Punjab, Dev Dharam Anand was one of nine children. His father Peshauri Mal Anand, a prominent freedom fighter, was a leading criminal lawyer there. The world of cinema was not Dev Anand's first choice. Following in the footsteps of his elder brother, the late cineaste Chetan Anand, he went to the much-coveted Goverment College in Lahore, where he did his undergraduate degree in English literature. This was the abode of the elite where ambitions were seeded; but when they were not realized lifelong frustrations followed.

Inspired by Eric Dickenson, the erudite head of the English department of this prestigious college, Dev Anand planned to do a masters in English literature here before going to England to study at Cambridge University. He wanted to join the elite Indian

Civil Services (ICS) and become a pucca brown sahib. But when the time for him to enrol for his masters came, his father, on a financial downslide at the time, could no longer afford to support his third son's education.

Dev Anand also failed to realize his second choice of career. He was rejected for a commission in the Royal Indian Navy of the British Armed Forces. Interestingly enough, Raj Kapoor, attracted by the super-white smart naval uniform, too tried to join the Navy but failed to get selected. The glamour of the uniform attracted both men: they were good-looking men touched by narcissism—perhaps an essential ingredient for most actors. The Navy would have allowed them an entrée into a larger, more sophisticated and Westernized world.

Thwarted ambitions can be powerful spurs. When Dev Anand's father suggested he get a clerical job in a bank, he balked at the prospect. 'I shed a silent tear. A blank wall rose in front of me. It seemed that the river Ravi, on the banks of which Lahore prospered, had stopped flowing, and I was besieged by the thought of an empty abyss that was waiting to suck up a nonentity, who, before he could blossom, was about to fade away into nothingness forever. My mind revolted. My dreams took charge of the reins of my decision-making.'[1]

The dreams were larger than life. The Mecca of films was not waiting for him with open arms. However, unlike many aspiring actors he had somebody waiting for him at Bombay Central Station when he stepped off the Frontier Mail. Chetan Anand, master in Doon School in Dehradun, was visiting Bombay, and showed his younger brother the sights of the cosmopolitan city in a Victoria.

Success took its time coming. Like the other hopefuls lured by Bombay's Tinseltown, Dev Anand hung round the usual places, waiting to be discovered. Meanwhile, homeless and hungry,

[1] See Dev Anand, *Romancing with Life: An Autobiography* (Penguin Viking, 2007). All further quotes by Dev Anand, unless otherwise specified, have also been taken from this book.

he sold his precious stamp collection for Rs 30 to buy food. He worked briefly as a clerk in an accountancy firm and stayed in a chawl before finding a job in the Military Censor Office at Flora Fountain, where he earned Rs 165 a month, back then a respectable salary for a middle-class gentleman.

His job was to read the letters the Army officers wrote. One day he came across one in which the officer had told his wife that he wanted to quit: 'I wish I could chuck this job right now and rush straightaway into your arms.' That was the exit cue for the actor-in-waiting. He immediately resigned to, as he puts it, 'woo his destiny'.

Dev Anand started with a series of flops. His debut film, *Hum Ek Hain* (1946) was directed by P.L. Santoshi and had Durga Khote as his leading lady for Prabhat Film Company in Pune. The second film he acted in, *Aage Badho* (1947), was directed by Yashwant Pethkar. Four other rather indifferent films followed in Bombay, including Girish Trivedi's *Vidya* (1948) on the sets of which he met actress-singer Suraiya, the great love of his life, before he finally got lucky in 1948 with *Ziddi*.

Directed by Shahid Latif for Bombay Talkies and with Kamini Kaushal as the leading lady, the film was an instant success and Dev Anand came into the limelight as an actor—five years after he got off the Frontier Mail at Bombay Central. It was a chance encounter at Churchgate Station with Latif and his wife, novelist Ismat Chugtai (she wrote the script for the film), that led to his being cast in *Ziddi*.

More significantly, it brought him into touch with Ashok Kumar and his younger brother, Kishore Kumar, and Bombay Talkies. The partnership with Kishore Kumar was to be critical to the actor's success. Some of the most unforgettable romantic songs in Indian cinema are those he sang for Dev Anand. Interestingly, the first song of his career as a playback singer was for Dev Anand. He had just arrived in Bombay from Khanwa and *Ziddi* was his debut film. The first song he recorded was a ghazal composed by Prem Dhawan: 'Marne ki duayen kyun mangoon'.

Dev Anand's face and Kishore's voice fused amazingly in countless romantic songs. They 'complemented each other,' as Dev writes in his autobiography, adding, 'He always sang my songs with an eye on how I would perform them, and gave the necessary nuances to his voice with my acting style in mind.'

Prabhat Film Company might not have made Dev Anand a star, but it was here that he met and made friends with Guru Dutt, who was at the time assisting Vishram Bedekar at the Prabhat Studios. Curiously, a dhobi was responsible for the two becoming friends. He had mixed up their shirts. Theirs was another enduring creative partnership, one that was to serve both equally well. They shared a passion for cinema: Guru Dutt wanted to make great films and Dev Anand to become a great actor and star. The two even made a pact of sorts, solemnized by the clinking glasses of beer: Guru Dutt swore that Dev Anand would be his star when he became a director. The actor pledged in return that Guru Dutt would be the director of the first film he would produce.

And it happened, almost like that, some years later.

After *Ziddi* Dev Anand became a bankable star, with producers now seeking him. He asked one of them to give him an advance, which he used to launch Navketan, the film company he formed in 1949 with Chetan Anand. The elder brother's cinematic career had come to a standstill despite winning the Grand Prix for his debut film, *Neecha Nagar*, at the first International Cannes Film Festival in 1946—along with David Lean's *Brief Encounter* and Sven Nykvist's *Frenzy*. In the wake of the Partition, the film was not well received in India.

Certainly Dev Anand was ambitious for himself. But by unfurling a new banner he was not just repaying a debt to a brother who had helped him in his formative years, the actor was able to make Suraiya the first leading lady of the Navketan first production, *Afsar* (1949). An adaptation of Russian playwright Nikolai Gogol's *The Government Inspector General*, the film bombed at the box office.

Now at the helm of Navketan with his brother, the actor

also found the opportunity to deliver on his promise to Guru Dutt. He asked the director-in-waiting to direct Navketan's next film, *Baazi* (1951). Not only was the film a major commercial success—the first for the production house—it was a watershed role for Dev Anand. Clearly inspired by the film noir of '40s Hollywood, and based on a script written by the consummate actor Balraj Sahni, *Baazi* created the template for Dev Anand's ambiguous but charming trickster hero.

In this crime thriller he plays Madan, a small-time gambler, and somewhat of a low life. Drawn into the shady world of femmes fatales, gambling and night clubs, he becomes a sophisticated and rich gambler. He teeters on the wrong side of the law and allows pride and *la dolce vita* to get the better of him. But his heart is in the right place. And, of course, he redeems himself in the end.

Dev Anand's screen persona in *Baazi* of a likeable scoundrel, not to forget the cheekily placed beret on his head, went down well with the audience. The Indian film noir had found its hero. Not as sexily cynical as Robert Mitchum or sourly charismatic as Humphrey Bogart, Dev Anand managed to be 'dark enough' to make many of the desi noirs he acted in work. He acted in a spate of film noirs like *Jaal* (1952), *Pocket Maar* (1956), *C.I.D.* (1956), *Nau Do Gyarah* (1957), *Kala Bazar* (1960) and *Jaali Note* (1960).

After *Baazi*, Guru Dutt directed Dev Anand in *Jaal*, in which he plays a ruthless gold smuggler who disrupts the life of a peaceful community of fisherfolk in Goa. The protagonist's character in this film is not just dark but sinister. *Jaal* is based on an Italian film, *Bitter Rice*. The two friends had seen it together in 1949 and were impressed by the performance of Vittorio Gassman. The effervescent and sprightly Geeta Bali, who had acted in *Baazi*, starred in this film as well.

Guru Dutt's penchant for film noir and the anti-hero must have come from his mentor, Gyan Mukherjee, who had previously directed *Kismet* (1943), a phenomenal success with Ashok Kumar as arguably Hindi cinema's first anti-hero. Guru Dutt kept his side of the bargain by casting Dev Anand in *C.I.D.*, his first film as producer. Directed by Raj Khosla, the film in which Dev Anand plays a newspaper reporter accused of murder did well at the box office. The director effectively used some of the cinematic elements of film noir like chiaroscuro effects, low-key lighting and unusual camera angles.

Dev Anand has never been known as a great actor. However, he gave some very fine performances. He won a Filmfare Award for acting in Raj Khosla's *Kala Pani* in 1958; and he was riveting in *Guide* (1965), based on R.K. Narayan's novel of the same name. Dev Anand plays a guide in Udaipur with a gift of the gab who encourages a neglected wife (a sublime Waheeda Rehman) to realize her dream of becoming a dancer, only to exploit her when she becomes successful and rich. And, finally after being rejected by her, to find redemption by becoming a self-sacrificing guru.

Directed by his brilliant younger brother Vijay Anand, Dev Anand probably gave the best performance of his career, winning his second Filmfare Award for it. *Guide* also garnered several other Filmfare Awards, including Best Picture and Best Director. Dev Anand co-produced an English version of the film with Nobel Prize–winning American writer Pearl Buck.

Dev Anand's brothers directed some of Navketan's most memorable films. Chetan Anand's *Taxi Driver* (1954) and *Funtoosh*[2] (1956) were refreshingly different. *Taxi Driver* also broke new ground. On a shoestring budget, with no money for elaborate sets, Chetan Anand took the camera outdoors. It was a French Éclair camera. Since it was light they could attach it to the bumper of a taxi.

'Almost the entire story,' Uma Anand (née Chatterjee) writes in *Chetan Anand: The Poetics of Film*, was 'shot in the streets, on the beaches, through the palm groves and gullies of a remarkable

---

[2] The title of this black comedy was coined by Dev Anand; Kalpana Kartik and he call each other 'Funtoosh' in *Taxi Driver*.

character: the city of Bombay circa 1954. This feat earned the
city a separate mention in the titles.'

The film was immensely successful. Perhaps its very success
triggered the professional rift between the two brothers. Chetan
Anand wanted to form his own company and make his kind
of films. In his autobiography Dev Anand writes that Chetan's
'breaking away from the shackles of his younger brother's image,
desiring to achieve something on his own, was a natural corollary
that followed his acceptance as a viable box-office proposition.
Dev Anand had chanced upon an unposted letter Chetan Anand
intended for his wife in which he had written: 'There is a lot
I would like to do in this company, but Dev is my problem.'
Dev Anand then turned to Vijay Anand, and their fruitful
partnership began with the younger brother behind the camera.

The 1950s belonged to the triumvirate—Dilip Kumar, Raj
Kapoor and Dev Anand. They dominated the golden age of
Hindi cinema, dwarfing all the other actors who wanted to grab
a bit of the limelight. Dev Anand might not go down in the annals
of film history as a great thespian, unlike Dilip Kumar, the actor's
actor whose title of tragedy king has still not been usurped.
Nor was he a showman like Raj Kapoor, who was undoubtedly a
superior director and an actor known for the passion and intensity
he brought to his performances.

Dev Anand's enduring impact on cinema, however, is no less.
Inexplicably, Navketan Films didn't get the credit it deserves. The
Anand brothers (Chetan, Dev and Vijay) were responsible for
many of the memorable and path-breaking films that rolled out
from here. The production house brimmed with talent. But what
really sets Dev Anand apart from the others was his popularity
as a romantic hero, even one with dark sides to his character in
many of his early films.

The matinee idol was not only a crowd-puller; his persona
activated fantasy, allowed viewers to forget for a brief spell the
humdrumness of their own lives in entertaining films like *Paying
Guest* (1957), *Taxi Driver*, *C.I.D.*, *Jab Pyar Kisi Se Hota Hai* (1961),

Nau Do Gyarah, Tere Ghar Ke Samne (1963), *Jewel Thief* (1967), *Kala Bazar*, *Johnny Mera Naam* (1970) and *Hum Dono*.

Dev Anand incarnated the modern, urbane, Westernized and usually educated hero on screen. The country bumpkin or a variation of the Devdas prototype consumed by alcohol and obsessive love were not for him. There was a lightness of being in the way this gentleman-lover went about romancing his heroines. Most of his leading ladies from films of the black-and-white era had a certain lustre about them, one that had nothing to do with the lighting. Nutan, for example, has rarely glowed so ethereally, been so vivacious or appeared to be so charmed by a co-star as in *Tere Ghar Ke Samne*.

It wasn't just Dev Anand's textbook good looks. Tall, slight of build and handsome in his youth, he bore a nodding resemblance to American actor Gregory Peck. At least that is what Suraiya and many of his women fans believed. Nor was he dubbed 'debonair Dev' for nothing. Much of the persona that he evolved for himself had to do with his sartorial style: scarves tossed casually around his shoulders, full-sleeved, buttoned-up shirts, berets, all kinds of caps and, of course, his patented puff, which so many actors and young men emulated.

His mannerisms also set him apart from the others. Breezy, cocky and charming initially, these unfortunately fossilized into caricature. But at least through the '50s, '60s and a bit of the '70s this long-distance runner cast a spell with his charm. Nodding his head became second nature to Dev Anand's screen persona, an affectation picked up by many actors after him, notably Rajesh Khanna. He also evolved a different style of walking. Loping forward, he gives the impression of a man in a hurry to reach his destination or goal. Not blessed with dancing feet, he also walked through the song sequences, tilting forward and swinging his arms in tune to the music.

His signature mannerisms are also aural. The way he modulated his voice was distinctive: he often took it up to a pitch, and then slowly brought it down to enhance the intensity in his voice.

Dev Anand's rapid-fire dialogue delivery, like one of those rat-a-tat self-loading rifles, was also unique.

Dev Anand didn't just represent the quintessential modern, Westernized gentleman on the silver screen, he *was* one. Chetan Anand and his wife, Uma, who co-wrote the script for *Taxi Driver*, were significant influences in his life. The cosmopolitan couple opened up the rather conservative, small-town world he was born into. (His father was a strict Arya Samaji, and his mother had sent a five-year-old Chetan to a gurukul near Rishikesh for five years.)

The progressive couple's home at 41 Pali Hill in Bandra, where Dev Anand lived for a while and helped financially support, was a vibrant bit of Bohemia in the Bombay of the 1940s. A watering hole for intellectuals and artists, including those associated with the Indian People's Theatre Association (IPTA), it was also a chummery for those who had no place to stay. Zohra Sehgal lived here with her family, as did Balraj Sahni with his, for a brief spell.

Here Dev Anand must have heard Kafka, Sartre and Jean Genet discussed over daal chawal. Those who floated through included cineastes Guru Dutt, Mohan Sehgal, Raj Khosla, writer Raja Rao, poets Sahir Ludhianvi, Ali Sardar Jaffri, composers Ravi Shanker, S.D. Burman and a few disciples of Uday Shanker.

Modernity also manifested itself in the portrayal of women in Navketan Films, undoubtedly influencing Dev Anand's own take on women. The vamps were looked at with some measure of respect. Interestingly, the nightclub replaced the kotha as the site where the hero interacts with a non-conservative, non-familial world. Uma Anand puts it succinctly:

> The usual attitude towards women who dared, was conservative, even one might say, chauvinist. The vamp conjured up a vision of a short-skirted, cigarette-smoking, bob-haired, heavily made-up young woman named Molly or Maria who had a one-track mind: how to win by hook, but mainly by crook, the susceptible noble-minded hero. Not so with the Anand brothers. In *Baazi* with Geeta Bali, an actress of vital energy and flair, in Sheila Ramani in *Taxi Driver* and

much later with Waheeda Rehman in *Guide*, Navketan set the style of
the talented young woman of independent spirit, but more specially
of generosity of heart. In the actresses who played these roles they
were fortunate, being in their very different ways accomplished
performers, who often threatened to overshadow the insipid if more
respectable romantic heroine. They set the standard towards a
more sophisticated assessment on the left bank of society—the bohemian
or drop-out who gave herself the right to command the respect, if
not win the heart of the hero.[3]

Dev Anand has been described as a ladies' man. Justifiably, as
his uninhibited autobiography reveals. He is surprisingly explicit
about his sexual encounters with married women (on a train, in
a guest house, in the fields) during his early days in Bombay. It
did not take too long for him to shed his Arya Samaj conditioning.

The great love of his life was arguably Suraiya, the singing star
whom he met on the sets of Mohan Sinha's *Jeet* in 1949, and
later acted with in several films. He called her 'nosey', and she
called him Steve. Their 'love story' reads like a film about star-
crossed lovers. She was a Muslim, whose grandmother put an abrupt
end to the affair. Suraiya, who never married, threw the engagement
ring he had given to her into the sea to, as Dev Anand reminisces,
'sing songs about our romance to the rising and falling tides'.

Dev Anand met Mona Singh when *Baazi* was being made,
and famously married her about three years later by sneaking off
from the sets of *Taxi Driver* during a half-hour break. Chetan
Anand had discovered this sprightly young woman who had
graduated from St Bede's College in Simla, and renamed her Kalpana
Kartik. They acted in a few other films together—*Humsafar* (1953),
House No. 44 (1955) and *Nau Do Gyarah*—before she stopped
acting, called it a day, became a recluse—a bit like Garbo—and
disappeared into their home in Pali Hill.

Dev Anand's directorial debut with *Prem Pujari* in 1970, a

---

[3] Uma Anand and Ketan Anand, *Chetan Anand: The Poetics of Film*
(Himalaya Films Media entertainment, 2007) p. 59.

film he also produced and wrote, didn't fare too well, despite S.D. Burman's popular music and Waheeda Rehman as his co-star. However, the next film he directed *Hare Rama Hare Krishna* (1971) was a major success—as was Zeenat Aman. The film catapulted the former beauty, who had acted in a couple of indifferent films, to stardom.

Dev Anand introduced many actors, helped forge many careers, including Tina Munim's (the future Mrs Anil Ambani) in *Des Pardes* (1978). Sometimes, he fell in love en route. Zeenat Aman, with whom he worked in several films, was much more than a distraction. He was devastated when she pursued Raj Kapoor and snapped up the lead role in *Satyam Shivam Sundaram* (1978). He is quite candid regarding his feelings about her in his autobiography. 'While she as a person was God's creation, her image was of my making, and together we became inseparable in the public eye.' In his mind he was Professor Higgins, and she was his metamorphosing flower girl. Until Raj Kapoor came along.

Flops have never slowed down Dev Anand. The eternal optimist just picks himself up, dusts off his disappointments, both personal and professional, and continues to make film after film. Whatever the fate of his latest, *Chargesheet*, Dev Anand is already planning his next.

Sahir Ludhianvi's lyrics in *Hum Dono* aptly describe his philosophy of life:

Main zindagi ka saath nibhata chala gaya,
har phikr ko dhuen main udata chala gaya.

MY FIVE FAVOURITE DEV ANAND FILMS

1. *Guide* (1965). Directed by Vijay Anand. Co-stars: Waheeda Rahman, Leela Chitnis and Kishore Sahu. Inarguably a classic, Vijay Anand's inspired adaptation of R.K. Narayan's novel is an accomplished piece of story-telling that charts the journey to redemption of a small-town, glib guide with the gift of the gab and many grey shades in his character who accidentally

becomes a godman. With S.D. Burman's spellbinding music and memorable performances by Dev Anand and Waheeda Rehman, this classic film is also remarkable for its sensitive portrayal of a woman's need for sexual freedom. The songs remain etched in the mind: who can forget 'Gata rahe mera dil', 'Aaj phir jeene ki' or 'Din dhal jaye haye'?

2. *Taxi Driver* (1954). Directed by Chetan Anand. Co-stars: Kalpana Kartik, Sheila Ramani, Johnny Walker and Hamid Sayani. Necessity is also the mother of creative imagination. On a shoestring budget Chetan Anand, forced to dispense with expensive studio sets, took the film outdoors, using a light French camera attached to the bumper of the taxi Dev Anand drives. This immensely popular, quasi-neorealist film inspired by film noir, takes the viewers on a ride of the Bombay of the '50s, zooming in on its vibrant streetscapes, palm groves, beaches, gangsters and the working class—to the extent that the city almost becomes a character in the film and even appears in the closing credits. The film also has the unforgettable 'Jayen to jayen kahan' sung by Talat Mahmood. Zohra Sehgal choreographed this film, as she did many others for Navketan Films.

3. *Tere Ghar Ke Samne* (1963). Directed by Vijay Anand. Co-stars: Nutan, Rashid Khan and Harindranath Chattopadhyay. A delightful romantic comedy with Dev Anand at his debonair best, the film has an enviable lightness of touch, even while it addresses the gap between generations and the pas de deux between modern and traditional values—not to speak of the consequences of envy. Nutan is incandescent and uncharacteristically sprightly and coquettish, while Dev Anand (an architect in the film) is convincing as a romantic lover, with the chemistry between the lead pair charmingly palpable. Vijay Anand's genius is evident in the way he uses the camera, especially in the brilliantly filmed song sequences. Particularly memorable is the title song in which Dev Anand visualizes Nutan in a glass of whisky.

4. *C.I.D.* (1956). Directed by Raj Khosla. Co-stars: Shakila, Waheeda Rehman, Johnny Walker, K.N. Singh and Kum Kum. An accomplished nod to Hollywood film noir—chiaroscuro and dramatic camera angles—this stylishly shot urban crime thriller evocatively presents the demi-monde world of Bombay—its dark mean streets and dens of vice. There is even an ode to the city in the song, 'Ae dil hai mushkil', wonderfully enacted by Johnny Walker at his comic best. Waheeda Rehman makes her Hindi film debut as a vamp. O.P. Nayyar's music is exceptional as are Majnu Sultanpuri's lyrics, not to forget the voices of Geeta Dutt, Shamshad Begum and Mohammad Rafi in such timeless numbers as 'Aankhon hi aankhon mein ishara ho gaya', 'Kahin pe nigahen kahin pe nishana' and 'Leke pehla pehla pyaar'.

5. *Kala Pani* (1958). Directed by Raj Khosla. Co-stars: Madhubala, Nalini Jaywant and Sapru. Raj Khosla has brought out the real thespian in Dev Anand in this film which won the actor his first Filmfare Best Actor Award. The facile charm toned down, the mannerisms off-loaded, he brings intensity and conviction to his role of a son determined to clear the name of his father whom he believes was wrongly convicted for murder. Based on an A.J. Cronin novel, the film has some fine acting by Nalini Jaywant. Madhubala is effervescent, especially in the song sequence 'Achhaji main hari'. Like *C.I.D.*, the film is also inspired by film noir, with its effective use of low-key lighting and use of dark shadows.

MADHUBALA

ETHEREAL BEAUTY, ETERNAL ICON

URMILA LANBA

When I was invited to write about Madhubala I was delighted. Madhubala is one of my favourite actresses; my sister and I were only allowed to watch one movie a month and I recall we never missed her films, so we watched all her movies released between 1958 to 1960—*Ek Saal* (1957), *Chalti Ka Naam Gaadi* (1958), *Phagun* (1958), *Insan Jaag Utha* (1959), *Mughal-e-Azam* (1960) and *Barsat Ki Raat* (1960). She is perhaps the most beautiful actress of all time—her radiant smile not only lit up her face but her eyes as well. She also had a very attractive personality. I once met Raj Kapoor in 1963—it was before the release of his blockbuster *Sangam* (1964). On being asked whom he considered the most beautiful actress of the time, he said Madhubala. He said, 'She looks as if God has sculpted her from marble with perfection.' According to him she was a natural beauty who required no artificial aids to enhance her looks. I asked if he would take me to meet her when I came to visit Bombay (now Mumbai) and he was kind enough to say he would. I did not visit Bombay until the year 1980 and by then it had been almost twelve years since Madhubala passed away. Raj Kapoor made his debut along with Madhubala in Kidar Sharma's *Neel Kamal* (1947) when she was fourteen and he was twenty-three. The film did not create box-office history but gave Hindi cinema two great actors who ruled the silver screen for years to come. Even after their deaths both of them have gained iconic and legendary status—she as the most beautiful heroine ever and he as the greatest showman of Indian cinema.

Madhubala was born on 14 February 1933 to a Pathan couple, Ataullah Khan and Begum Ayeesha, in Delhi. She was their fifth child and altogether they had eleven children. Madhubala was originally named Mumtaz Jehan Begum Dehalvi. She was a beautiful child with a very happy disposition. She and her sisters loved dancing and spent their time enacting scenes from the latest films and imitating people to entertain themselves. Her father had lost his job with the Imperial Tobacco Company and was heavily in debt. One day he looked at young Madhubala and was struck by an idea—he would try to get his beautiful daughter to act in Hindi films. With this in mind he left for Bombay with his entire family. After many hardships and taking endless rounds of studios, Madhubala was given a chance by the then reigning queen of Bombay cinema, Devika Rani, the owner of Bombay Talkies. In 1942 her first film *Basant* was released. She played the daughter of Mumtaz Shanti, a very popular heroine of her time. The hero of the film was Ulhas. Madhubala was a beautiful child and had good screen presence; she was noticed and thus started her Hindi film career as Baby Mumtaz. She acted in several films as a child artiste—she got her break as the leading lady in Kidar Sharma's *Neel Kamal* opposite debutant actor Raj Kapoor. After that, she acted in twenty-four films in the first four years of her career—from 1947 to 1950—to take care of her family's financial needs. Her choice of films in this period was careless and many of these were rather forgettable films—*Chittor Vijay* and *Khubsurat Duniya* in 1947; *Amar Prem*, *Lal Dupatta*, *Parai Aag* in 1948.

But it was with Bombay Talkies's *Mahal* (1949)—a suspense thriller directed by the hugely talented Kamal Amrohi (his debut film as a director although he had established himself as a writer) and with haunting and melodious music by Khemchand

Prakash—that she became a star. Madhubala replaced the then reigning queen of Hindi cinema, Suriaya, who was charging a princely sum of forty thousand rupees. Madhubala was paid seven thousand rupees only for this film. *Mahal* was a huge success at the box office and is still a favourite that is regularly shown on TV as a classic while the music is still alive in the hearts of movie buffs.

The success of *Mahal* brought producers rushing to her with films opposite most of the big stars of that era—Rehman in *Pardes* (1950); Dev Anand in *Nirala* (1950), *Madhubala* (1950), *Aaram* (1951) and *Armaan* (1953); Prem Nath in *Badal* (1951) and *Saqi* (1952); and Dilip Kumar in *Tarana* (1951), *Sangdil* (1952) and *Amar* (1954). Unfortunately for Madhubala, although these films had the leading actors of that time, most of them failed at the box office. Even Mehboob Khan's *Amar*—despite boasting power-packed performances by Madhubala, Dilip Kumar, Nimmi and Jayant as well as very popular and melodious music by Naushad—failed at the box office. Madhubala went through a very bad period professionally and was labelled 'box-office poison'! She wanted to act in good films and with good directors. She was very keen to work with Bimal Roy, and was even considered for his *Biraj Bahu* (1955), based on Saratchandra's novel of the same title. She demanded her market price and Bimal Roy passed her over for Kamini Kaushal who received the Filmfare Best Actress Award for this film. Madhubala was very sorry and said she would have acted for free had she known she would lose the film for financial constraints!

Madhubala was a versatile actor and she proved her mettle in almost all genres of films being made at that time. She played a conventional lady in the swashbuckler film *Badal*, while in *Tarana* she played an uninhibited village girl romancing the heartthrob of millions and the reigning superstar of the time, Dilip Kumar. In this film, the two share some of the most romantic scenes seen on Hindi cinema. When I mentioned this to Dilip Kumar's brother, Ahsan Khan, he said that Yusuf Bhai was deeply in love with Madhubala at that time, so it was natural for the romance to transcend to the screen as well. She played the traditional Indian woman in *Sangdil*, an adaptation of Charlotte Bronte's *Jane Eyre*. Till date the song 'Ye hawa ye raat ye chandani' is remembered by music lovers, but Dilip Kumar serenaded the actress Shammi and not his lady love Madhubala in the song! Madhubala was appreciated for her comic performance in Guru Dutt's *Mr and Mrs 55* (1955). *Shirin Farhad* (1956) and *Rajhath* (1956) saw her in period get-up. She even played a double role in *Kal Hamara Hai* (1959), a tale of two sisters diversely different in character. One sister is the smoking-and-drinking dancer while the other is the conventional Indian girl, a paragon of virtue.

Madhubala was not the conventional goodie-goodie type of heroine of that era. She was natural and sensuous, she had glamour, she was coquettish and yet had a childlike vulnerability which was irresistible. She proved this in Shakti Samanta's *Howrah Bridge* (1958) with Ashok Kumar, where she played Edna, a club dancer who helps her beloved to avenge his brother's murder. In this film she spoke an Anglo-Indian type of lingo and projected a very Westernized image of a woman with open hair who wore deep-cut blouses, capri pants, Chinese-cut dresses. Madhubala's song 'Ayiye meherban', sensuously sung by Asha Bhonsle and equally seductively performed by Madhubala, was a big rage. In *Chalti Ka Naam Gaadi* she drives a car into a garage in the middle of the night completely drenched while looking sensuous and totally fearless of her vulnerability. In *Kala Pani* (1958) she played a daredevil, never-say-die journalist who helps her hero to prove his father innocent of murder charges with great spunk.

These films were followed by a string of hits like *Insan Jaag Utha* with Sunil Dutt, *Phagun* with Bharat Bhushan, *Chalti Ka Naam Gaadi* with Kishore Kumar, *Ek Saal* with Ashok Kumar and *Barsat Ki Raat* with Bharat Bhushan. But her ultimate brilliance came with the super success of *Mughal-e-Azam*. She reached the pinnacle of her career with this mega epic, acclaimed by critics and the public at large. *Mughal-e-Azam* ran for five years, a record which was broken only fifteen years later by *Sholay* in

1975. Subhash Ghai, the well-known film director, was attending a celebration of the fifty years of *Mughal-e-Azam* and he said, 'Till today there is no match to Dilip Kumar and Madhubala's ultimate chemistry on screen as the love legends.' The film, even after half a century, created box-office history when it was re-released in colour and stood its own against Yash Chopra's superhit *Veer–Zaara* (2004). Madhubala in black-and-white was magic but in colour she was stunning beyond words and breathtakingly beautiful. In 2011 Shahrukh Khan made a well-received documentary on the making of *Mughal-e-Azam* which shows the continued interest of moviegoers in the epic even after fifty years.

Although Madhubala was and is considered one of the most beautiful artistes ever seen on the Indian screen, she is also one of the most underrated actresses, as her beauty attracted more attention than her talent. She was a very fine artiste and could easily slip from playing a club dancer (*Howrah Bridge*) to a historical character (*Rajhath*), from a village girl (*Tarana*) to a modern girl (*Kala Pani*) with equal ease. She was good with comic roles in films like *Chalti Ka Naam Gaadi* to highly dramatic roles in *Amar* and finally her unforgettable performance as the doomed Anarkali in *Mughal-e-Azam*. That she never got recognition for her immense talent as an actress is evident by the fact that despite her power-packed performance in *Mughal-e-Azam* she was not given the Best Actress Award by Filmfare for this film; rather, it was given to Bina Rai for an average performance in the film *Ghunghat*.

Dilip Kumar felt that had Madhubala lived longer and selected her films with greater care, she would have been far superior to her contemporaries. Apart from being very versatile and an excellent artiste, she had a warm and cheerful nature. God had gifted Madhubala with so many things. Alas, God did not bless her with health and long life. However, she lives on in the hearts of film lovers even generations after her death.

Madhubala, who came from a humble background with no

formal education or any training in acting, became one of the most sought-after actresses in the early 1950s. She was avid about watching films; she would watch most of the good Hollywood films as well and taught herself to speak English. The early 1950s were glorious years for Madhubala. Her fame rose not only in India but she was also noticed by Hollywood and appeared in many American magazines. One magazine in August 1952, *Theatre Arts*, published an article about her that showed her as a mysterious and ethereal woman of mystical beauty with legions of fans. The article was titled 'Biggest Star in the World (And she's not in Beverly Hills)'.

During this period American film-maker Frank Capra visited Bombay and was wined and dined by all the important film personalities but he was looking for Madhubala. He wanted to meet her with the prospect of discussing an opening for her in Hollywood. Madhubala's father declined and put an end to her potential Hollywood career.

Madhubala's father never allowed her to make any public appearances, to the extent that she was not even allowed to attend the premieres of her films. He believed that actors should not appear too much in public so as to keep their magic alive. Perhaps it was this very elusiveness—the rare public appearances, her untimely death and breathtaking beauty—which has kept the magic of Madhubala still alive even forty-two years after her death.

Even today, Madhubala's name is synonymous with beauty. Till date one hears people exclaiming dialogues like 'Does she think she is Madhubala?' or 'She is certainly no Madhubala!' The name Madhubala in this context implies beauty—a beauty unmatched to date on the Indian screen, known as the Venus of the Indian screen. Her glamour, beauty and her smile have led to people comparing her with Marilyn Monroe. Perhaps her death at a young age, her unparallel good looks, keep her alive in the hearts of filmgoers and is remembered by film buffs as the most beautiful actress of her time and even today her fans remember her as the most beautiful, seductive woman with a million-dollar smile. The only other film actress who comes somewhat near her is Madhuri Dixit who also has a magical smile. When I was researching for Dilip Kumar's biography I had met the late Amjad Khan and he said, 'Yusuf Bhai and Madhubala had beautiful smiles and they made a great couple on and off screen.'

Madhubala's beauty touched whoever met her. Recently, Balasaheb Thackeray blessed his grandson Rahul, son of Smita Thackeray, whose directorial debut, the Marathi film *Raada Rox*, was going to be released. On this occasion he shared stories from his early years when he worked as production assistant. He said, 'On one occasion, while I was busy with my work, Madhubala happened to pass by me. I was dumbstruck and stared at her like a zombie. That one incident made my day and my work as an assistant worthwhile!' Such was the impact of her beauty on people.

Shammi Kapoor's first film with Madhubala was *Rail Ka Dibba* (1953). He once recalled with a sigh, 'She was beautiful, beautiful, beautiful!' He added that simply looking at her made him forget his dialogues more than once!

Madhubala lived with her parents and sisters in a large bungalow called Arabian Villa in Bandra. According to late C.V.K. Sastry of B.R. Films, Madhubala's father was very strict with his daughters and talked about them in a very derogatory manner. He said Ataullah Khan kept track of the dates of his daughters' menstrual cycles and hell would break loose if, heaven forbid, the girls were late even by a couple of days!

Madhubala, a warm-hearted, fun-loving girl, was always cheerful and laughing. Dev Anand did a total number of seven films with her and her last film to release in her lifetime, *Sharabi* (1964), was also with him. Dev Anand once told me that Madhubala was always laughing on the sets. When he asked her why she laughed so much, she would giggle even more and say 'I don't know!' Dev Anand said she looked happy and in good health and that he had no inkling of her illness during the making of *Kala Pani*.

Her much-publicized romance with Dilip Kumar—or Yusuf Khan, as he was actually known, the legendry superstar who ruled the Indian film industry for over five decades, the handsome, intense romantic—is still a topic of discussion among their fans and movie buffs. Perhaps this legendary romance is discussed as much as her beauty is talked about. Their romance is one of the enduring legends of Hindi cinema. It lasted for five years, from 1951 to 1956, beginning on the sets of *Tarana* and ending on the sets of B.R. Chopra's *Naya Daur* (1957). This fairlytale romance ended in a highly emotional and much-publicized court case pertaining to *Naya Daur* when Madhubala's father would not allow her to go for the shoot. He did not want his daughter to be away from Bombay for a long period with Dilip Kumar. So B.R. Chopra replaced Madhubala with Vyjayanthimala and Ataullah Khan then took B.R. Chopra to court. Dilip Kumar gave evidence in favour of the Chopras and against Madhubala. Madhubala was shattered—she could not believe that her beloved would go against her. But Dilip Kumar said that he took the side of the truth and the truth was with the Chopras. This love saga had all the ingredients that make a blockbuster film—drama, romance, conflict and tragedy. Two fascinating people loved and lost; and their love ended with Dilip Kumar's intense declaration in court that he loved Madhubala and that he would love her till his dying day! The press had a field day—never in the history of cinema had a top actor declared his love for a leading actress in a courtroom for all to hear!

Although Dilip Kumar and Madhubala fell in love at a time when film stars had some privacy and publicity was avoided, the fact remains that their love for each other was clearly visible on the screen—in Madhubala's eager eyes, her demeanor and body language—for all to see.

Prior to meeting Dilip Kumar, Madhubala was reportedly always falling in love. In fact they say she seemed to be in love with Love itself. Her name was linked with Kamal Amrohi, director of her first hit film, *Mahal*. Madhubala met Dilip Kumar on the sets of *Tarana*; Dilip Kumar was recovering from an intense and unfulfilled relationship with his beautiful co-star, a beauty with brains, Kamini Kaushal. Madhubala was just the kind of person he needed. She was like sunshine, a breath of fresh air, bubbling with life and totally bewitching. In turn Madhubala was swept off her feet by the handsome, romantic Pathan—totally in awe of him. You have but to see *Tarana* and it becomes obvious how involved the two of them were. He looks besotted, and she madly in love. Madly and passionately in love she was. It was not just good acting but something more; the sheer magic of their love comes through the screen for the world to see. Despite her laughter and playfulness, she loved Dilip deeply, although there were reports of her flirting with the dashing Prem Nath, her co-star of the film *Badal*, prior to this but her true love was Dilip Kumar. Prem Nath, a friend of Dilip Kumar, just moved away when he realized that Madhubala was seeing Dilip Kumar. Madhubala just adored Dilip; she was totally and madly in love with him and naturally Dilip Kumar found this irresistible. Gulshan Ewing recalls that in the early 1950s Madhubala thrust upon her the mantle of confidante. The many whispered conversations she had with her were all rustling with the same rhythm—Yusuf, Yusuf, Yusuf. She was so besotted the light of her love leapt out and dazzled everyone. She would squeal when his name was mentioned, she would blush and perspire when his presence was imminent.

Shammi Kapoor says that when he was shooting with Madhubala for the film *Naqab* (1955), Dilip Kumar would often drive in from Bombay with his friend K. Asif to be with her. He even came and spent Eid with her.

Although Madhubala never attended film premieres, not even her own, she did make an exception in 1955 for the premiere of Dilip Kumar's *Insaniyat*, which she attended with Dilip as her escort, thus making their romance public.

It was widely believed in the Hindi film industry that the stunning couple would eventually get married. *Filmindia* had even commented: 'Madhubala has found her soul at last in the company of Dilip Kumar.' Yash Chopra, the assistant director of *Naya Daur* who became a very good friend of Dilip Kumar, said it was a well-known fact that Dilip and Madhubala were in love, and that all believed that sooner or later they would get married. Madhubala had in no uncertain terms expressed her feelings for Dilip to Yash Chopra during the making of *Naya Daur*.

During the making of *Mughal-e-Azam* Dilip Kumar was in the habit of dropping in to see Madhubala even though he was not required for the shoot. If she was working, nothing was said and he stood watching; wordless glances were exchanged and he would leave, but his very presence was enough to make Madhubala happy. She looked forward to these moments with all her heart, her eyes searching for him constantly. And when she saw him, her day was made! Towards the latter part of the making of this film Dilip Kumar and Madhubala were not on talking terms—it is said that their most well-known and highly regarded love scenes were shot during this period of their conflict. Ajit, who had acted in many films with Madhubala and was a good friend of hers, told me of the shooting of a famous scene between Anarkali (Madhubala) and Salim (Dilip Kumar). In the scene Prince Salim is very angry with Anarkali and he slaps her. Dilip Kumar got carried away and slapped Madhubala vey hard. The slap brought tears to her eyes—she was not only in physical pain but was emotionally hurt as well. She complained to K. Asif, a good friend of Dilip's who knew about the love affair and stormy break-up of this star pair. He consoled her by saying, 'Yusuf must still love you; it was the action of a man in love expressing his anger!' Madhubala was pacified and perhaps happy that maybe Yufuf still loved her!

If romantic scenes of *Mughal-e-Azam* stand out as a class apart and continue to weave a spell on viewers even today, it is largely due to that spark of truth which runs through them and manifests itself via palpable undercurrent of passion. The same could be said of *Tarana, Sangdil* and *Amar*.

Madhubala loved only one man till the day she died, said her sister, Kaneez Fatima—and that was Dilip Kumar.[1]

---

[1] It was this tempestuous, larger-than-life romance that has kept the on-screen association of this couple alive in the public memory even today.

It was fairly easy for Dilip Kumar and Madhubala to meet each other as they were working together in a number of films. Soon, however, Madhubala's father heard about their romance and was not happy about it. Amjad Khan highlighted the irony of this: 'If anybody were to object about family background then it should have been Yusuf Bhai and certainly not Ataullah Khan. Madhubala's maternal grandmother was a dancing girl, so the objections probably had nothing to do with his eligibility but with the fact that Madhubala was supporting her family.' Dilip Kumar was not on good terms with Ataullah Khan. Madhubala and Dilip wanted to get married but her father opposed it. Dilip even agreed to take care of her family's financial needs on the condition that she break all ties with her father but Madhubala, although passionately in love with him, was hesitant to do so. On the sets of the film *Dhake Ki Malmal* (1956), Dilip Kumar called the late Om Prakash to be a witness to his proposal. He said, 'I have the qazi waiting at home, come with me now. I will marry you; my only condition is that you break all ties with your father.' Madhubala started weeping, recalled Om Prakash, and Dilip walked off in anger. Apparently this was not the first time she had let him down. He had now had enough and after this incident he never went back to Madhubala.

Madhubala did try to meet him again but Dilip Kumar was unrelenting and thus ended their love story. Bunny Reuben has said that when he went to meet Madhubala to write an article on her for *Filmfare*, she cried her heart out to him. When Reuben tried to convey this to Dilip Kumar, telling him that she still carried a torch for him, Dilip snapped, 'What bloody torch!' A friend of Dilip's sister's said that once when she was in the Khan

---

There is a website created by fans of Madhubala and Dilip Kumar called 'DilipKumarMadhubalaeternallyunited.tk' which contains many pictures of both stars together, as well as pictures cut and pasted from films in which they have acted with other artistes but which have been spliced together here! There are comments by their fans about them which are regularly updated.

home and heard that Yusuf Bhai had fever, she rushed to see him. When Apaji, Dilip Kumar's elder sister, came to tell him that Madhubala had also come to meet him, he was very angry and refused to meet her although Apaji requested him to see her for a few minutes.

After her break-up from Dilip Kumar, Madhubala moved on with other actors very reluctantly, and it was rumoured that Pradeep Kumar, Bharat Bhushan and Kishore Kumar were all trying to woo her and, as she could not have Yusuf but was keen to marry nonetheless, she chose Kishore Kumar. It was a disaster from day one and soon Madhubala was back home with her family. Her illness was first reported in the mid-1950s on the sets of S.S. Vasan's *Bahut Din Huwe* (1959) in Madras (now Chennai). She became ill and reportedly vomited blood in 1954. The incident was played down and soon forgotten. Ajit told me that while shooting for *Mughal-e-Azam*—in the scene when Anarkali runs away from Prince Salim after hearing that Akbar was approaching them and then runs back into the prince's arms—Madhubala fainted in Dilip Kumar's arms. They had to send for a doctor. The doctor who came to the sets and examined her diagnosed that she was suffering from a heart ailment.

Shammi Kapoor said that Madhubala was very sick while shooting for their last film *Boy Friend* (1961). As a matter of fact, she was not able to complete the film and her sister Chanchal had to step in to do her scenes. Shammi Kapoor also recalled how she matched her dance steps with him, and when Asif dropped in to meet her on the sets she apparently told him, 'Look at this boy's energy; even I get enthused to perform to his tune!'

After *Mughal-e-Azam*, Madhubala was offered a string of author-backed roles but her health had deteriorated so much that she was unable to accept any new assignments. She even went to London for treatment but the doctors there told her that they could not operate on her as her illness had advanced severely and that she had only one or two years left to live. Madhubala was devastated. She wanted to live and she did live for nine years after the doctors' verdict but the quality of her life was not good—she was lonely and virtually abandoned by the same film industry that used to surround her. Now, only few people came to visit her.

Sayeeda Khan, Dilip Kumar's sister, remembers Madhubala with great affection. She remembers her as a beautiful, slightly plump girl who was always smiling. She had been to see Madhubala a day before she died and she recalls Madhubala pleading with the doctors that she wanted to live, and that they should save her and not let her die. Sayeeda says she looked beautiful even in death; her skin, although pale with the strain of prolonged illness, glowed with inner beauty. Shakti Samanta, one of her favourite directors, later recalled that when he visited her he was really surprised to see her all decked up (usually she never wore any make-up). She told him that the illness had taken a toll on her looks and that she wanted him to see her looking good, hence the make-up. She cried her heart out to him and the next day Samanta read that she had passed away.

Madhubala acted in seventy films in her short life. She has often been compared with Marilyn Monroe, perhaps because, like Monroe, she too was a radiant film icon who died very young. Madhubala is one of the most enduring figures of Hindi cinema. In 1990, almost twenty-one years after her death, a poll was conducted by the magazine *Movie* in which Madhubala polled 58 per cent as the most popular actress of all times. More recently, i.e., in 2007, Rediff.com conducted a poll for the top ten actresses of Hindi cinema and Madhubala ranked second. The first place was marginally won by Madhuri Dixit. These actresses that made the final list were voted for on the basis of 'acting skills, glamour, box-office appeal, versatility and iconic status'.

Madhubala was honoured by Indian Postal Services on 18 March 2008 when a stamp was released in her memory. After Nargis, Madhubala was the second Indian actress to have a stamp dedicated to her. On this occasion, veteran actor Manoj Kumar said, 'Madhubala is the face of the country. There can be only one

Madhubala in one century. Every time I would see her, my heart would start singing ghazals. I am extremely lucky that I had the pleasure of working with her. I am happy and want to thank the department for their initiative.'

MY FIVE FAVOURITE MADHUBALA FILMS

1. *Mughal-e-Azam* (1960). Directed by K. Asif. Co-stars: Prithviraj Kapoor, Dilip Kumar, Nigar, Ajit and Durga Khote. One of my all-time favourite films, K. Asif's magnum opus took ten years in the making, with the actors being replaced several times. Now widely hailed as a classic, this is a heartrending love story in which everything—the music, sets, dialogues, costumes, power-packed scenes between Prithviraj and Dilip Kumar, the mesmerizing love scenes between Madhubala and Dilip Kumar—overwhelms the viewer. Madhubala performed beautifully as the lovelorn courtesan. The songs picturized on her have become legendary—'Pyar kiya to darna kya', in which she artfully questions the emperor, and the haunting 'Mohabbat ki jhuti kahani pe roye', which she sings in prison, as she is being enclosed in the wall. Truly mesmerizing!

2. *Mahal* (1949). Directed by Kamal Amrohi. Co-stars: Ashok Kumar, Vijayalakshmi and Kanu Roy. The film that shot Madhubala to fame in which she holds her own against polished actors like Ashok Kumar. Considered one of the first suspense/ghost films of the Hindi cinema, this was a very different film for its time—a tragic psycho-drama, a thriller which kept the audiences gripped till the very end. What remains astonishing is the film's visuals, unique use of lights and sounds, its alluring ambiguity and haunting music composed by Khemchand Prakash and ably sung by Lata Mangeshkar, Rajkumari and Zohra Bai.

3. *Tarana* (1951). Directed by Ram Daryani. Co-star: Dilip Kumar. I loved this film for its sheer magic and chemistry between the two leads—Dilip Kumar and Madhubala. This was the first

film that paired them together. A young doctor who finds himself in a village when his plane crashes there. He then meets the beautiful village girl who steals his heart. What follows is an exciting tale of romance. The film had some unforgettable songs by the talented Anil Biswas like 'Seena main sulag te hain arman' and 'Baiman tore naina'.

4. *Kala Pani* (1958). Directed by Raj Khosla. Co-stars: Dev Anand and Nalini Jaywant. Loosely based on a novel by A.J. Cronin, the film depicts a young man's crusade for justice to free his father from imprisonment. Madhubala plays a lovely and spirited news reporter who aids him. Brilliant performances and songs are the highlight of this film. Madhubala's song 'Achaji main hari' with Dev, sung by Asha Bhonsle and M. Rafi, was beautifully filmed. She also danced memorably in 'Dilwale ab teri gali thak aa pahunche'.

5. *Mr and Mrs 55* (1955). Directed by Guru Dutt. Co-stars: Guru Dutt, Lalita Pawar and Johnny Walker. A sophisticated romantic comedy, this film ably depicted the social concerns of the time—the Western influence on traditional Indian values. The film had sparkling wit and relied on intelligent repartee rather than buffoonery and slapstick comedy which was prevalent during this period in Hindi cinema. Madhubala displayed a flair for comedy and looked very beautiful as a young modern girl with her traditional values still intact.

MEENA KUMARI

POETRY ON CELLULOID

PAVAN K. VARMA

W hy do those who achieve unprecedented stardom have such abysmally unhappy lives? Born to an impoverished father, who left her momentarily in an orphanage after her birth, Meena Kumari wanted to go to school but was forced at the tender age of seven to become an actress; at twenty she fell in love with and married Kamal Amrohi, who was already married and fifteen years her senior, but it was a spectacularly unhappy marriage; she never had a child; divorced when not yet thirty, she had an unfulfilled liaison with two younger men, Dharmendra and Gulzar, both of whom 'respected' her, looked upon her as an idol rather than a partner, and moved on with their lives; she became an alcoholic and died of cirrhosis of the liver at the age of thirty-nine, heartbroken and penniless, with not enough money to even pay for her hospital bills.

Against this stark background of loss and deprivation, her cinematic career was dazzlingly successful. She acted in more than ninety films and achieved cult status in her own lifetime. Beginning with mythological and fantasy films while still in her teens, real fame came to her for her portrayal of the self-negating woman in *Baiju Bawra* (1952), for which she became the first

actress to win the Filmfare Best Actress Award in 1953. A series
of highly successful films followed, including *Parineeta* (1953),
Ek Hi Rasta (1956), *Dil Apna Aur Preet Parayi* (1960) and
Kohinoor (1960), to name just a few. 1962 saw her at her peak—
she was nominated for all three Best Actress awards for her role
in the films *Aarti, Main Chup Rahoongi* and the legendary *Sahib
Bibi Aur Ghulam*, a record never equalled since.

I have watched *Sahib Bibi Aur Ghulam* several times. It is a
deeply haunting story of a zamindar family unable to cope
with changing times, and of the personal relationships within that
family. Meena Kumari's role as the 'chhoti bahu', socially imprisoned
within the four walls of the haveli, will remain perhaps her
most powerful portrayal. In particular, her attempt to seduce her
philandering husband away from visiting the kotha—the traditional
and socially sanctioned pursuit of established and wealthy men—
has a sensual pathos to it that will never be forgotten. When she
sings 'Na jao sainya chhuda ke baiyyan' to her husband—played
by Rehman in the film—she is required to project a complex
duality: firstly, her lack of acquiescence in his being in the company
of other women, but, even more crucially, her own sense of
loneliness, frustration and sexual need. The message of physical
intimacy and need can be played with ease by a vamp. But for a
wife to convey it, especially in the claustrophobic and structured
confines of traditional society, required two opposites to come
together: explosively pent-up desire and minimalistic depiction,
uncharacteristic assertion and abject devotion. Under the directorial
genius of Guru Dutt, the scene where, after she has forced herself
to drink in order to dilute her inhibition and please her husband,
she lies in bed with her hair open, holding on to Rehman's
hand or throwing flowers at him to attract his attention, not entirely
in her senses but not beyond the pain of unrequited love and
physical longing, will forever remain a tribute to Meena Kumari's
prowess as an actress.

In all her films, the strength of Meena Kumari's acting was
understatement. For the many roles she played of the sacrificing

and exploited woman, she came to be regarded as the reigning tragedienne of her era. However, in all these portrayals there is a sense of restraint, of deliberately holding emotions in abeyance, of conveying more by doing less. Critics may even argue that this strength was her weakness, limiting her repertoire to the intense, controlled and emotionally underplayed actress. This becomes clearer if one compares her artistic canvas to the other reigning actresses of her era: Nargis was capable of greater histrionics (*Mother India*), Madhubala of lovable mischief (*Chalti Ka Naam Gaadi*), Nutan of playful dalliance (*Tere Ghar Ke Saamne*) and Waheeda Rehman of both ethereal beauty and anguish (*Chaudhvin Ka Chand, Pyaasa, Kaagaz Ke Phool*).

Did Meena Kumari allow herself to be typecast as the mascot of tragic roles? Commercial cinema is undeniably driven to replicate an actor's role if it is perceived to be attractive to audiences. Starting with *Baiju Bawra*, a series of films—of which the more notable were *Ek Hi Rasta, Bhabhi Ki Chudiyan* (1961) and *Dil Ek Mandir* (1963)—saw Meena Kumari extracting copious amounts of tears from an audience convinced that to suffer was her ordained destiny. Undoubtedly, she was good in this genre. Noted critic Bhawana Somaaya once said that she was one of the rare actresses who could look beautiful even when crying, and, even more importantly, could effectively deliver her dialogues with tears rolling down her face. Other actresses sought to emulate her or were in competition for such roles. It is believed that Waheeda Rehman wanted to play the chhoti bahu in *Sahib Bibi Aur Ghulam*, but Guru Dutt rightly felt that an older woman was more suited for the role, and only Meena Kumari could bring to the character the sense of doomed melancholy it required.

And yet, the truth is that when required, or when given the chance, Meena Kumari was more than capable of excelling in romantic and effervescent roles, including comic ones. Those who have seen her opposite the thespian Dilip Kumar in *Azaad* (1950) and *Kohinoor* (1960), or co-starring with Kishore Kumar in *Mem Sahib* (1956), or as the lead character in *Miss Mary* (1957), would vouch for the fact that the happier Meena Kumari had a light-hearted touch which was quite irresistible. It is a pity, therefore, that the appellation of 'Tragedy Queen' became attached to this actress, merging her reel life with the undeniable sorrows of her real world.

In any role—tragic, romantic, seductive or comic—Meena Kumari's strength was her almost perfect beauty. Her eyes, whether swimming in glycerine or radiant with laughter, were gazelle-like and remarkably expressive; her nose was chiselled to just the right dimension; her lips, full yet reticent, were the closest approximation to a rose bud; her complexion was pearl white. The result was poetry on celluloid. Perhaps the most evocative depiction of her beauty is seen in the song 'Piya aise jiya mein sama gayo re' in *Sahib Bibi Aur Ghulam*. She is in her boudoir completing her make-up and adornment in anticipation of her husband's arrival. The camera literally drinks in the perfect symmetry of her face, closing in on every detail, while two maids straighten her hair and wash her feet and assist her in wearing her jewellery. The most enduringly lyrical tribute to her looks was in *Aarti* (1962), where Pradeep Kumar sings these lines in the moving voice of Mohammad Rafi:

Ab kya misaal doon main tumhare shabaab ki,
Insaan ban gayi hai kiran aaftaab ki.

To my mind there is only one other portrayal in Indian cinema which so powerfully combines melody and poetry in evoking the mesmerizing appeal of a woman: the title song of *Chaudhvin Ka Chand*, again sung by Mohammad Rafi, in which Guru Dutt showers justified praise for an absolutely stunning Waheeda Rehman.

Interestingly, apart from her riveting face, there was little else physically to commend Meena Kumari. She was not fashionably tall, nor particularly buxom, and had put on too much weight much too fast on her hips. Without the beauty of her face, she would be considered, by the standard of today's actresses, to be almost dowdy. It was perhaps for this reason that in almost all her films she was 'overdressed', with the pallu of her sari round her shoulders or over her head, or in a gharara and kurta with even her hands covered. Even when this was not the case, the camera preferred to focus less on her physicality and more on the near ethereal beauty of her face. It was her face, and the expressions she could bring to it, that could launch a thousand films; and in the cinematic era of which she was the crowning jewel, audiences did not demand anything more, and considered even the asking to be vulgar.

Of course, like in any life, luck and happenstance were a part of Meena's life too. The lead role in *Baiju Bawra*, the film that catapulted her to fame, was first offered to Nargis. For some reason, Nargis turned it down, and by good fortune it fell into Meena Kumari's lap. She was lucky too to be picked up by directors who knew how to read the commercial pulse. But most importantly, almost every film that she acted in had a musical score that cast a spell over the nation. Every song of *Baiju Bawra* was a hit. It was the same with *Parineeta, Azaad, Ek Hi Rasta, Yahudi* (1958), *Savera* (1958), *Kohinoor, Dil Apna Aur Preet Parayi, Bhabi Ki Chudiyan, Sahib Bibi Aur Ghulam, Aarti, Dil Ek Mandir, Sanjh Aur Savera* (1964), *Chitralekha* (1964), *Bheegi Raat* (1965) and *Bahu Begum* (1967). It is important to remember that such musical megahits followed in quick succession, sometimes as many as two or three a year. In the space of this essay it is not possible to enumerate all the evergreen melodies, but to give just one example, who can ever forget Meena Kumari in *Dil Apna Aur Preet Parayi*, when she sings 'Ajeeb daastaan hai ye, kahaan shuru kahaan khatam?' It was a powerful scene, and her portrayal was not wanting; but it was the song that lifted her role on to the lips of every Indian, and ensured that both she and the film would remain part of cinematic history in perpetuity.

An important asset for Meena Kumari was her knowledge of and interest in Urdu and Urdu poetry. In the Urdu *tehzibiyat* that mostly defined the films of her era, this gave to her dialogue deliveries a chaste conviction often lacking in other heroines. In fact, she was a poet herself, and a collection of her writings was published, including an album, *I Write, I Recite*, where she has herself sung her compositions to the music of Khayyam. Not surprisingly, many of the most well-known ghazals of Hindi films have been filmed on her, and are memorable not only for their intrinsic worth but for their portrayal by an artiste who could effectively emote their meaning given her own deep understanding of the language and also the tradition and canvas of Urdu poetry. The lyrics she penned herself provide a window to an extremely sensitive, intelligent yet tortured soul. The compositions no doubt mirrored the anguish of her personal life and, in particular, her search for fulfilment in love. But they also indicate a high level of literary dexterity, quite amazing for a person who never really had formal education or respite from her frenetic shooting schedules. In fact, it is said that many of the leading actors of her time were wary of her intellectual high ground, and often found reason not to accept roles with her. She did act in some films with the ruling triumvirate of that period—Dilip Kumar, Raj Kapoor and Dev Anand—but a great many of her films are with B-grade heroes, of whom the one most often paired with her was Pradeep Kumar.

By 1964, Meena Kumari's personal life was in a shambles. She was already drinking heavily, a problem accentuated by her marital problems which culminated in a divorce with Kamal Amrohi. Ironically, this was the time when she was at the peak of her cinematic career. Two years earlier she had been nominated for the Filmfare Best Actress Award for three superb performances simultaneously, a feat never repeated since. But the growing hiatus between her glamorous public persona and her personal traumas were beginning to surface. It is useful to remember that although she had gone through so much, both in terms of her personal life and her film career, she was only thirty-two years old. Her decline had begun at an age when most people are as yet only preparing to lay the foundations of their future.

While her addiction to alcohol increased after her divorce, she continued to work in films, and added several successes to an already glittering career. These included *Sanjh Aur Savera*, *Kaajal* (1965), *Bheegi Raat* and *Phool Aur Patthar* (1966). *Kaajal* won her the Filmfare Best Actress Award for the fourth and final time, although she was subsequently nominated for *Phool Aur Patthar*, and posthumously for *Pakeezah* (1972). Her liver was badly affected by her excessive drinking, and in 1968 she fell seriously ill. She was taken to London and Switzerland for treatment, and this brought some respite but she could not give up her addiction. In fact, at the pathetically young age of thirty-six, she seemed to have realized she would not live much longer. On returning to Bombay (now Mumbai), she settled her debts and made up with her sister, Madhu, with whom she had broken all relations for several years.

But Meena Kumari did not fade away unnoticed into the dark night. Her final years were remarkable for her friendship with two younger men, the actor Dharmendra, and the writer-lyricist-director Gulzar. Dharmendra was her co-star in the box-office hit *Phool Aur Patthar*, and Gulzar invited her to act in his directorial debut *Mere Apne* (1971). The nature of her closeness to Dharmendra and Gulzar has never really emerged from the shroud of mystery and speculation. Dharmendra was young, good-looking and combined a certain rustic innocence with the sensitivity of a good man, which must have appealed to her. He was at the threshold of his career and she was the goddess on the final pedestal. If she took him under her wings and was willing to make public her partiality for him, he could hardly protest. It is equally likely that he was drawn to her as a human being, and was in awe of her. With Gulzar, poetry must have been the undoubted bridge. Racked with illness and the frustrations of an unhappy life, she found increasing solace in her poetic pursuits, and Gulzar, a man of extraordinary compassion and literary sensitivity, still working to find his feet in Bombay's very own Tinseltown, would have given her all the time he could provide.

Whatever the relationship, it is undeniable that both these men were an important influence in her final years, and must have brought her some glimpses of the happiness she always yearned for.

Two films will always define the dramatic swan song destined for Meena Kumari. The first was *Mere Apne* in which she played an elderly woman caught between two gangs of angry and frustrated young men, who finally make peace and shun violence as a result of her getting killed. For a woman not yet forty, who was until recently playing romantic roles, it was an amazing transformation to don a white wig, and play with conviction the part of an ageing matron. When asked about this in an interview she simply said, '*Main bohot jaldi boodhi ho gayi.*' (I just aged too soon.)

Pakeezah was Meena Kumari's final triumph. Directed by her former husband Kamal Amrohi, it was first planned as far back as 1958, and was even partially shot in 1964. However the split between the two canned the project for the next several years. Luck again played a role in reviving the project. Sunil Dutt and Nargis saw some of the incomplete footage and persuaded the estranged couple to complete it. The Dutts arranged for Kamal and Meena to meet; tears were shed as two people, once so close, looked back to the lost opportunities of their past. Amrohi gave her a gold guinea as a token payment, and reportedly promised he would make her look as beautiful as the day when the film was first conceived.

Meena Kumari's role in *Pakeezah* was of a pure-hearted courtesan who dared to dream of a married life. It would have been a challenging role in any circumstance for any actress, but for Meena Kumari, who was grievously ill by this time, the commitment to complete the film was nothing short of heroic. The film was crafted with lyrical and extravagant beauty by Amrohi. Each scene was like a painting; the dialogues and lyrics captured the imagination of a nation; and the music, composed by Ghulam Mohammad, was an instant and superhit. Meena Kumari lived to see the release of the film. She was aware of its success when, two months later, she died. After her death, and in memory of her, the film became one of Bollywood's greatest box-office successes. In time, it acquired the status of a classic, and Meena Kumari, in her last role, became a cult figure. No heroine could have asked for a more triumphant culmination to her career.

On 31 March 1972, when not yet forty, Meena Kumari passed away at a private hospital in Bombay. Few actresses could claim to come close to the success and popularity she achieved. And even fewer could confess to lives even remotely as unhappy as hers. This was the triumph and tragedy of the legend of Meena Kumari. She ruled the world on the screen, but away from the arc lights, led a deeply unfulfilled and anguished life. I suppose, in the final balance sheet, this is an unfair summation: unimagined success at one level, and unacceptable tragedy at another. She did not want her life to be like this, but probably in her final years, through the haze of alcohol, accepted that for some people balance sheets are congenitally awry. As she so poignantly wrote:

Chand tanha hai aasmaan tanha
Dil mera hai kahan kahan tanha
Ham safar koi ghar mile bhi kahain
Donon jalte rahe tanha tanha

(The moon is alone, the sky is alone,
In so many places, my heart is alone;
Even if I were to find a companion somewhere,
Both of us would burn, alone, alone.)

MY FIVE FAVOURITE MEENA KUMARI FILMS

1. *Sahib Bibi Aur Ghulam* (1962). Directed by Abrar Alvi. Co-stars: Guru Dutt, Waheeda Rehman and Rehman. The role Meena Kumari plays in this film has few parallels in Hindi cinema. The pathos and anguish she brings to her depiction of chhoti bahu, and the manner in which she projects her personal yearnings, including the need for physical fulfilment, makes for compelling viewing.

2. *Mere Apne* (1971). Directed by Gulzar. Co-stars: Vinod Khanna and Shatrughan Sinha. In this film Meena Kumari plays with great conviction the pivotal role of an ageing woman. It is an unconventional role, which few heroines would accept when still as young as Meena was then. Under the direction of Gulzar, the film also fully taps Meena Kumari's acting potential.

3. *Pakeezah* (1972). Directed by Kamal Amrohi. Co-stars: Ashok Kumar and Raaj Kumar. This film is one of my favourites, not because of Meena Kumari's acting alone but because of Kamal Amrohi's spectacular sets and the authenticity which he brings to recreating the period and the milieu. Besides, it remains nothing short of amazing that Meena Kumari looked so beautiful, even when she was almost terminally ill. It was a heroic effort on her part, and the film will remain a classic.

4. *Kohinoor* (1960). Directed by S.U. Sunny. Co-star: Dilip Kumar. This delightful film, made with a lightness of touch, allowed Meena Kumari to break out of her stereotypical tragedienne mould. It has provided a new insight to the range of her acting potential, and has always left me wishing for her to have done more such roles. Naushad's music adds another unforgettable dimension to why this film will always remain a pleasure to watch.

5. *Bhabhi Ki Chudiyan* (1961). Directed by Sadashiv J. Row. Co-star: Balraj Sahni. While Meena Kumari played a great many roles of sacrifice and feminine deprivation, her character in this story, which she portrays with genuine empathy, is truly heart-wrenching. If I have to choose a film in which I would be happy to shed tears with Meena Kumari, this would have to be the one. Two songs in this film, 'Jyoyi kalash chalke' and 'Lau laga ke, geet ga ke', also happen to be my all-time favourites.

SHAMMI KAPOOR

A STAR LIKE NO OTHER

NASREEN MUNNI KABIR

The very history of Hindi film could be told through the story of the Kapoor family, starting with the charismatic Prithviraj from whom a river of talent flowed. He was a colossus of a man and a most accomplished stage and cinema actor. In 1944, he started Prithvi Theatres and many members of his family joined his prestigious theatre company at various points. Nearly all the Kapoors, including Prithviraj's three sons—Raj, Shammi and Shashi—grandsons, great-grandsons, and great-granddaughters have made (and continue to make) a significant mark on Hindi film. But it is Prithviraj's second son, Shammi Kapoor, who, through his sheer ingenuity and matchless style, made a very different kind of contribution.

Shamsher Raj Kapoor, affectionately called 'Shammi,' was born on 21 October 1931 at Ajinkya Hospital on Charni Road in Bombay (now Mumbai). He brought great joy to his parents and brother Raj, as his birth followed the death of his two infant brothers. In Shammi Kapoor's words, he was 'the child looked forward to.'

Soon after he was born, Prithviraj Kapoor joined the Grand Anderson Company, an English theatre group, and toured

India. But the company went bankrupt by the time they arrived in Calcutta (now Kolkata); nevertheless Prithviraj and his wife, Ramasarni Devi, decided to live there with their young family. He joined New Theatres and acted in many important films. A few years later, the Kapoors had a daughter who was named Urmila and with whom Shammiji formed a close bond. He went to kindergarten in that great city and on 18 March 1938, his younger brother Shashi was born.

In 1939, the Kapoors moved back to Bombay where they settled for good and lived in a comfortable five-room flat in a building called 'Kumkum' on College Road in Matunga. Raj, Shammi and Urmila had an idyllic childhood: 'We lived in Matunga in a quiet lane. I knew everyone around. There were just three cars in our lane. All day long we would play cricket, seven tiles with balls so hard that if you didn't duck in time, you'd go home with a fracture.'[1]

Very early in Shammi Kapoor's life, he understood that his father was a talent impossible to outshine, and that his brother Raj, seven years his elder, already showed signs of exceptional creativity. 'I grew up inheriting not only big brother's hand-me-downs but also his shadow. All through childhood, I never strayed from it.'[2]

In spite of the inevitable comparisons that would be made, Shammi Kapoor's urge to act surfaced at thirteen when he won the first prize for his performance in *Dick Whittington Goes to Town*, a school play. While still at school, he went on to play minor roles in Prithvi Theatres' productions, including the character of Bharat in *Shakuntala*.

Young Shammi once expressed a wish to become a scientist, but the desire to act dominated all other ambitions. He left school in 1947 and joined Ruia College in 1948. He did not stay there long, having decided that the stage was far more

[1] Kapoor, *Filmfare*, 1–15 May 1986.
[2] Ibid.

appealing. By 1948, at seventeen, he joined Prithvi Theatres, earning fifty rupees a month. Working there was hugely beneficial. He learned the art of dialogue delivery and received a thorough training in acting. He met many leading writers and actors of the period and developed a natural connection with the audience.

In 1951, producer A.R. Kardar offered Shammi Kapoor a role in *Jeevan Jyoti*, and it was then that he decided to give up the stage for the screen. His brother Raj Kapoor's *Awara* had been released that same year, and this brilliant film signalled that Hindi cinema was entering a new and exciting phase. Unsurprisingly Shammi Kapoor was drawn to films in the belief that they would provide greater opportunities for a young actor.

Jeevan Jyoti was released in 1953 and directed by Mahesh Kaul. Cast in the lead role opposite newcomer Chand Usmani, young Kapoor was undoubtedly dashing and attractive, but the character he played impressed no one. Neither did his subsequent films do much for his career or for his self-esteem.

In April 1955, during the location shooting of *Rangeen Raaten* in Ranikhet, a hill station, Shammi Kapoor fell in love with the beautiful Geeta Bali, who appeared in a cameo role in the film. They shared the same interest in music and got on famously. From April to July that year, he pursued Geeta relentlessly, proposing to her several times. But she refused to marry him, explaining that her first responsibility was caring for her family. They met again in Bombay in August, during the monsoons, and on the spur of the moment, Geeta Bali agreed to marry Shammi Kapoor on condition that they would marry at once. 'My parents were in Bhopal touring with their theatre group, and I was at a loss to know what to do. So we went over to my friend Johnny Walker's house. We figured he could tell us how we could marry that very day because he had married Noor just the week before. Johnny said: "Have you gone crazy? I'm a Muslim and we were married in a mosque, you are Hindus, so go to a temple." The difference between Hindu and Muslim hadn't even occurred to us, we were so much in love. We then met the producer

Hari Walia and he said we could marry immediately if we went to Banganga.'[3]

They rushed over to Banganga and chose one of the many temples there. But the doors of the temple were closed and the priest told them the gods were resting and that they should return the next day at 4 a.m. They then went to the Kapoor's family flat in Matunga and had dinner prepared by the cook. At four the next morning, on 24 August 1955, they returned to Banganga to find 'the Gods waiting for them' and were married in a simple ceremony.

Shammi Kapoor and Geeta Bali had a happy married life and soon became proud parents of two children, Aditya (born in 1956) and Kanchan (born in 1961). While home life was good, Shammiji had started to tire of acting in uninspiring melodramas, and wearing silly wigs and riding horses in stunt movies. He was well aware that the doors of opportunity had initially opened for him primarily because of his surname, but this came laden with other pressures: 'Being the son of Prithviraj Kapoor and the brother of Raj Kapoor, people were bound to expect great things from you and set you up against the standards they had already achieved. I still remember a review of my second picture *Rail ka Dibba*. It said: "Shammi Kapoor apes Raj Kapoor." It hurt a lot because I didn't understand what it meant to ape somebody because I wasn't aping. I came from the same school of acting. We were from the same stage and had done the same roles. But it made me realize that it was going to be tough. When I married the star Geeta Bali, I was in even deeper trouble. Then I was no longer only the son of Prithviraj Kapoor, and brother of Raj Kapoor, but I was also the husband of Geeta Bali. That's three-to-one. It gave me a challenge, an incentive to go out there and prove myself.'[4]

---

[3] Kapoor, *Filmfare*, 20 May 1960.

[4] This and all subsequent quotes are by Shammi Kapoor from the television programme "Shammi Kapoor, Always in Time," featured in the series

It also did not help that the 1950s belonged chiefly to three actors: Dilip Kumar, Raj Kapoor and Dev Anand. The best roles were tailor-made for them, and all other actors were routinely considered second choice. At one point, Shammi Kapoor even thought of (stacking, thought of instead of considering to avoid stacking) giving up films and finding a job as a manager on a tea plantation in Assam. His wife, Geeta Bali, advised him against making any hasty decision and persuaded him to stick it out in films.

The opportunity of turning things round was at last on the horizon thanks to Sasadhar Mukherjee, Filmistan's co-owner. Mukherjee had decided to give his writer Nasir Hussain a break as a director. They had finalized the title of the film, *Tumsa Nahin Dekha*, but had not cast the lead actor. 'Nasir Hussain wanted Mr Dev Anand but didn't get him. He wanted Sunil Dutt, but didn't get him either. So Mr Sasadhar Mukherjee thrust me on Nasir Hussain and said: "Try this lad. Let's see how it works out. I see some greatness in him." I don't know how he saw any greatness in me, but that inspired me a lot. I had nothing to lose, so I went all out, changed my image, shaved off my moustache, got myself a crew cut, and there grew the yahoo image.'

When *Tumsa Nahin Dekha* was released in 1957, cast opposite Ameeta, Shammi Kapoor made a strong impression with his fresh acting, playfulness and great physical agility, which involved jumping, leaping and general cavorting. Most importantly, he exuded an unabashed and irresistible sexuality that was far from the heroes of the time, who projected romanticism but rarely sexuality. With his dreamy eyes, soft voice, charming dialogue delivery and arresting personality, Shammi Kapoor radiated the raw appeal of an Elvis Presley—especially evident when performing songs.

Movie Mahal, produced by Hyphen films for Channel 4 TV, UK. Interview by Nasreen Munni Kabir, 1987.

Nearly four years after his first film and nineteen flops later, this essentially girl-meets-boy story catapulted the hazel-eyed Kapoor into an overnight star. He instantly won an army of fans from all walks of life, and everyone from the frontbenchers to the elite took a shine to his fantasy character. The title of the film, *Tumsa Nahin Dekha*, was undoubtedly meant to describe the hero's sweetheart, but it was Shammi Kapoor who was the one never seen before.

Watch 'Tumsa nahin dekha' (written by Sahir Ludhianvi) or 'Chupne waale saamne aa' (by Majrooh Sultanpuri) on YouTube and the excitement he generated is quite understandable. Even Mohammad Rafi, who sang these fabulous numbers, sounded more youthful and flirty than ever before, because he was singing for Shammi Kapoor.

The next big hit was *Dil Deke Dekho* (1959), also directed by Nasir Hussain. In this light-hearted romance, he was cast opposite newcomer Asha Parekh. The film proved that Shammi Kapoor had lasting talent. He was quickly dubbed a dancing hero and a rebel star. These descriptions, credited to L.P. Rao, the then *Filmfare* editor, were in direct contrast to the ruling trio—Dilip, Raj and Dev—who were not considered for the most part dancing heroes or rebellious. Shammi Kapoor did not have the brooding quality of James Dean, the famous Hollywood rebel, but in the Indian context, he was a rule-breaker with a brazen attitude towards prudishness as well as a light disdain for parental authority and conventional behaviour. The young urban middle classes of the 1950s became fascinated by him because they too longed for an individual voice, and yearned to be like him, free of the dos and don'ts of traditional society.

Shammi Kapoor did not seriously dent the popularity of the great trio of Hindi cinema, yet nevertheless he was the only actor who carved out a separate space for himself at the height of the trio's reign. Another important difference was that 'the triumvirate,' as Dilip Kumar, Raj Kapoor and Dev Anand were called, were considered by audiences as 'men'—similar to

Poster of *Durga* starring Devika Rani

Ashok Kumar and Meena Kumari in *Parineeta*

Vyjayanthimala and Dilip Kumar in *Devdas*

K.L. Saigal

Nargis and Raj Kapoor in *Shree 420*

Waheeda Rehman and Dev Anand in *Guide*

Amitabh Bachchan and Rajesh Khanna in *Anand*

Aamir Khan in *Qayamat Se Qayamat Tak*

Kajol and Shahrukh Khan in
Dilwale Dulhania Le Jayenge

Hrithik Roshan and Kareena Kapoor in
Kabhi Khushi Kabhie Gham

Suraiya

Madhubala

Meena Kumari

Nargis

Waheeda Rehman   Madhuri Dixit

Grateful acknowledgement is made to the following for their kind permission to reproduce copyrighted material:

- The Osian's Archive and Library Collection for the *Durga* poster featuring Devika Rani, the *Andaz* poster featuring Shammi Kapoor and Hema Malini and the still from *Anand* with Amitabh Bachchan and Rajesh Khanna.

- The estate of B.D. Garga for the following film stills: Raj Kapoor and Nargis in *Awara*; Waheeda Rehman and Dev Anand in *Guide*; Shahrukh Khan and Kajol in *Dilwale Dulhania Le Jayenge*; Kareena Kapoor and Hrithik Roshan in *Kabhi Khushi Kabhie Gham*.

- Rinki Roy Bhattacharya for the *Parineeta* poster featuring Ashok Kumar as well as for the still from *Devdas* with Dilip Kumar and Vyjayanthimala.

- Pran Nevile for the photograph of K.L. Saigal.

- Bhaichand Patel for the six portraits—of Madhubala, Madhuri Dixit, Meena Kumari, Nargis, Suraiya and Waheeda Rehman—from his private collection. These stars as well as many others posed for the renowned photographer, Jethalal H. Thakker (1923–2003) in his India Photo Studio in Dadar, Mumbai.

Poster of *Andaz* starring Hema Malini and Shammi Kapoor

the way their Hollywood counterparts like Gregory Peck, Gary Cooper or Clarke Gable were regarded. In addition, the famous three were usually seen in mature and solemn roles—often playing characters burdened by duty towards family, or struggling against repressive social norms that came in the way of their ambitions and romantic choices. On the other hand, Shammi Kapoor stirred in the audience a great appetite for hip, affluent and carefree heroes—good-looking 'boys' who brazenly stole hearts and whose stories were just fun to watch.

In 1961, Subodh Mukherjee's *Junglee* gave him a career-defining role. In this wonderful film, he plays the wealthy Chandrashekhar, a dour man transformed by his love for a young woman whom he meets in Kashmir. The film was originally titled *Mr Hitler* and when Dev Anand said no to the project, it went to Shammi Kapoor. Once again, he was cast opposite a newcomer, the beautiful Saira Banu. In fact, he was often cast with newcomers, including Ragini in *Mujrim* (1958) and Kalpana in *Professor* (1962). Sharmila Tagore's debut in Hindi cinema was also as Kapoor's screen sweetheart in *Kashmir Ki Kali* (1964).

Junglee was unusual for another reason. In the early 1960s, colour photography was just too expensive and regarded as something reserved for the historical or mythological film. Even the budget of the majestic *Mughal-e-Azam,* released in 1960, only permitted the filming of four reels in colour. Subodh Mukherjee, however, believed completely in *Junglee* and it gave him the courage to make this typical musical romance in colour. 'The very idea of *Junglee* was so different. Everyone thought it was a big risk. We were taking Shammi Kapoor, an actor identified with singing songs and jumping about; could he do the serious role of a big industrialist who doesn't smile, who belongs to a very strict, orthodox and disciplined family?'

He proved the sceptics wrong. He not only knew how to perform songs, had smart comic timing, but could also go from serious to light-hearted, as required by the hero's character. He delivered his finest performance in *Junglee,* and the title song

with its yahoo cry (famously recorded by his friend, the actor/
writer Prayag Raj) firmly established him as a youth icon.

Shammi Kapoor became an important role model in the 1960s,
and a major inspiration for future generations of stars, especially
the Khans, whose early personae and films bear great resemblance
to the characters he personified and the feel-good stories he
validated. 'The type of movies I worked in were simple musical-
comedies: boy meets girl, boy woos girl, chases girl, girl turns
down boy, boy sings to her, gets her into situations, then she
eventually accepts boy. The villain drops in, takes the girl away,
then the boy brings the girl back. And that was that. In between
you sang eight or nine songs. It was a complete movie that you
could enjoy with all your family and kids, eat popcorn and come
home and say, "Aha, what splendid work!"'

In a cinema entirely dependent on song and dance, his
understanding of music, including Western classical, was
an additional asset. He had no formal training in dance, yet
rarely needed a choreographer to guide him. One could
easily imagine that he was unable to give retakes because his
dancing just came out of him as reactions to rhythm rather
than practised dance steps.

Less discussed is Shammi Kapoor's grasp of the language of
cinema. He understood the camera perfectly—and knew how to
stay in character in long shot and mid-shot and how to hold
attention in a close-up through his mobile face and expressive
eyes. He was at his most astute in understanding film editing.
This particular talent, unusual for an actor, gave his dance numbers
an unrivalled originality. Even his directors may not have been
fully aware of the subtle editing pattern that he imposed on
his song sequences. 'You wanted to know why I made my exit
from a particular shot the way I did. My dancing was not only on
the beat but off beat, half beat, quarter beat and a lot of my
own beats. And if I were to leave the shot in a haphazard manner,
leave it loose, they would cut it incorrectly. So I would leave the
shot exactly where I thought it should be cut. They had to cut,

because I wasn't there. I would turn my back, or jump out of the frame. But I would always leave the frame on the beat, knowing they would have to use this particular beat only up to here, no more, no less.'

In the years that followed, Shammi Kapoor continued to be the crowd-puller of many hit films with hugely popular music, including *Professor, China Town* (1962), *Rajkumar* (1964), *Kashmir Ki Kali, Budtameez* (1966), as well as the crime thriller *Teesri Manzil* (1966), directed by the exceptional Vijay Anand.

During the making of *Teesri Manzil*, personal tragedy turned Shammi Kapoor's world upside down when his wife Geeta Bali died of smallpox on 21 January 1965. 'I went through a very traumatic experience in 1965. I lost my wife and that left me quite berserk. It left me without moorings. I drifted and drank. I went haywire for nearly four years. Then in 1969, I got married again. I had to change certain things in my life, throw away my little black book, settle down and bring up my two children. We became a family all over again. It was as though life had given me another chance.'

His marriage in 1969 to Neila Devi Gohil, who belonged to a royal family of Gujarat, brought him great stability and happiness. He was thirty-eight and had begun to put on weight. Years of strenuous filming had also taken their toll. 'Both my knees had given way five or six times during the filming of the "yahoo" song, falling over in the snow on tree stumps; jumping off a cliff into a lake for *Laat Saheb* and landing on an underwater rock on both knees; or sitting on the back of an elephant and singing in *Rajkumar*, and the elephant decides to make an about turn and crushes my knee against a boulder. I hear my knee go crack, crack, crack. So I thought: enough is enough and I closed shop.'

The 1971 film *Andaz* was one of his last successes as romantic hero. No longer fitting the bill, he gracefully slipped into supporting roles. He even directed two films, *Manoranjan* (1974) and *Bandalbaaz* (1976), but neither met with any success. By the late 1990s, he decided to stop acting altogether. 'I've been fortunate in more ways than one. I've been able to get the right people around me at the time I wanted them. When I wanted inspiration in my life, I married Geeta. She contributed a lot to what I eventually became in life. My second wife, Neila, brought me a great deal of strength when I needed it the most, a lot of stability and character. She brought up my children like her own till they got married and settled down. We're grandparents now. I found my spiritual guru when I needed one. He guided me and showed me the great light. I am not in the rat race anymore. I've seen it all. I've done it all and don't feel the need to do anything or go anywhere. It's very peaceful where I am.'

A retired life and Shammi Kapoor were not a likely pair. His alert and ever curious mind soon developed new interests and he became one of India's first leading Internet users. This was twenty-three years ago, and till the end of his days, he continued to maintain a website dedicated to the Kapoor family. A must-watch is his online series 'Shammi Kapoor Unplugged', in which he takes us on a fascinating journey through his life.

In his last years, he suffered very poor health and was on dialysis three times a week. His doctors, nurses and ward boys—all die-hard fans—would look forward to his hospital visits, and much to his amusement, they would sing his old songs to him. He never complained or made a big show of his physical suffering. Instead he believed that he was better off than his doctors who had to be at the hospital seven days a week while he only needed to be there on Mondays, Wednesdays and Fridays.

Shammi Kapoor sadly passed away on 14 August 2011 at the age of seventy-nine. The entire film industry expressed their deep sorrow at his passing. His big personality, lively spirit and love of life, so manifest in his work, has forever assured him a place in Indian film history. Behind the flamboyant star persona was also a gentle and marvellous man with spiritual depth, mind and heart.

EPILOGUE

This article draws extensively and quotes from a filmed interview with Shammi Kapoor that took place in 1987 for a special programme featured in *Movie Mahal,* the twenty-eight-part television series on Hindi cinema that I produced and directed for Channel 4 TV, UK.

Discovering the personality of stars through filmed interviews was rare till the early 1990s. Until that time mainstream television in the West showed no interest at all in Hindi popular cinema, and the numerous Indian television and satellite channels were yet to exist. We mostly knew about actors through their screen characters, popular gossip and second-hand accounts in film magazines or newspaper articles. There existed very little filmed interviews. So we were keen to persuade Shammi Kapoor to let us record his story.

It was in this connection that I met him for the first time at his south Mumbai home in February 1987. When we entered his private world, the first thing that struck us was the pervading sense of peace. The quiet grace of his home came from Neilaji, his warm and welcoming wife. She was clearly someone who had spent her life placing the needs of others before her own. Neilaji led us into a room where the large and bearded Shammiji was waiting for us. Sitting on a chair and looking splendidly grand, he had a glint in his eye and an imposing bead necklace around his neck—a photograph of his young guru hung on a wall behind him. While Neilaji graciously served us tea and sandwiches, Shammiji agreed to us making a programme on him, which was titled: *Shammi Kapoor, Always in Time.*

The filming of the Channel 4 interview took place on 18 April 1987. When the camera rolled, the soft-spoken star answered each question with focused attention, recounting the many ups and downs of his life. He came across as a generous man of great humility and personal reserve. He was honest and freely admitted to his flaws and failings. The pauses he took in speech, his lively eyes and terrific sense of timing made him a natural and riveting storyteller. Recording Shammi Kapoor tell his own story, as he remembered it in 1987, was a very special privilege.

MY FIVE FAVOURITE SHAMMI KAPOOR FILMS

1. *Junglee* (1961). Directed by Subodh Mukherji. Co-stars: Saira Banu, Shashikala, Lalita Pawar and Anoop Kumar. Kashmir in glorious colour, great comedy, fabulous songs, and the introduction of a beautiful young actress, *Junglee* is Shammi Kapoor's best calling card.

2. *Teesri Manzil* (1966). Directed by Vijay Anand. Co-stars: Asha Parekh, Prem Nath, Prem Chopra and Helen. A must-see example of screen sparkle provided by its stars in this great crime thriller directed by Vijay Anand. It also has a brilliant soundtrack by the exceptional R.D. Burman and brilliant lyricist Majrooh Sultanpuri.

3. *Tumsa Nahin Dekha* (1957). Directed by Nasir Hussain. Co-stars: Ameeta, Pran and Raj Mehra. A lost-and-found story provides the backdrop to Shammi Kapoor's big makeover. Nineteen films after his first movie was released, he emerges here as a bolder, sexier and vibrant star.

4. *China Town* (1962). Directed by Shakti Samanta. Co-stars: Shakila, Helen and Madan Puri. Some say this film inspired *Don,* as Kapoor plays the double role of hero and gangster. A special treat is 'Baar baar dekho' sung to perfection by Mohammad Rafi.

5. *Bluff Master* (1963). Directed by Manmohan Desai. Co-stars: Saira Banu, Pran, Mohan Choti and Lalita Pawar. All the trademarks of Desai are present here: the importance of national integration, drama and comedy. The film is also remembered for the 'Govinda alaa re alaa' song, highlighting real Mumbai locations.

WAHEEDA REHMAN

THE IMAGE OF FEMALE GRAVITAS

JERRY PINTO

What did Waheeda Rehman think, I wonder, when she was asked to star in *Guide* (1965)? When they came to narrate the story to her, how did they present Rosie, a woman of uncertain origin, a tearaway considerably before her time, a woman who refuses to sacrifice her life for the men she loves? I do know that she had been a little apprehensive about the film when it was released; she told Nasreen Munni Kabir she was. I do know that she knew that Tad Danielewski, the director of the English version, did not want her for the role; she told journalist Mohan Bawa that he wanted Leela Naidu. In his turn, Dev Anand tells us that he stuck to his guns and so Waheeda Rehman got to star in one of those startling films which should never have been a hit.

Consider what the story says: Raju (Dev Anand) wanders around the ruins of Rajasthan, telling tall tales to startled tourists. One day, he encounters an archaeologist Marco (Kishore Sahu) and his wife (Waheeda Rehman). The archaeologist is a bit of a stuffed shirt; he has made his wife hang up her ghungroos. The guide slowly brings the woman to life; she leaves her husband and moves in with him and his mother. She begins to dance again and gradually Raju finds himself a supernumerary in her world. His self-esteem begins to slide and he ends up in prison for forging a cheque. This is where we meet him, leaving jail, while in the background S.D. Burman asks one of those philosophical questions that Bollywood sangeet no longer cares about: '*Wahaan kaun hai tera musafir, jaayega kahaan?*' (When there is no one who awaits you, traveller, where will you go?)

Rosie manages a double whammy, bloodying the nose of the image of the Hindi film heroine. She does not stand by her husband. She does not stand by her second chance at love. She is, in other words, a woman who puts her own interests first. Marco buys her respectability. Raju gives her freedom. She takes both and moves on.

It is not quite the kind of role that established women stars took on easily in 1965. That was the year in which Meena Kumari was weeping her eyes out again in *Kaajal*, because Raaj Kumar insisted on drinking and dancing with his inamorata Helen, even after he had married her. It was the year in which *Waqt* brought us the first multi-starrer and the Yash Chopra version of life among the upper classes. But whether in the mansions or in the hutments, all the women who walked through Hindi films were putative virgins. No one even talked about this but it was assumed that they were pure. The non-virgins were vamps and fallen women. The heroine might drink—these were the silly sixties, after all—but only in the safety of her bedroom with the encouragement of Kitty Kelly (Helen), as Nanda did in *Gumnaam*.

Thus '*Kaaton se kheenchke yeh aanchal*' can be read as an anthem of women's liberation. The words might suggest a tentativeness—'*dar hai ki safar mein kahin kho na jaaoon main*' (I fear I might lose myself on this journey)—but Rosie did not lose her way. Raju may end up a reluctant hero, sacrificing himself for the common weal. Rosie does no such thing. She enjoys her worldly success. She gets on with the business of living.

But then the cinematic Waheeda Rehman had a way of getting on with it.

*

You can't talk about the cinematic Waheeda Rehman without mentioning Guru Dutt who is always credited with discovering her. He didn't discover her. Telugu cinema had already done that. She had acted in two films and was something of a star already. She told Mohan Bawa the story in *Actors and Acting* (India Book House, 1975):

> When *Rojulu Marai* was celebrating its silver jubilee Guru Dutt happened to be in Hyderabad. He met me at the function and we talked for half an hour. He told me that he was looking for a new girl in Bombay and would I care to come over to that city for a screen test? I said yes, but I thought it was one of those passing fancies. When he would return to Bombay he would probably forget all about me. Then while making a Telugu film in Madras two friends of Guru Dutt came over to take us to Bombay.

Abrar Alvi, with a little help from journalist Sathya Saran, fleshes it all out in *Ten Years with Guru Dutt: Abrar Alvi's Journey* (Penguin Viking, 2008). 'Waheeda has a buffalo to thank for the fact that we signed her on,' says Alvi. In his version of events, *Missiamma* (1955) had been a huge hit and a distributor, Manu Bhai, suggested that a remake might give Guru Dutt another hit. Since no airplane or train tickets were available, the director decided to drive to Hyderabad and invited Alvi along. Alvi managed to hit a buffalo, after driving all night. The group did reach Hyderabad and did see *Missiamma* but the film left the director cold. This was when they decided to visit a distributor.

> We were idly looking out of the door and talking among ourselves when a car drew up with a group of urchins trailing behind it. A woman got out and, avoiding the young boys crowding around her, entered the building opposite ours. I asked the distributor, "Is there an office there, who is that woman?" He replied, "She is a dancer in a Telugu film, *Rojulu Marayi*, which is a superhit thanks to her dance number." The film was celebrating its hundredth day and the starlet had become so popular that filmgoers had started recognizing her, which was also the reason the urchins were running after her car, he explained.

But she did not impress anyone. Alvi says:

> It was an anticlimax. She was very plainly dressed, without even lipstick to relieve the monotony of her face, strangely reserved, and spoke softly in near monosyllables to our small talk and queries. Then, getting up abruptly, she folded her hands into a namaste, and said, 'Ab main chaloongi,' in a markedly south Indian accent, and turned and left.

Perhaps this was because she had always had a problem about her speaking voice.

'You see,' she told Mohan Bawa, 'in the early stages, I was convinced that I did not have a good speaking voice. Guru Dutt kept telling me to get rid of this notion but it was not so easy to erase. I would talk in such a whisper that the sound recordist could hear nothing at all! It took me several films to get over this difficulty.'

Her accent and her voice seem perfectly competent in *C.I.D.* (1956), her first Hindi film. What seems all wrong is her character. She plays Kamini and when we meet her, you can see Guru Dutt trying to turn her into a Veronica Lake–style noir woman. The problem was, of course, that Indian noir had no place for such dangerous women. Our version of noir posits the woman as the positive moral pole of a binary universe. The hero will be lured into a life of crime, but it is the love of a good woman which will draw him back. Raj Kapoor defined this well in *Shree 420* (1955)—Nadira, in league with the bad boys and stitched into her dress, was Maya; Nargis, teaching children riddles about peacocks and chillies, is Vidya. In *Kala Bazaar* (1960), Waheeda Rehman would play Alka, the kind of girl who would tear up cinema tickets that were bought on the black market. Seeing this, Raghu would turn from his own black marketing *dhandha* and begin to read poetry. That was what women—Hindu women, good women—did for their men.

The problem was there was already a good woman in *C.I.D.*, the heroine Rekha (Shakila). Who was Kamini, then? We know that the name does not bode well. No Kamini ever came to a good end. Most Kaminis were played by Helen or Bindu. They were the kind to chase blind men on horseback or lure the hero into a bad marriage and then mock the old folks by saying that Hindu *strees* don't divorce their husbands, *na*?

Waheeda would only come into her own in *Pyaasa* (1957) where she would play a sex worker. You know *Pyaasa*. If you don't, you should put down this book and go and see it and then come back. If you do, you remember that the plot pivots on Vijay (Guru Dutt), from the moment he wakes up in some sylvan spot and begins to hum a line of poetry to the moment he walks off into the sunset. The women of *Pyaasa* are incidental. Meena (Mala Sinha) spurns him but it is the contumely of the poet's evil brothers that stings much more. If Gulabo (Waheeda Rehman) saves his poems by buying them from the *raddiwala*, she will also cause them to be saved again when, after his assumed death—a contrivance borrowed from Preston Sturges's *Sullivan's Travels*—she gets them published. But centrally, *Pyaasa* is a film about the creative man and his position in society. Meena and Gulabo are mirror images of each other. Meena throws away love in order to climb the social ladder. Gulabo puts her all into saving the poetry of a dead man. And in the end when Vijay walks away with Gulabo, you are never sure whether he has chosen her for her integrity and for what she represents or because he loves her.

In *Kaagaz Ke Phool* (1959), the martyr complex that drove Guru Dutt—his use of the imagery of the crucifixion in the climax of *Pyaasa* has not gone unnoticed—was allowed full play. It was here that he prefigured his own end but he worked backwards from the beginning. Now Suresh Sinha, as the central protagonist was called, would discover his beautiful protégée all over again, simply for the pleasure of making his claim. In that famous camera chase, we watch as Dutt sends up his own predatoriness: the camera swoops down on Shanti (the twenty-one-year-old Waheeda Rehman), who, in the film, has only come to return a coat and ends up a star. As Sinha wanes, his discovery grows and once again, she moves on as alcohol and failure claim him.

Is Shanti important in the film? Is Suresh Sinha's daughter important? Both serve a purpose. The contrived scene in which Sinha's daughter attacks a classmate was probably put in only to show that no crime of love goes unpunished. Shanti too is needed only to provide a counterpoint, a figure to emerge from the gloom of the deserted studio set, as that single ray of light cuts through the gloom and the strains of 'Waqt ne kiya kyaa haseen sitam' begin to play.

There are only two more films in which Waheeda Rehman and Guru Dutt shared screen time. *Chaudhvin Ka Chand* (1960) was a potboiler. Badly stung by the failure of *Kaagaz Ke Phool*, Dutt decided to make a safe Muslim social in which two young men fall for the same woman. The central theme is therefore a nawabi struggle, each man trying to prove himself the nobler of the two, each trying to sacrifice his love for the happiness of his friend.

And then came *Sahib Bibi Aur Ghulam* (1962). You know that one too. You ought to. You know who dominates it. Meena Kumari as Chhoti Bahu is one of the most bizarre and beguiling of women to have lit up the screen. It helps that she was never more beautiful than in this film. It helps that we know how much she suffered playing the role: 'This woman is troubling me a great deal. All day long—and a good part of the night—it is nothing else but Chhoti Bahu's helplessness, Chhoti Bahu's sorrows, Chhoti Bahu's smiles, Chhoti Bahu's hopes, Chhoti Bahu's tribulations, Chhoti Bahu's endurance, Chhoti Bahu's, Chhoti Bahu's . . .' she is said to have written in her diary.

And yet when she sings, '*More angna mein jab purvaiyya chali, more dwaare ki khul gayi kiwaadiyaan,*' she is resplendent. The metaphors do their work. And this makes her signature song, 'Na jaao saiyyaan chudaake baiyyaan', almost post-modern in its irony. She doesn't really want her husband (Rehman) any longer. This unnamed woman, known only by her position in the

household, has swallowed herself. She has tried every remedy
including Mohini Sindoor to keep her husband from going to the
kotha. He has explained his position as well. It is a matter of
masculine pride. He might love his wife but she cannot drink with
him and he cannot be seen as a henpecked husband.

And so in an act of despair, Chhoti Bahu begins to drink. And
where '*Piya aiso jiya mein samaaye gayo re*' begins with the slow
combing of hair, here she will talk of her *bikhri zulfein*, her *gulta
kajra*, her *meheki chunri* and her *man ki madira*. What began in
shringara has ended in decadence.

What weapons could the gamine, the ingénue, bring to bear
against this trajectory beginning in beauty and adornment
ending in death and 'dishonour'? Jaba, and was there ever such
an ugly name, gets Bhootnath (Guru Dutt) to be sure but it is
Chhoti Bahu whose bangles will still clink from beyond the grave,
who will stir Bhootnath in his sleep with '*Koi door se aawaaz
de chale aao*'. Jaba sings '*Bhanwra bada naadaan hai*' and has to
stick out her tongue to show how innocent she is. Why does this
even count as a Waheeda Rehman film?

Because you have '*Meri baat rahi mere man mein*' and
suddenly all is forgiven. Suddenly, you see just how beautiful
Waheeda Rehman could be. As a restless chiaroscuro passes over
her tormented face, it does seem to turn into a moon. This is
one of the few times when the hyperbole of Hindi film lyrics is
justified: she is a *chaudhvin ka chand*. In the tight close-ups, all
the unsaid words, all the dammed-up love is expressed by a tear
glistening in an eye, a crease in the brow. This is not acting; it is
melodrama but it works because it is pure and perfect and
unselfconscious. It is about making you cry. '*Jiya mora pyaasa
rahaa saawan mein*' brings back the other passionate song, '*Aaj
sajan mohe ang laga le janam safal ho jaaye*' in *Pyaasa*, where the
jogan demands union with the godhead and the poet watches her
yearning even as he is watched in his turn by the sex worker
who yearns for him. Note the links in the chain: God to seeker
to poet to prostitute to us.

For we yearn for Waheeda Rehman; at last, in *Pyaasa*, the putative virgin has been put to flight. We know what respectable girls do. They choose the security of society. It is the streetwalker who stands by her man. Saratchandra knew this instinctively. For every man has his dream of Chandramukhi, even if he has a Paro at home.

*

So why aren't there more great Waheeda Rehman films?

I can think of the camp *Neel Kamal* (1968)—but then what reincarnation film is not camp?—and Satyajit Ray's *Abhijan* (1962), where she is wasted, and *Reshma Aur Shera* (1971), which flopped perhaps because it was ahead of its time. Where was she otherwise? Why did she do so many pointless films with spineless men?

We know why Dilip Kumar didn't act with her. There just wasn't enough chemistry even though Bunny Reuben suggests that many hoped the two Muslim actors would get together. After the failure of *Dil Diya Dard Liya* (1966) and *Aadmi* (1968)—in which Dilip Kumar is obsessed with a doll, making it the first film that looked at fetishism—they came together next in *Mashaal* (1984), where her death offered the thespian one of his most magnificent grandstanding sequences—and then he got to do it twice over in the same film.

Why didn't Raj Kapoor act with her? There's only *Teesri Kasam* (1966), magnificently shot by Subroto Mitra, where she plays Hirabai, another woman who gets on with it while Hiraman (Kapoor) swears his third promise: never to take a woman passenger again.

There is a scene in it which is perhaps telling. An ant is climbing on the sleeping Hirabai's leg and Hiraman watches it with that mixture of concern and voyeurism that was so pitch perfect for the kind of male Kapoor enjoyed playing: not quite sexually mature on screen while calling all the shots off it. He tries to dust it off and wakes her up.

'*Cheenti*,' he says and his voice is a plea for forgiveness.

Perhaps *Phagun* (1973) has something to tell us. Here was another strange film that few other actresses would have accepted. *Phagun* paired her with Dharmendra, a rich girl who marries a poor boy. On Holi, he throws colour on her and ruins her sari. She berates him for not knowing the value of an expensive sari and he leaves her and the house and walks away. She gives birth to their child, Santoshi/Toshi (Jaya Bhaduri), and when her daughter gets married, goes to live with the young couple. The presence of masculine energy (in the form of Vijay Arora) awakens something in her, suggesting, horror of horrors, that a mature woman might have some spark of the sexual alive in her.

The film flopped. Discussing it, she asked Bawa rhetorically,

> What went wrong with *Phagun*? Here is the story of a mother who has still retained her sexuality and womanhood. Meeting her daughter's young husband-to-be comes as a shock to her. He reminds her of her own husband who has disappeared. This is the essence of the story that Rajendra Singh Bedi was trying to tell. But somewhere along the way *kuch garbar ho gayee*. He messed things up. Frankly speaking, Rajendra Singh Bedi is a brilliant screenplay writer but director he is not. He should stick to the writing of scripts. I was thinking, the other day, if Raj Kapoor had directed this film what a brilliant film would have resulted!

Perhaps we needed Waheeda to grow old so that we could conceal her status as a fully grown and challenging female presence behind a silvery bouffant. That's how you see her in *Kabhi Kabhie* (1976), in a wonderful performance as the woman who gets the poet once the poetry has been drained out of him. That's how you see her in *Delhi 6* (2009), this time as the grandmother of the poet's son.

Today, there is something about Waheeda Rehman that suggests royalty. Perhaps it was because, very early on, she knew her mind. Abrar Alvi wanted her to change her name. They felt Waheeda was not a good screen name. A film magazine had

called her Wadia Rehman and so a list of possible names was drawn
up. 'But Waheeda was a girl with a mind of her own,' Alvi told
Sathya Saran. 'She refused to look at the list and was adamant
about not changing her name!' (Many years later, Dino Morea
did not have as much courage of conviction. His first film lists
him as Siddhanth, his screen name in *Pyaar Mein Kabhi Kabhi*
(1999). No offence to Dino but for a newcomer who says that
she and her mother were terrified of Bombay, refusing to even
look at the list shows class.)

Perhaps it has to do with the ability to laugh at herself, a very
rare thing in Bollywood. There was a time when Mehmood
asked Waheeda Rehman to do a guest appearance in his film *Sadhu
Aur Shaitan* (1968). She didn't want to do any guest appearances
and told him that she would do an important role if he would
write one for her. Mehmood was offended and so when he made
Kunwara Baap, some time later, he put in a line where he goes
up to a junior artiste who is washing clothes at a well and
says, '*Eh, Waheeda Rehman, yeh bachche ka moonh dhona hai.
Thoda sa paani loon kya?*'

When the film was released, several of Waheeda Rehman's friends
rang her up. But she had seen the film and she laughed.

She laughed?

You can see why the film industry uses her when it needs a
female presence of some gravitas. Because that's what Waheeda
Rehman has: the ability to conjure up the best of womanhood.

MY FIVE FAVOURITE WAHEEDA REHMAN FILMS

1. *Guide* (1965). Directed by Vijay Anand. Co-star: Dev Anand.
   Dev Anand made this film in two languages. The English version
   has completely vanished. What has remained in the Hindi
   version is the unforgettable figure of Rosie, a woman who
   broke free from a miserable marriage and then cuts loose
   from a loser lover.
2. *Teesri Kasam* (1966). Directed by Basu Bhattacharya. Co-star:

Raj Kapoor. Hirabai is to Hiraman as fire is to water. They don't mix but that only adds a hint of tragedy to this beautifully shot road movie.

3. *Kaagaz Ke Phool* (1959). Directed by Guru Dutt. Co-star: Guru Dutt. Once more, Waheeda Rehman plays a movie star. And a woman who can move on when the situation demands it. Couple that with a hero who loses and you have a recipe for disaster. Waheeda herself didn't think so. She thought it was about the audience's refusal to admit that its celluloid dreams were built on a substratum of failure and misery.

4. *Pyaasa* (1957). Directed by Guru Dutt. Co-stars: Guru Dutt and Mala Sinha. Gulabo may have been based on a real woman, Gulabo, who Abrar Alvi knew. But this sex worker with a heart of gold may have even given birth to Gulabi of *Abhijan*. The missed opportunity was the cigarette Alvi wanted to place in Gulabo's hands, the streetwalker language he wanted to give her. Guru Dutt refused and the first hard-talking sex worker was Sharmila Tagore in *Mausam*.

5. *Reshma Aur Shera* (1971). Directed by Sunil Dutt. Co-stars: Sunil Dutt, Amitabh Bachchan, Vinod Khanna and Rakhee. Waheeda Rehman was nominated six times for Filmfare awards but she won the National Award for her performance in this film, which she told Mohan Bawa was based on a mixture of imagination and observation.

HEMA MALINI

Dream Girl to Dream Woman

Bhawana Somaaya

I t is said that when Jaya Chakravarthy was pregnant she had a recurrent dream of the goddess Lakshmi visiting her home. That is how she began painting the goddess on her walls and, at midnight on 16 October 1948—it was Dussehra—Jaya delivered her third child, a divinely beautiful daughter. She called her Hema Malini, a name derived from a Lakshmi *sutram*.

As Hema grew older, she discovered that her mother nursed special dreams for her future. They were perhaps remains of Jaya's own dormant desires sacrificed at the altar of marriage, which she now hoped to realize through her daughter.

Jaya enrolled her little girl for formal training in Bharatanatyam, under the tutelage of Guru Tara Ramaswamy. The first time Hema was demonstrated the *adavus* her knees hurt terribly but she was not allowed to give up. 'You will get used to it,' her mother explained gently and she was right. Within a few weeks, Hema was dancing in the posture without complaints and before the end of the year, even performing at public gatherings.

Based in Delhi, opportunities to perform before ministers came frequently. These included the then President Rajendra Prasad and other dignitaries like Queen Elizabeth II. There were not too many young performers in those days, and as a result Hema was amongst the most talked about child dancers in the capital.

'I relished the attention and for the time being forgot the aching knees,' recalls Hema Malini today.

Hema's father served with the Employees' State Insurance Corporation (ESIC) and they lived in the official government row houses in the colony near Gole Market in Delhi. The family seldom had social outings but they never missed an opportunity to attend a dance concert. Once Hindi cinema's reigning star, Vyjayanthimala, was performing at Sapru House in Delhi and the Chakravarthys had gone to watch her perform.

Vyjayanthimala was electric on stage and even today, Hema Malini remembers her shining black eyes. 'She looked ethereal. After the show, she shook hands with me and spoke a few encouraging words. That was a magical moment for me and more so for my mother,' she adds.

Unlike other dancers who go through a lifetime devoted to just one guru, Hema had the rare opportunity of learning from a number of teachers in her long, artistic career. In time to come Jaya convinced her husband that the spark she saw in her daughter could be fanned into a blazing talent only if the family shifted to Madras (now Chennai). The decision involved Hema's father, Chakravarthy, seeking a transfer from his ESIC office and uprooting his two sons—Kannan and Jagannath—who then completed college and school in Madras.

It was the summer of 1962 when the Chakravarthys shifted bag and baggage to make a home out of Madras. Hema was admitted in her new school, Rosary Matriculation. Thus began a new phase of Hema learning a deeper and more concentrated form of Bharatanatyam dance and for the first time in several years, Jaya did not feel the need to replace her teacher. Finally, her search for the perfect tutor was over. Kitappa Pillai continued to teach Hema dance all through his life till he passed away more than a decade ago.

Interestingly film producers started to approach Hema when she was barely fourteen. It is a common practice for film-makers to pick up stage artistes and give them a break in films and Hema was considerably well known in the art circle. Her first offer to do a dance item in a south Indian film came from producer Vellu Mani, followed by another dance item for a Telugu film. Jaya wanted her daughter to become a dancer. She had never dreamt of a career in films for her but destiny had different plans.

One day, a Tamil producer arrived at the Chakravarthy residence with a proposal to launch Hema as a heroine. Chakravarthy was not enticed by the offer and rejected the idea outright. Jaya suggested, however, that there was no harm in exploring the possibilities. The producer made a grand announcement and spoke in glorious terms about his two heroines, Hema and Jayalalitha (the latter went on to become the chief minister of Tamil Nadu).

Then, a few months after the first schedule of the laborious shooting in Madurai, the Chakravarthys read in the paper that the film producer had dropped Hema from the project and replaced her with someone else. Hema recalls: 'It was a rude shock and it was not as if we had gone seeking for a role. He had made the overture and now suddenly, he had thrown me out of the film.'

Hema's godfather, Anantha Swamy, walked into their lives out of the blue. It was as if his entry coincided with the infamous producer's exit. Destiny was playing its cards for the Chakravarthys and they merely had to toe the line. The following events occurred so rapidly that there was no time for reflection.

Anantha Swamy spotted Hema Malini for the first time at a dance concert and he was impressed. He later visited the Chakravarthys and informed them that he was making a Hindi film and asked whether Hema would be interested to work as a heroine opposite Hindi cinema's superstar Raj Kapoor. While Jaya and Chakravarthy appeared at a loss for words, Hema, without consulting her parents, promptly replied 'yes'. Anantha Swamy was taken aback by her bravado. The family wondered if he was a conman but when Anantha Swamy appeared a few days later with three air tickets to fly them to Bombay (now Mumbai) to meet the showman there was no reason for suspicion. He made it clear from the beginning that Raj Kapoor would be the one to make the decision.

The screen test was conducted at R.K. Films, the studio that Raj Kapoor owned in Deonar, and Hema was understandably nervous. Raj Kapoor was behind the camera and was so reassuring that Hema lost all her inhibitions. Shot over, Raj Kapoor turned to director K. Asif and music director Shankar present in the studio and said, 'She is going to be the biggest star of the Indian screen.'

As luck would have it, Hema was subsequently signed up for all the top banners. She did Madan's Mohla's *Sharafat* (1970), where she played the role of a courtesan, and Vijay Anand's *Johny Mera Naam* (1970), where she posed as a female don, and both were huge successes. Dev Anand and Hema paired in eight films after *Johny Mera Naam—Tere Mere Sapne* (1971), *Shareef Budmaash* (1973), *Chupa Rustam* (1973), *Joshila* (1973), *Amir Garib* (1974), *Jaaneman* (1976), *Sachche Ka Bol Bala* (1989) and decades later *Censor* (2001)—but somehow none could match the magic of *Johny Mera Naam*.

She was the Dream Girl and the reigning queen of Hindi cinema and almost all the leading heroes of that time—Dharmendra, Jeetendra and Sanjeev Kumar, to name a few—held a torch for the dazzling beauty. They say that Hema Malini saw Dharmendra for the first time at a film premiere in 1969. It was a coincidence that the two signed four films together in the same year—*Sharafat* (1970), *Tum Haseen Main Jawan* (1970), *Naya Zamana* (1971) and *Raja Jani* (1972). Cupid struck his arrow fiercely and on the sets of *Seeta Aur Geeta* (1972) director Ramesh Sippy was the common confidant. Dharmendra has said that it was Hema's beauty and simplicity that he found endearing, while Hema confessed that she felt reassured in Dharmendra's presence.

Two years later, during the shooting of *Sholay* (1975), the chemistry between the lead pair was palpable to everyone on the sets. Both were madly attractive and successful. He was Hindi cinema's reigning star. She was the country's most eligible beauty. The film took a long time to be completed and this helped the blossoming of their relationship. They made a phenomenal pair and film-makers loved casting them together. Pramod Chakraborty cast them in four films—*Naya Zamana, Jugnu* (1973), *Dream Girl*

(1977) and *Azaad* (1978)—while Dulal Guha did so in three—
Dost (1974), *Pratiggya* (1975) and *Dil Ka Hira* (1979). The other
directors who cast the pair together were Ramanand Sagar in *Charas*
(1976), M.A. Thirumugam in *Maa* (1976), Manmohan Desai in
Chacha Bhatija (1977), Ravi Chopra in *The Burning Train* (1980),
Basu Chatterjee in *Dillagi* (1978), Mohan Sehgal in *Raja Jani*
and *Samraat* (1982), Harmesh Malhotra in *Patthar Aur Payal*
(1974), Umesh Mehra in *Alibaba Aur 40 Chor* (1980) and Biswajeet
Chatterjee in *Kahte Hai Mujhko Raja* (1975). There was a magical
chemistry about their pairing but Hema Malini was as much in
demand as a solo star and the first choice for all prestigious projects.

The critics failed to be impressed by her acting prowess but
film-makers touted her as an immensely lucky and dependable
star. Two mega films, *Meera* (1979) and *Razia Sultan* (1983), altered
her image as an actress and both have interesting background
stories. One evening Hema returned from Pune and discovered
film-maker Premji waiting for her at home. Premji had been
keen to start a film with Hema for many years but nothing had
worked out. 'If you would be interested in making a film on
Meera I would love to play the part,' she told Premji. The next
day, Premji had signed up Gulzar to write and direct the film.
Hema remembers Gulzar telling her that it would be a film she
would be proud to watch with her children and grandchildren—
and he was right. Hema is proud of her performance in *Meera* and
has no regrets that the film didn't fare well at the box office.

Kamal Amrohi considered Hema for *Razia Sultan* even though
she was not well versed in the Urdu language, a basic requirement
for the character. He felt Hema had all the other personality
traits important for an empress. She had a regal bearing and a
superstar stature essential to make a heroine-oriented project
feasible. There is another reason why Amrohi cast Hema. While
researching in the Turkistan Archives he came across a portrait of
Razia that bore a striking resemblance to Hema Malini. Amrohi
is supposed to have told her that if she trusted him he would give
her a performance of a lifetime. She did. She walked on hot sands,

rode elephants and horses, enacted sword fights and wore uncomfortable crowns and costumes. Learning Urdu dialogues was a tough proposition but Amrohi hired a special tutor to supervise her diction. It was a milestone year for the actress who was simultaneously shooting for the two most important films of her career—*Meera* in the day and *Razia Sultan* in the evening.

Hema tied the knot with Dharmendra in 1980. Considering the complex circumstances surrounding their union, the couple sought dignity in silence. Part of the credit for this goes to them and the other part, to their good fortune that they managed to survive the controversies. Marriage did not affect her stardom. Hema was pregnant with Esha during the shooting of *Rajput* (1982) and *Satte Pe Satta* (1982), both picturized during the final months of her pregnancy. Four years later Hema was pregnant for the second time, this time with Ahana.

Despite a glorious film career Hema continued to perform her dance shows on stage. Initially she performed only pure Bharatanatyam dances but gradually, as her shows became more popular, the promoters put pressure on her to include different dance forms and expand the shows into mega ballets about legendary women like Savitri, Durga, Meera and Draupadi. Performances of this kind were to become her signature tune in time to come. In fact, Hema considers dance as an important factor in her rise to superstardom. Over her four-decade-long film career, Hema Malini got dance opportunities depicting every mood and moment in Hindi films. In *Charas* she did a Cleopatra-style dance, in *Dus Numbri* (1976) she was a bartender. In *Jaaneman* she did a mujra and in *Swami* (1977), a nautanki. In *Meera*, she swayed with a tanpura inside a temple and in *Alibaba Aur 40 Chor*, for the first time, she did an Arabic belly dance. In *The Burning Train*, Parveen Babi and she compete between Eastern and Western dance traditions. In *Jyoti* (1981), she performed the dandiya raas and in *Sharara* (1984) she danced the waltz with Raaj Kumar.

Directors opined that her classical dance background helped her performances. Gulzar offered her *Kinara* (1977), about a dancer who loses eyesight in an accident. The film focused on her struggle to conquer her fears and return to the stage. It is a performance Hema remains proud of. Of the 100-plus films she did in her four-decade-long career, her choices can be divided between the commercial and the creative. Compared to any other heroine of her generation, her record of hits at the box office is rather enviable. *Seeta Aur Geeta*, *Haath Ki Safai* (1974), *Prem Nagar* (1974), *Dharmatma* (1975), *Sholay* and *Trishul* (1978) in the '70s; *Do Aur Do Paanch* (1980), *Naseeb* (1981), *Satte Pe Satta*, *Rajput* and *Andhaa Kanoon* (1983) in the '80s; right up to *Baabul* (2005), she was privileged to be offered a variety of roles with different directors and genres.

She was self-righteous in *Prem Nagar*, a free spirit in *Dharmatma*, progressive in *Trishul* and the matriarch in *Satte Pe Satta*. Similarly she was timid and shy in *Jahan Pyar Mile* (1969), mischievous in *Waris* (1969), romantic in *Abhinetri* (1970), running scared in *Aansoo Aur Muskaan* (1970) and flamboyant in *Tum Haseen Main Jawan* (1970). Every decade offered her landmark projects that escalated her stardom a few rungs higher. Ramesh Sippy's *Andaz* (1971) generated a lot of interest because Rajesh Khanna, a rage in those days, was coming together with the dream girl for the first time. F.C. Mehra's original choice for the 'other' woman in the costume drama *Lal Patthar* (1971) was Vyjayanthimala but hero Raaj Kumar was very keen that it had to be Hema Malini. F.C. Mehra was unsure if Hema, still a newcomer then, would be able to portray such a complex role but Raaj Kumar was persistent and guided the young actress at every stage. 'For this film I received maximum appreciation from my colleagues,' says Hema.

Dulhan (1974) was a typical family drama where she transforms from a radiant bride to a reluctant widow. Hema says everything about Gulzar's *Khushboo* (1975) was just perfect—the characterization, the timing of the film, the casting and, most important, the costumes. This was the first time Hema was draped in cotton-crumpled sarees with unmatched blouses, sporting her natural hair tied in a simple braid and her face devoid of make-up. Based on Saratchandra's story 'Pandit Moshai', the film proved a milestone in Hema's career. So did *Dharmatma* and Hema gives full credit to Feroze Khan's packaging of the film. When Ramesh Sippy narrated the role of Basanti to Hema, she was not impressed. She could not fathom why the director who cast her in *Andaz* and *Seeta Aur Geeta* wanted to cast her as a *tangewali*, but since he had given her two big hits it was difficult to refuse him and she agreed half-heartedly. It is a different story that after the release of *Sholay* Hema was identified as Basanti wherever she travelled.

Hema remained the first choice for all big banners—B.R. Chopra's *The Burning Train*, F.C. Mehra's *Ali Baba Aur 40 Chor*, Manmohan Desai's *Naseeb*, Ramanand Sagar's *Baghavat* (1982) and R. Sippy's *Satte Pe Satta*. She was the first choice of all the independent directors as well—Rakesh Kumar's *Do Aur Do Paanch*, Subhash Ghai's *Krodhi* (1981), Chetan Anand's *Kudrat* (1981) and it is to her credit that she juggled the artistic *Ratnadeep* (1979), *Jyoti* and *Dard* (1981) with mainstream movies *Bandish* (1980), *Aas Paas* (1981) and *Samraat* with equal ease.

Andhaa Kanoon was produced by A. Purnachandra Rao and directed by T. Rama Rao and was a super-duper hit all over India. This was the first time Hema appeared as a police inspector and played sister to south Indian superstar Rajnikanth who essayed the role of a criminal. Earlier she had played sister to Amitabh Bachchan in *Gehri Chaal* (1973). In Hindi films it is believed that if the lead pair is cast as siblings they will not be accepted as a romantic pair. Amitabh and Hema did innumerable romantic films in their career from *Kasauti* (1974) to *Baghban* (2003).

Hema thought of her debut film production when she was reading Irwing Wallace's *The Second Lady*. *Sharara* was released in 1984 and starred herself, Raaj Kumar, Shatrughan Sinha and Mithun Chakraborty. The film did not fare well at the box office but was appreciated for its production values and gripping plot. She was inspired to launch her first tele-serial *Noopur*, produced by HM Creations in 1990. It was about a classical dancer who travels in search of a guru. The story was Hema's and the serial was scripted by Gulzar.

She was going through a transit phase as an actor and Hema decided it was the right time to experiment with parallel cinema. For the first time critics lauded her choices as an actor. She had earlier worked with middle-of-the-road film directors like Basu Chatterjee and Gulzar, and now she agreed to do a cameo role in *Lekin* . . . (1990), played a Punjabi widow in Sukhwant Dadda's *Ek Chadar Maili Si* (1986) and a feisty woman in Aruna Raje's *Rihaee* (1988), all of which proved to be liberating experiences for her, both as an actress and as a woman.

After much deliberation Hema took the plunge and launched herself as a feature-film director. *Dil Aashna Hai* released in 1991 and suddenly Hema found herself approached with only directorial assignments. This is not what Hema wanted and until she got what she desired, Hema explored multiple options. She edited a magazine *Meri Saheli*, directed a TV film *Mohini*, acted in tele-serials *Yug* and *Women Of India*. She was comfortably settled in her new world when Kamal Haasan offered her a role in his home production *Hey Ram* (2000). After their romantic pairing in *Ek Nai Paheli* (1984) the two came together a decade later as mother- and son-in-law.

It was in the winter session of 2003 that the actress was honoured with the Padma Shri award by the Government of India and consequently sworn into the Rajya Sabha. When Ravi Chopra visited Hema Malini's home to narrate the story of *Baghban* Hema knew it was the role of a lifetime and for a change even the critics appreciated her moving performance as much as her stunning beauty. Amitabh Bachchan and she last starred in *Satte Pe Satta* in 1981, and after the success of *Baghban* did *Veer–Zaara* (2004), *Gangotri* (2007) and *Baabul*.

Today Hema Malini is the only actress of her generation who is active on the big screen with Prakash Jha's *Aarakshan* (2011) as well as on the small screen with her occasional serial and several brand endorsements. She continues her stint as a politician (with the BJP) and remains a favourite for brand endorsements in addition to her various dance shows. At the end of 2011 she released *Tell Me O Kkhudda*, her second film as a director, starring daughter Esha Deol.

Hema Malini was launched as the Dream Girl in *Sapnon ka Saudagar* (1968) and after forty-plus years remains the Dream Woman both on and off screen.

MY FIVE FAVOURITE HEMA MALINI FILMS

1. *Lal Patthar* (1971). Directed by Sushil Majumdar. Co-stars: Raaj Kumar, Raakhee and Vinod Mehra. Set in Bengal this period film revolves around a young widow living in abject poverty in the temples of Benaras. She is spotted by a feudal lord who makes her the mistress of his palace. Raja saab (Raaj Kumar) loves her but not enough to marry her. He marries an intelligent, well-bred, gifted artiste who has to constantly vie with the 'other woman' for her husband's attention. As the fiery, alluring, wicked and suddenly insecure mistress Hema lent a regal bearing to her character Saudamini. The scene when Raja saab walks past her chamber to be with his wife and Hema is consumed with rage, standing beside the tigress, is an unforgettable moment.

2. *Meera* (1979). Directed by Gulzar. Co-stars: Shammi Kapoor and Vinod Khanna. It is said that Mani Kaul asked Gulzar why he cast Hema Malini as Meera and Gulzar responded, 'Because she has a peaceful face.' *Meera* was the right role at the right time in her career. The extravagant project demanded a numero uno star and Hema absorbed the various phases of the beggar princess's life. As Meera transforms from the radiant bride to the deity-obsessed saint, she drops her *shringara* and vibrant costumes to first flaming red, then saffron, yellow, brown, beige and finally pristine white apparel to embrace her lord. Throughout this transformation, she has you hooked to the character. My favourite scene is the one where she tells the guru

Surdas not to mention Radha in her presence because, as she put it, '*Main Radha se jalti hoon.*' Delicious.

3. *Seeta Aur Geeta* (1972) Directed by Ramesh Sippy. Co-stars: Dharmendra, Amitabh Bachchan and Jaya Bachchan. A masala film where two twin sisters separated in childhood live diametrically different destinies. One day fate intervenes and the twins trade places. While the director had no doubts about her projection of the timid sister Seeta, Ramesh Sippy was unsure of her playing Geeta. But Hema surprised him with her abandon and energy in the role of the extroverted sister. The power and force exhibited through her expressions and body language when she cracks the whip on her wicked relatives as Geeta is awesome!

4. *Khushboo* (1975). Directed by Gulzar. Co-star: Jeetendra. Adapted from a story by renowned Bengali writer Samresh Basu, the film revolves around a child bride whose groom never returns to take her home. Years pass by and Kusum, now past her prime, is still waiting for her husband but will not contact him. As the proud and dignified bride who makes no claims on her husband, Hema Malini adds many colours to her character. The last scene of the film—my favourite— where the husband asks her to specify his failings, is heart-breaking. She may not be a histrionic actress but her simplicity and submission to her director's sensibility is touching.

5. *Prem Nagar* (1974). Directed by K.S. Prakash Rao. Co-star: Rajesh Khanna. A remake of a highly melodramatic south Indian film. Hema plays Lata, the secretary of an unhappy and alcoholic rich man (Rajesh Khanna). She takes it upon herself to heal him and in the process loses her heart to him. He is complex and arrogant but likeable and Lata understands him. She is wholesome and upright and will not compromise on her values. In a specific scene where she is suspected of robbery in the mansion and Rajesh Khanna confronts her in private, so as not to embarrass her, Hema's moment of outrage and hurt is a scene to remember.

RAJESH KHANNA

THE GOD OF ROMANCE

AVIJIT GHOSH

A lot happened in Bombay cinema in 1966. Dharmendra bared his beefcake torso and scored both at the box office and with heroine Meena Kumari in *Phool Aur Pathar*. Shammi Kapoor, despite a protruding paunch, danced like a dervish to the boisterous tunes of R.D. Burman in *Teesri Manzil*. And lyricist Shailendra produced a classic, *Teesri Kasam*; the movie's failure broke his heart, took his life.

Few paid attention to *Aakhri Khat*, a low-budget quickie that, in hindsight, appears to be a precursor to Hollywood's cutesy 1994 box-office smash, *Baby's Day Out*. Directed by Chetan Anand (of *Neecha Nagar* and *Haqeeqat* fame), the movie was weaved around the escapades of a fifteen-month-old wandering the city streets and vanished like smoke in the wind. The only thing that endures in popular memory is the melodious track, 'Baharon mera jeewan bhi sanwaron' (gorgeously rendered by the combined talents of Lata Mangeshkar, Kaifi Azmi and Khayyam), that Vividh Bharati plays to this day.

The film's hero was a twenty-three-year-old debutant named Rajesh Khanna; it was his reward for winning the United Producers Talent Contest. He played a city-based sculptor who falls in love with a *gaon ki gori*. She conceives after a hesitant sexual union—as innocent belles invariably did in 1960s' Hindi movies. Complications arise; they separate. When the hero comes to know through her *aakhri khat* that his beloved is somewhere in the city with his child, he desperately looks around. The role required the young actor to showcase an array of emotions—tenderness, anxiety, guilt, frustration—and he wasn't found wanting.

But the following year when he starred in three more box-office turkeys—*Raaz* (the movie's opening credits says, G.P. Sippy proudly presents Rajesh Khanna), *Baharon Ke Sapne* (superhit director Nasir Hussain's first flop) and *Aurat*—one wondered whether the judges who declared him a winner had made a serious error of judgement.

Then, much like a blizzard without advance warning, director Shakti Samanta's *Aradhana* arrived on 7 November 1969. A goulash of drama, romance and some of the finest music that S.D. Burman ever composed, the movie turned out to be a monster hit. A month later another romantic family drama created a similar box-office tsunami: director Raj Khosla's *Do Raaste* with Mumtaz as the young hero's leading lady. But the impact of these two movies was much more than the megabucks raked in. Together they unleashed the Rajesh Khanna phenomenon, creating a fresh hierarchy of stardom in Bombay (now Mumbai). One shake of his head was enough for financiers to write out blank cheques for distributors to buy a movie before a single shot was canned. Producers, directors, writers—everyone became secondary to his star power.

The route to the audience's heart is complicated and mysterious. Nobody really knows how an actor—of ordinary build, average height and a face often sprinkled with pimples—induced such messianic mania and hypnotized an entire nation. Groping for a phrase to capture the zeitgeist, the industry finally coined a new term: superstar. Rajesh Khanna had become the omphalos of a new world order in the Hindi film industry.

Born in Amritsar on 29 December 1942, Rajesh (his original

name was Jatin) was adopted by a childless couple related to his own parents who were more affluent than them and lived near Girgaum, Bombay. By all accounts, he was pampered as a child. As a teenager he was interested in theatre. When he wanted to join films, the young actor went around asking for roles in 'an MG sports car', say Dinesh Raheja and Jitendra Kothari in *The Hundred Luminaries of Hindi Cinema*.

Maybe it was written. *Aradhana* came at a time when Bombay cinema badly needed a fresh face. Raj Kapoor, Dilip Kumar and Dev Anand had aged, though the last two were still playing lead roles. Shammi Kapoor had grown obese and Rajendra Kumar's appeal had gone stale. True, Dharmendra, Manoj Kumar and Jeetendra had delivered runaway hits but there was still plenty of room at the top.

And when Rajesh, sporting a black Nepalese cap, rode an open jeep and serenaded heroine Sharmila Tagore with the song, 'Mere sapnon ki rani kab aayegi tu', a generation of girls had found their pin code to heaven. Women now in their fifties claim they got the biggest O of their lives when the film's second Rajesh Khanna made his entry in the famous airport scene. Dressed in a flight-lieutenant uniform, the actor looks arresting as he walks towards girlfriend Farida Jalal, muttering words of love, and takes her in his arms. Few women wouldn't have liked to swap places with Jalal. If there was one game-changing moment in his career, this was it.

They say shrieking college girls smeared his car with lipstick, wrote letters in blood, married his photograph. Once when he had fever, a group of college students spent hours taking turns to put ice water on his forehead in a photograph, as the actor recalled in an interview to Gulf News in October 2007.

Men admired and aped everything he did. When he slapped a belt over his shirt for Binaca Geetmala's top 1971 track, 'Zindagi ik safar hai suhana', it spawned a million imitators. His round-collared guru kurtas, an intelligent fashion ploy that also hid an expanding waistline, too became a rage. Even kids, especially after *Haathi Mere Saathi* (1971), adored him. His smile sold toothpastes (Macleans), a rare case of celebrity endorsement those days.

Navin Nischol, a star in his own right, had a first-hand experience of the frenzy. He told the *Star and Style* in the September–October 1980 issue: 'Believe me, the kind of mass hysteria he aroused in his day, I don't think even Amitabh has seen. And I was a witness to it. I had gone for a wedding reception at the Taj. Kaka [Rajesh was nicknamed Kaka much before a Brazilian footballer got that name] was coming out of the hall while I was going in. We crossed each other on the way, and—this is the incredible part—the whole damn hall walked out behind that guy! It was such a stunning sight—that whole sea of humanity simply following him as he made his way out. It was unforgettable . . . Look I'm getting goose pimples just talking about it.'

That's why Jack Pizzey's 1973 BBC film documentary on Rajesh Khanna, *Bombay Superstar*, introduces him 'as the biggest star of the biggest film industry of the world.' He is described as someone with 'the charisma of Rudolph Valentino and arrogance of Napoleon'. You can understand where the last bit came from: the filmstar cancelled five appointments with the makers of the documentary—including inviting the crew home and promptly forgetting—before giving them audience.

He was acting big because, strictly going by box-office statistics, he was the biggest thing to have happened to mainstream Hindi cinema. His finest hits came with Sharmila Tagore, Mumtaz and Asha Parekh (in that order), although overall, he did a dozen movies with Hema Malini too. Statistics put out by Boxofficeindia.com show that between 1969 and 1971, Rajesh Khanna delivered superhits by the sackful. In 1969, apart from *Aradhana* and *Do Raaste*, the year's two top grossers, *Bandhan* was another big box-office smash, while even *Doli* and *Ittefaq*, a songless murder mystery, earned profits. In 1970 the superstar had four of the year's top-ten winners: *Sachaa Jhutha*, *Aan Milo Sajna*, *Kati Patang* and *Safar*. That year *The Train* and *Anand* also earned profits. The next year he bettered himself delivering four of the year's five biggest hits: *Haathi Mere Saathi*, *Dushman*, *Maryada* and *Andaz*. Among the other of his films released that year, *Amar Prem* finished eighth. Everything he touched turned to box-office gold. The dream run was finally broken when *Mehboob Ki Mehndi* (1971) collapsed at the cash counters.

Few top actors till then, with the exception of Ashok Kumar and Dilip Kumar, had endeared themselves in equal measure to the masses, the classes as well as the critics. Rajesh Khanna found that fine balance. In his early days, he displayed a penchant for intelligent, off-beat movies such as *Ittefaq* and *Aavishkar* (1974). Barring Dharmendra, no other big hero took such risks in the late 1960s and early 1970s. There was symmetry to his performances in *Khamoshi* (1969), *Safar*, *Anand* and *Amar Prem* that won him critical accolades. He surprisingly got the Filmfare Best Actor Award for *Sachaa Jhutha* and, more deservingly, the following year for *Anand*. In the awards ceremony held in 1973, despite two impressive performances in *Dushman* and *Amar Prem*, he lost out to Manoj Kumar's thoroughly forgettable *Be-imaan*. That was also the year when Hema Malini's *Seeta Aur Geeta* was preferred to Meena Kumari's *Pakeezah* for the Best Actress Award. And incredibly, *Be-imaan* also swept the Best Film, Best Director and Best Music categories over contenders from *Pakeezah*, *Shor*, *Amar Prem*. So much for Filmfare being India's answer to the Oscars!

Songs were the soul of Rajesh Khanna's movies. And he enacted them in his trademark style: rhythmically shaking the head and gently lowering the eyelids as if offering an invitation. His hands would often go up in the air as if striking a mudra. Even flops such as *Mehboob Ki Mehndi*, *Mere Jeevan Sathi* (1972), *Mehbooba* (1976) and *Aashiq Hoon Baharon Ka* (1977) had chartbusting tracks. His career thrived on some of the most popular numbers composed by R.D. Burman—in films like *Kati Patang*, *Amar Prem*, *Namak Haraam* (1973), *Aap Ki Kasam* (1974)—and Laxmikant–Pyarelal—in movies like *Do Raaste*, *Haathi Mere Saathi*, *Dushman*. The two music directors, along with

Kishore Kumar whose singing career was revived by *Aradhana*, synergized Rajesh's movies. They invariably reserved their best for the superstar. Once the slide began, the songs ceased to be as great as before. Without them, Rajesh Khanna became an actor without his best lines.

Romance was his core competence. As the 1973 BBC documentary noted, 'Rajesh has found more ways of implying love than the Kama Sutra has of making it.' But the truth is that the actor brought no revolution to the art; he just gently tweaked the existing formulas. He blended the playfulness of Dev Anand with a fraction of Dilip Kumar's intensity; to this he added his own charm and style. The characters he played had a touch of poet-philosophers. The forest officer of *Kati Patang*, with eyes clearer than spring water, recites poems to a 'widow' he has fallen in love with. As a man, the actor evoked a mélange of possibilities. He could be a sensitive lover, a naughty but reliable husband, an eye-candy neighbour, an indulgent brother, even a great lover, if you wanted a 'Roop tera mastana' moment. He could be intense without being suffocating.

Which is why few actors profited more from a broken heart. It is easy to empathize with the smiling–laughing cancer patient Anand. The melancholia of Anand babu in *Amar Prem* seeps to the audience. You understand why the bhadralok visits the brothels. And you know he is not lying when he tells the golden-hearted prostitute (played by Sharmila Tagore), '*Tumne is kamre ko mandir bana diya.*' There is a style with which he says: I hate tears. Rajesh's acting was defined by style.

He wooed both urban and rural India, playing characters from the city as well as the hinterland; sometimes both in the same film as in Manmohan Desai's *Sachaa Jhutha*. He looked dapper in finely tailored suits; he could also carry off a dhoti-kurta-tabeez with ease. Just watch him play the country bumpkin in *Bandhan* (written by Salim–Javed) and dance to the paisa vasool track, 'Bin badra ke bijuriya kaise chamke'.

In his biggest hits, the characters he generally played belonged to the comfortable side of middle class: the flight lieutenant of *Aradhana*, the forest officer of *Kati Patang*, the bhadralok of *Amar Prem*. Some characters he played also came from the underclass. In the title role of *Bawarchi* (1972), he cooked food and served love in the mode of a proto-Munnabhai. The honest clerk of *Apna Desh* (1972), the rustic musician of *Sachaa Jhutha*, the unemployed youth of *Baharon Ke Sapne*, the working-class hero of *Namak Haraam* were again lower-middle-class representations. But Rajesh's strength lay in his ability to represent things he didn't even seek to. In the best tradition of the 1970s' hero, he was always pro-poor, a do-gooder. In *Aan Milo Sajna*, he pulls a horse-cart out of the mud to help an old gentleman and his five daughters. That's typical of the screen image he carefully fashioned.

The 1973 BBC documentary provides delightful fodder to a psychologist looking for insight into the superstar's emotional world. To the question 'Do you have to fight to stay at the top?' Rajesh cryptically admitted that one had to be 'a little cruel', without expanding on what he exactly meant by cruelty. He went on to say, 'One has to fight and fight well and win the battle.' In reply to a question, he admitted to using the smile to attract his female fans and doing things 'intuitionally' and 'impulsively'.

One of the actor's more impulsive decisions was marrying Dimple Kapadia, the fifteen-year-old star of the 1973 blockbuster *Bobby*, after breaking up with Anju Mahendru, his long-time girlfriend. Poison-penned gossip columnist Devyani Chaubal, with whom he shared an intimate relationship, was among the first whom Rajesh rang up at 3 a.m. to break the news. 'He was absolutely drunk,' Chaubal said in the same BBC interview.

The marriage was construed by his critics as a way of staying in the news after a row of flops. In the interview, during a moment of extreme honesty, Rajesh admitted to being nervous before the release of Yash Chopra's *Daag* on 27 April 1973. It was a big banner release and the superstar, now on shaky ground, was hoping for a blockbuster that would stop the slide. Rajesh confessed that after having been a superstar, when one falls a little, one wonders how deep the fall is going to be. 'One is scared,' he said. It is in these moments of candour that the star is also the most endearing. 'He is so insecure, so complex,' Chaubal said.

Contrary to what the documentary predicts, *Daag* raked in the moolah. After *Bobby* and *Jugnu*, it was the year's third biggest grosser. But it was *Zanjeer* (1973), starring a tall, brooding young man, that fired the imagination of the youth at a time of student unrest. Rajesh's soft romantic musicals suddenly seemed an idea past their expiry date. Amitabh Bachchan's flamboyant rich industrialist overshadowed his gentle working-class hero in *Namak Haraam* the same year. In public perception, Rajesh had lost the on-screen battle against someone already being touted as the next big thing. With teenage girls having found a fresh vanilla of the season in *Bobby*'s hero Rishi Kapoor, it was double jeopardy for the superstar.

In 1974, Rajesh roared back into contention with three hits: *Prem Nagar*, *Roti* and *Aap Ki Kasam*. In *Prem Nagar*, he played a playboy prince; in *Aap Ki Kasam*, a suspicious husband. *Roti*, where he played a fugitive who falls in love, was more in tune with the times. But unlike Big B's Vijay in *Zanjeer*, who was so angry that he wanted to tear the world down, Rajesh's Mangal in *Roti* seems to be mocking at destiny. He is simply not angry enough at a time when the fight master was becoming more important than the music director. The times were a-changing and Rajesh had no answer.

Barring the mind-boggling success of the mythological *Jai Santoshi Maa*, most big hits of 1975 underlined the new box-office behaviour. *Sholay*, *Deewar* and *Pratiggya* were bursting with knuckle-crunching action and peppered with characters seething with rage. Rajesh Khanna's reply, Raj Khosla's *Prem Kahani*, a freedom fighter's love story, sank without a trace.

The actor's last attempt to recapture the glory days was *Mehbooba*. Based on popular pulp romance writer Gulshan Nanda's novel, the movie was directed by Shakti Samanta, who had collaborated with him in his most memorable movies such as *Aradhana, Kati Patang* and *Amar Prem*. But reincarnation as romance failed to rekindle the dying flame at the box office. Maybe it would have worked five years earlier or five years later. Despite competent work by the actor and classy music by R.D. Burman, the movie bombed. Rajesh Khanna, the superstar, was buried forever.

By this time, Rajesh seemed to be totally unsure of what his fans wanted from him. He was even trying out adventure-fantasies like *Bundal Baaz* (1976), directed by Shammi Kapoor, perhaps hoping the kids will like it. Ironically, the only film that modestly worked for him in 1977 was Joy Mukerji's *Chhailla Babu*, a racy thriller. That would have confused the romantic hero even more. Much of the superstar's rise to the top could be attributed to charm and charisma. But the same mannerisms that had the girls swooning five years ago now seemed comical in films like *Anurodh, Karm* and *Aashiq Hoon Baharon Ka*. With every passing year, he not only became increasingly theatrical but also a bigger prisoner of mannerisms. By the 1980s, it was this exaggerated, imagined sense of himself that the actor kept believing to be the real Rajesh Khanna. He was becoming his own parody.

Film magazines in the 1970s wrote copious gossip items about his bloated king-sized ego. In 1977, Manmohan Desai delivered a remarkable quartet of box-office hits—*Dharamveer, Chacha Bhatija, Amar Akbar Anthony* and *Parvarish*. The multi-starrer era had truly begun. But the actor initially refused to work in them. Rajesh felt he was still good enough to deliver solo hits. It is better to have one horse than four bullocks in a movie, he once told a Hindi newsmagazine. By the time realization dawned on him—two multi-starrers where he held his own, *Kudrat* (1981) and *Rajput* (1982)—the golden moment was gone.

All this, combined with his 'attitude' problems (he was unable to get along with co-stars and was coming late on the sets), meant he had few backers once the chips were down. Premier directors like Yash Chopra and Manmohan Desai, who had regularly worked with him in the past, stopped doing so after *Daag* and *Roti*. And he fought with Salim–Javed, the premier scriptwriting pair of the era.

But just when everybody was busy writing off the ex-superstar, Rajesh made a stirring comeback with *Amardeep* (1979), playing a playboy on the mend. But by now, with a receding hairline and a burgeoning backside, he was genuinely looking middle-aged. In the Danny-directed *Phir Wohi Raat* (1980), the crowd often whistled in derision as he shook his substantial hips to the number, 'Sang mere nikle thhe saajan'. What kept him in business was the occasional hit—*Thodi Si Bewafai* (1980), *Ashanti* (1982)—and the occasional off-beat flick where his performance was talked about. In *Red Rose* (1980) he played a psychotic killer who hates women. His performance as a barber who becomes a chief minister in *Aaj Ka MLA Ramavtar* (1984) was again much discussed and appreciated.

The actor's main competitor now was Jeetendra, whom he is said to have coached once for auditions. With half Rajesh's acting ability, one-third his waistline and four times the discipline, Jeetendra comfortably ensconsed himself as the director's favourite for weepy socials or mindless entertainers made down South. Rajesh could only watch the water flow.

In 1983 Rajesh confounded everybody again, including his most trenchant critics, with a roaring solo superhit after nearly a decade: *Avtaar*. The Mohan Kumar movie, a forerunner of *Baghban* (2003), saw him in a stand-out performance as an ageing egoistic mechanic who is deserted by his sons and daughters-in-law only to build his own industrial empire. In an age when elderly parents are often left to fend for themselves, the movie touched a hidden chord in the audience.

The same year, he paired with Tina Munim in another box-office success, *Souten*. Rajesh, who was paired with Tina in real life too, once said, 'We share our toothbrushes,' making it the yuckiest romantic quote of all time. The next year, he had another box-office smash, *Maqsad*, which had some of the dirtiest double-meaning songs and dialogues that the censors ever passed. In pursuit of success, Kaka had become Kaka Kondke.

But between 1985 and 1991, he kept lurching from one disastrous film to another, films that can only be categorized as avoidable footnotes in an otherwise illustrious career. Some exceptions were: *Aakhir Kyon* (1985), *Zamana* (1985, where he worked with Salim–Javed after a long gap) and David Dhawan's *Swarg* (1990, where as an ageing patriarch, he played second fiddle to Govinda). The superstar was now like a millionaire fallen into middle-class days.

Joining the Congress party in 1991 was a good career move. As a politician, the film star's high point came the same year when he contested the Lok Sabha election against the BJP leader L.K. Advani, then gloating from his Ayodhya rath-yatra high. A political greenhorn, Rajesh Khanna gave Advani the fright of his life, losing by only 1,589 votes from the New Delhi Lok Sabha constituency. A few months later he comfortably won the by-election beating fellow actor Shatrughan Sinha by over 28,000 votes in June 1992. In politics, the actor sparkled like a shooting star only to disappear with the same speed.

The last two decades have been pretty disappointing for the actor. In 1999 he played a father in the R.K. Films production, *Aa Ab Laut Chalein*. He also acted in serials such as *Ittefaq*. Nobody noticed. At one point, he even considered doing *Bigg Boss 4*. Imagine the ex-superstar doing the same thing as Dolly Bindra! Of late, like Dev Anand, Rajesh too has acted in movies that would make his daughters squirm.

In *Wafaa* (2008), for instance, he played an ageing husband whose wife is having an affair with the driver and plots his killing. In the film's opening scene, Rajesh, in his henna-coloured hair and beard, is shown cleaning a gun by the poolside, wearing a red kurta and sunglasses, looking every inch Shakti Kapoor's elder brother. Soon a sex kitten, old enough to be his granddaughter, emerges from the water in a woefully inadequate bikini. She turns out to be his wife. And when Rajesh rubs her back with suntan cream, she moans vigorously as they generally do in soft-porn movies. Watching the scene one wonders if any of his original female fans have watched the movie and what their reaction might be. As the scene unfolds, Rajesh begins screaming like a part-time Ramleela performer. What on earth was he thinking when he accepted the part?

Yet nothing—nothing—can take away what Rajesh Khanna achieved in his prime. Over the decades, Bollywood has seen plenty of stars. But nobody has captured the nation's collective mindspace like him. What really made him such a frighteningly popular social phenomenon can be the subject of any doctoral thesis in sociology. Let us just say that at a time when young India was slowly getting angry about unemployment and price rise, the actor temporarily provided a welcome diversion. He was perhaps a hyphen between the innocence of the past and the uncertainty of the future.

But what a hyphen he was! During the 2009 IIFA ceremony in Macau, where Rajesh received the Lifetime Achievement Award, host Amitabh Bachchan introduced him, saying, 'The Indian film industry had never seen superstardom like they had of Rajesh Khanna and probably never will.' Dressed in a saffron-coloured silk kurta and pyjama, the actor behaved like a superstar frozen in time. He was exceedingly theatrical but as he spoke in a voice overwhelmed with emotion, the actor formed an immediate connect with the audience. When he referred to Big B as Babu Moshai and recited a couplet that ended with the line, '*Yeh bhi ek daur hai, woh bhi ek daur tha*,' they clapped uproariously. They may not have seen his movies but, at that moment, they knew by instinct what the man would have been in his prime. They understood: once a superstar, always a superstar.

MY FIVE FAVOURITE RAJESH KHANNA FILMS

1. *Amar Prem* (1971). Directed by Shakti Samanta. Co-star: Sharmila Tagore. Nobody could have made Anand babu

as likeable as the superstar. And few songs have been as evocatively picturized as 'Yeh kya hua'.

2. *Avishkaar* (1973). Directed by Basu Bhattacharya. Co-star: Sharmila Tagore. As an egoist husband, Rajesh displays remarkable control over his craft missing from his later work.

3. *Dhanwan* (1981). Directed by Surendra Mohan. Co-stars: Reena Roy and Rakesh Roshan. The actor is brilliant as the arrogant industrialist with negative shades in this lesser-known film.

4. *Kati Patang* (1970). Directed by Shakti Samanta. Co-star: Asha Parekh. The ultimate romantic movie. The filmstar looks good, acts great. The film has a superb soundtrack too.

5. *Haathi Mere Saathi* (1971). Directed by M. Thirumugam. Co-star: Tanuja. The movie that introduced me to the movies. Every kid loved the title song.

AMITABH BACHCHAN

FROM ANGRY YOUNG MAN TO PATERFAMILIAS

SIDHARTH BHATIA

Film stars can never be divorced from their screen personas. A star persona takes time to emerge, but once it does, it becomes the definitive image associated with the star. So Dilip Kumar will forever remain the Tragedy King though he has done many comedy roles, and done them rather well, too. Amitabh Bachchan is an exception of sorts—he has managed to shed off his earlier persona as the Angry Young Man fighting a venal establishment and smoothly transited to become the exact opposite—the settled establishment man. That speaks as much about his own craft as also his ability to keep himself relevant. Most of all, it tells us about how India itself has changed and how the most durable star in Indian cinematic history has kept himself relevant with changing mores.

Bachchan has been part of our national consciousness for four full decades and, moreover, is one of those rare actors who inhabit several worlds at the same time. He has meant different things to different generations. He has segued from being a young man with the anger of a generation simmering inside him to being a kind of father figure, in a manner of speaking, who has your best interests at heart. Through this, it bears mentioning that Bachchan himself always remained an establishment man—how could he be otherwise, given his personal background—but he successfully articulated the angst of his fellow Indians by portraying characters who were angry with the system.

He has not only followed trends but created them too. He became a television host at a time when movie stars hesitated to appear on the small screen, which they felt diminished their glamour. He joined politics along with Rajiv Gandhi's corporate baba log before film stars discovered politics, was a corporate tycoon in tune with economic liberalization before the suits entered the film industry and a model long before other stars realized their brand equity could be monetized. Today he is an ambassador for a variety of products ranging from cement to chocolate, where he stands for trust and durability, light years away from an earlier era when he saw—on the screen at least—capital as untrustworthy and exploitative.

Less remarked upon but equally significant is his effortless switch into the new social media. He is a regular blogger, writing a few hundred words every night and tweeting his views to a loyal fan following. This allows him to communicate directly with his fans, bypassing all traditional channels like media interviews and surprisingly, instead of diluting his mystique, it has served to further enhance his appeal. Stars usually tolerate their fans with the barest pretence of patience and goodwill; Bachchan actually enjoys it. Young pups have come and even gone, but Bachchan, the colossus, goes on forever—a reminder of stability in the time of uncertainty and quick change. It is tempting to say that Amitabh Bachchan is not simply a man of the times; he symbolizes the times.

Clearly then, Bachchan is unique; even if he had done a fraction of these things, he would still be the dominating presence of our age, looming large over our collective consciousness. He is not merely a cultural totem but a social phenomenon, telling us something about ourselves, mirroring our concerns and our hopes. When we were frustrated at the drift in our nation— strikes, riots, the Emergency—he was angry; and now when we are getting rich, comfortable and global, he is our wise elder assuring us of the genuineness of our aspirations.

What makes Bachchan even more remarkable is that he has warded off the challenge of two, if not three, generations of stars. His peers of course have all disappeared into the sunset, but even those who came later have had to deal with him as a credible opponent, fighting if not for the same roles at least for screen domination. Acting opposite Bachchan puts everyone, from newbie to veteran, on his or her guard; his screen presence and, increasingly, his legacy can be intimidating.

Even if the world has moved on and new kinds of cinema have emerged which do not necessarily revolve around him (unlike in the 1970s and 1980s), Bachchan is still a player. He retains the ability to pull in the crowds; in his heyday, his name was enough to sell the film and ensure its success. Today, his name in the cast gives it the additional boost a film needs. Admittedly, many, if not most, of his films in the last decade or so have been flops, but it has not made the slightest difference to his standing. Anyone else would have been quietly put out to pasture by an industry whose only loyalty is to the box-office gods, but the queue outside his door remains as long as ever.

What explains this longevity and enduring appeal across generations, eras and cinematic styles? Audiences are fickle—they are quick to discard the old and embrace the new, and are also quick to move on. Yet they have been kind to the actor.

It is not as if Bachchan has not felt the heat of audience disapproval; in the 1980s, soon after he resigned from Parliament after his brief and not-too-successful stint as an MP, he acted in a seemingly never-ending series of rank bad films. Even his two favourite directors of the time, Manmohan Desai and Prakash Mehra, with whom he had successfully paired for some of his most popular films, could not recreate the magic—their latter-day outings, such as *Gunga Jumna Saraswathi* (1988) or *Jaadugar* (1989) were disasters, commercially and critically. Film-makers of all kinds were taking the lazy way out by producing formulaic Bachchan films, with a dash of action, a lot of comedy and ever-younger heroines. Who can recall (and who wants to recall) *Inquilaab* (1984), *Geraftaar* (1985), *Aaj Ka Arjun* (1990) or *Indrajeet* (1991)? He inevitably played the cop, the vigilante, or the ordinary man who stands up for justice. In most of those films, Bachchan looked jaded and desperate, as only a fading star can. It was all tiresome to watch and presumably tiring to do. The audiences pointedly stayed away.

Bachchan was professionally finished—that was the common consensus. The man described as the 'one to ten' in any listing of male stars of the '70s was now a washed-out has-been. A newer generation was emerging. His off-screen activities too were failures, the most high-profile of them being his business venture, the not-so-modestly named Amitabh Bachchan Corporation Limited (ABCL), set up to bring corporate culture to the notoriously chaotic and unorganized film business. The company went bankrupt. With huge debts piled up and with no roles worth the name in his hand, Bachchan's downfall looked imminent. And yet, at the beginning of the second decade of the twenty-first century, he straddles the universe, so to speak, working non-stop in films and elsewhere, putting in as many hours as his far younger contemporaries. Nor are his activities limited to entertainment—he writes a hugely popular blog and tweets incessantly, thus not only creating an online diary of his activities but also keeping in direct touch with his legions of fans for whom he continues to be a divinity. Not all of his films, especially his recent ones, have done him any credit or will enhance his CV, but there is no denying that Bachchan is now the most important film personality of the last 100-plus years of Indian cinema.

Some part of Bachchan's remarkable ability to re-invent himself and show an uncommon resilience can be traced back to his beginnings in the Hindi film industry. In the late 1960s, the leading man was usually a soft-faced, well-fed type, adept at wooing the heroine in lush, mountainous locales. He had to know how to smile but also to cry, to dance and sing but also look melancholy. The romantic dramas of the 1960s centred around the trials and tribulations of young love, inevitably set in the midst of some family drama—lost fortunes or lost children. The conflicts, such as they were, revolved around mistaken identities and chicanery by nasty relatives out to appropriate inheritances. The hero, more often than not the missing heir himself, had to fight these evil forces, but that was only in the last reel. Through most of the film he was romancing the girl.

In such a scenario, for a tall, gangly, unconventional-looking (by Hindi cinema standards) man to aspire to become an actor was itself an act of great faith, or great foolhardiness. Hailing from a prominent literary family and having grown up with proximity to power—the family was close to the Nehrus—and with what could be called a posh public-school education, the administrative services or the multinational corporate sector should have been the career of choice. Bachchan has on occasion also said that popular Hindi cinema was looked down upon by his high-minded academic father Harivansh Rai Bachchan, one of India's foremost poets. To merely consider it as a career option therefore was a revolutionary idea.

But the young man, with some English theatre behind him, made his way to Bombay (now Mumbai) with a letter in hand from Prime Minister Indira Gandhi herself and met up with Nargis and Sunil Dutt, who was then making *Reshma Aur Shera* (1971). They gave him a bit role but ironically, given that his deep baritone became his signature, made the character mute. Another film *Saat Hindustani* (1969), made by K.A. Abbas, another Nehru–Gandhi family friend, saw Bachchan as one of seven young revolutionaries. In neither did he show any spectacular acting talent, though seeing them now, the contours of his impressive screen presence can be discerned.

These films did little to convince producers that he had the potential to become a leading man. A few films did come his way but nothing that stood out then or has more than mere curiosity value now. Except *Anand* (1971). Hrishikesh Mukherjee immediately grasped the possibilities of Bachchan's smouldering presence, casting him as the intense Dr Bhasker Bannerjee, the perfect foil to the ebullient Anand, played by the then reigning superstar Rajesh Khanna. The cards were all stacked in Rajesh Khanna's favour, but Bachchan managed to stand out. But for the most part he got eminently forgettable film parts though it is intriguing to note that (even in those days) he was mainly offered roles of an outsider, someone who could never be part of the mainstream.

His was an angular personality, even literally so, and right from the beginning, he was cast in villainous roles, which, in Hindi cinema, marks you for life. The crossover from negative characters to more heroic ones is difficult in a business where the duality of bad and good is very clearly demarcated. Audiences, and therefore producers, do not want their preconceived notions disturbed by a popular villain suddenly becoming the noble hero. Very few have crossed over, but typecasting is a professional hazard in an industry where formula is king.

Bachchan, of course, was more interested in getting work rather than worried about what kind of work it was. There is a story about him once landing up for a crowd scene in a Merchant Ivory film. During the editing, the film's hero, Shashi Kapoor, spotted him as a face in a funeral and got the bit cut out to save the young actor from embarrassment.

That was in 1970–71. But in the three years that followed, Bachchan had ten releases (including guest roles) of which one, *Bombay to Goa* (1972) gave him an opportunity to play the typical romantic lead, complete with fights, comedy sequences and a chance to wear good clothes and woo the heroine. It is an awkward performance and the heroine, Aruna Irani, was not one of the top-flight leads of her time but Bachchan shows aplomb and flair. He is making the most of this chance.

Then his luck turned—two of the bigger stars of the time,

Dev Anand and Raaj Kumar, both declined to act as a police officer in *Zanjeer* (1973). It was easy to see why. Though it was a meaty enough role, the film had no songs or romance and the hero had no soft sides to his personality; he was angry all the time. Taking Bachchan was a leap of faith; he had no real success to his name until then, at least not as a solo lead. Perhaps it was his brooding rendition as Dr Bhasker Bannerjee in *Anand* that worked in his favour, though long-time Bachchan watchers have also pointed out that he had done a fine job as a villain in the relatively lesser-known *Parwana* (1971).

Much has been made of the fact that the explosive hero, the so-called Angry Young Man, was a hero of his times. India was passing through a particularly turbulent phase, with student unrest and the threat of massive strikes in the air, and the afterglow of 1971—when Mrs Indira Gandhi triumphed in the elections and directed a victory against Pakistan in the battlefield—had worn off. Indians were angry and they needed someone to articulate that anger. In Bachchan's Inspector Vijay, who takes on powerful smugglers posing as respectable businessmen, India found the perfect hero. The fact that Bachchan followed it up with similar roles consolidated that image and that theory.

But take a look at the other films released along with *Zanjeer* in 1973. It is the usual mix of romance, drama, suspense and thriller movies—the whole gamut of Hindi cinematic formulas which have not changed in decades. From *Bobby*, a pretty film on young love to *Yaadon Ki Baraat*, a lost-and-found drama with plenty of romance and violence to *Heera Panna*, with a bikini-clad Zeenat Aman displaying plenty of oomph, the year saw it all. Even Bachchan had two other films that year—*Namak Haraam*, an Indian take on Beckett, where he got an opportunity to rave and rant, and *Abhimaan*, a much softer film in which he was an envious husband going to seed with jealousy because of his wife's success.

All the three films were hugely successful—it was a breakthrough year for the actor. Though it is *Zanjeer* which is remembered as the film that gave him the initial fillip that launched him into the successful phase of his career, the two Hrishikesh Mukherjee vehicles contributed a lot to the industry perception about the emergence of a versatile actor who had star power too. Good actors in the Indian film industry have come and gone and many a star has faded away rapidly after one success or two; rarely does someone who combines both qualities emerge. Bachchan, with his tremendous screen presence and his intelligent understanding of the character's motivations, was a godsend for the industry.

In a short period he became, in the memorable words of one of his peers, 'the number one-to-ten actor' of Hindi cinema. Producers were literally queuing up outside his home with proposals; it is sobering to note that in the 1970s, he acted in over 55 films as the hero. That is more than five films a year, more than any other actor in Hindi films ever.

Intriguingly, this profligacy, if one could call it that, did not in any way impact the quality of his performances. Bachchan's '70s' films stand tall even today, as opposed to much that came after, from the rotten 1980s onwards. *Anand* or *Amar Akbar Anthony* (1977), *Deewar* (1975) or *Chupke Chupke* (1975), *Abhimaan* or *Kabhi Kabhie* (1976)—he was in top form in each of those varied roles that demanded anger, humour, romance or just quiet intensity. Even in a relatively less famous film like *Zameer* (1975), Bachchan effortlessly stood out. The occasional flop came and went with hardly a dent in his reputation or commercial value. Untouched by failure, he became bigger and bigger and an entire nation prayed for him when he was on life support after an injury in 1982, during the shooting of *Coolie* (1983).

After reaching such peaks, it was natural that he move into politics when his childhood friend Rajiv Gandhi, the new prime minister, called for elections in 1984. Bachchan won handsomely in Allahabad, his birthplace. Gandhi held out the promise of a new beginning for an India brutalized after the assassination of his mother Indira Gandhi, and Bachchan was to be among the young Indians by his side, leading the country to prosperity. Bachchan, the anti-establishment man on screen, was gravitating towards his natural habitat, the high table of power.

The law of averages had to catch up some time. The political career went bust when he quit in 1987 after describing politics as a cesspool. His name got sucked into the controversy over commissions paid for the sale of Bofors guns to India. And the films too began to flop, even those made by his two favourite directors, Prakash Mehra and Manmohan Desai. By the early 1990s, he was making a film a year—it is a period when he took a 'hiatus' from his career, as he says. The return was anything but encouraging; his big comeback film, *Mrityudaata* (1997)—in which he inexplicably played a doctor turned vengeance-seeker—showed that he, or at least his angry persona, was way past its sell-by date. Interestingly, by this time he had also broken away from the Gandhis. And his dream venture, ABCL, which was to bring corporate culture into the film industry, failed. It must have been a time of acute loneliness and self-doubt.

A new generation of directors, actors and viewers had emerged. India too had changed. It was not in an angry mood any more. Soft romance was slowly creeping back on the screen. Three young actors, who collectively came to be known as the Khans, were knocking on the doors of stardom, waiting to be let in. Both Aamir Khan and Salman Khan began their careers with love stories, but even Shahrukh Khan—whose first big hits (*Baazigar* and *Darr* in 1993) were in the Bachchan mould, except that he was a love-struck crazy—eventually found superstardom only with a love story. Post-liberalization India was in a happy mood, eager to embrace prosperity and join the rest of the world and those who still wanted to use Bachchan in his old mould were wasting their time.

It is at this juncture that the actor showed that he was capable of remaining relevant to changing mores and tastes. Accepting that audience tastes had changed, Bachchan readily accepted an assignment as a quiz master in a television show. It was a risky decision, since the small screen was considered a refuse dump, a potential graveyard where one-time stars went quietly to die. *Kaun Banega Crorepati* was a desperate bid to survive by Star TV which was floundering, but it was also a do-or-die gamble for Bachchan, who had no worthwhile films (and by all accounts, no money) in hand. That the foray into television was lucky, or prescient even, has now been borne out by the amazing growth of the medium in the country and the manner in which every actor, big and small, is doing something or the other on the small screen.

Slowly he clawed back into the mainstream, this time in roles that correctly reflected his own age. At the same time, he suddenly developed a willingness to take risks, something that was ironically missing during the peak of his stardom. So while he was happy to act in a *Mohabbatein* (2000) or *Kabhi Khushi Kabhie Gham* (2001) or even *Kabhi Alvida Naa Kehna* (2006)— films that were lavishly mounted and reflected the emergent upper-class India—he was also happy pursuing a *Black* (2005) or a *Sarkar* (2005), both somewhat off-beat films albeit in the commercial mould. One of the criticisms against Bachchan has been that he has stayed away from the so-called 'art cinema' circuit (and it cannot be for the lack of offers from film-makers). Yet, for all the dross he has worked in—and in recent years that side of the ledger has filled up fast—he has taken his chances. Regrettably, at the time when he was on top and parallel cinema was a credible alternative, he firmly turned his back on it. That will remain an intriguing question mark over his career.

That, in sum, could be his legacy. In his forty-year-long career, with over 160 films behind him and countless 'guest appearances', voiceovers and cameos, with a public life that has been more wide-ranging and intensely scrutinized than that of most other personalities, in films or outside, Amitabh Bachchan is a presence that dominates our consciousness in many different ways. But of this prodigious output, it would be hard to come up with ten truly great—or even remarkable—films that will remain with us for all time to come. That is not necessarily his failure alone, considering that he has acted well even in forgettable and embarrassing films; but he cannot escape blame because it was he who made those choices. It is remarkable that despite this kind of a professional record, he is still admired, respected and deeply loved by his fans not only for his on-screen acting but also his off-screen persona. Bachchan has now become, even more firmly, a pan-nation presence, a paterfamilias to middle India, loved and revered as much for his long career as for his wisdom. He is a wise old man but also young at heart, in tune with the new gung-ho mood which sees India's inevitable rise to superpowerdom. His is not the transitory success of the film star, but the permanent achievement of the icon.

MY FIVE FAVOURITE AMITABH BACHCHAN FILMS

1. *Deewar* (1975). Directed by Yash Chopra. Co-stars: Shashi Kapoor, Neetu Singh, Parveen Babi and Nirupa Roy. Though *Zanjeer* is said to be Bachchan's breakthrough film that positioned him as the intense, angry man at war with a corrupt establishment, *Deewar* is a far more nuanced portrayal by the actor. Where *Zanjeer* has its cheesy moments, *Deewar* is a much more complex story and the actor too is more sure-footed, fully internalizing the dilemma and angst of a man forced into crime by circumstances. He remains cool and detached through the film but comes up trumps in the emotional scenes too. It will forever remain his signature performance.
2. *Amar Akbar Anthony* (1977). Directed by Manmohan Desai. Co-stars: Rishi Kapoor, Vinod Khanna, Neetu Singh, Parveen Babi and Shabana Azmi. Bachchan had consolidated his 'angry young man' image when he took on this role which was totally different from anything he had ever done before. As the street-smart bootlegger Anthony Gonsalves, who is frivolous, romantic, tough and vulnerable at the same time, Bachchan completely overhauled his image, creating an

entirely new persona which he then was made to repeat in many films. This was a risky move by a superstar with a confirmed fan base but he took it head on, even getting beaten up on screen, not once but twice. After this it became apparent that he was a versatile actor who could manage any kind of role he was offered.

3. *Anand* (1970). Directed by Hrishikesh Mukherjee. Co-star: Rajesh Khanna. Everything was against him in this film—a reigning superstar with all the best moments and lines, a side role which could easily be relegated into the background. And yet Bachchan infused it with much simmering intensity, proving to be the perfect foil to the chirpy and cheerful Rajesh Khanna. He grasped every opportunity the script gave him to show his inner turmoil, all the while making sure it did not turn into a hammy performance. That he did it so early in his career showed that he was already on the path to greater things in the years to come.

4. *Shakti* (1982). Directed by Ramesh Sippy. Co-stars: Dilip Kumar and Rakhee. It was billed as a clash between two acting greats and it lived up to expectations. The tension between the honest cop, Dilip Kumar, and his wayward son, Amitabh Bachchan, representing two different eras and generations of the Bombay film industry lit the screen, with both vying equally for the acting honours. Dilip Kumar was understated and in full control and Bachchan, though undoubtedly conscious of what he was up against, stood his ground. Rakhee provided the bridge between the alienated father and son. This is an underrated film but bears repeated viewing to see how top-class actors handle dramatic moments without screaming their lungs out.

5. *Black* (2005). Directed by Sanjay Leela Bhansali. Co-star: Rani Mukherji. Much of what Bachchan did in the 1980s and 1990s was dross. He just coasted along, taking on meaningless films and delivering competent, copybook performances with no heart or soul. In *Black*, he got an opportunity to play a complicated character and he took to it with gusto. As Debraj Sahai,

the inspired but bitter teacher, he seem to bring years of grief and melancholy into the role. There were overwrought moments too, but on the whole he was in flowing form as he cajoled, fought and shook up the blind girl to rise above her handicap, while all the time himself slipping into his own dark abyss.

MADHURI DIXIT

MOHINI OF THE SILVER SCREEN

SHEFALEE VASUDEV

It is a sapphire evening in December 2010. The sky itself seems contemplative when you glance at it through the window. For it to reveal more, you must stay with it longer. But it is 9 p.m. and much is going on, on prime-time television. The shade card of the optical field changes with chameleon urgency. Pink, tack and bling fade in on the sets of *Jhalak Dikhla Jaa*, a dance show on Sony, now in its fourth season. Multi-coloured lights, gaudy props, a large, hired audience, too much noise. The anchors have been styled to look compatible with the overdone sets. Unblessed by articulation, they whip up the obligatory excitement to raise attention anxiety. They stumble on their act and feign a fainting fit as Madhuri Dixit, the star judge of the show emerges from backstage, the strobe lights on her face. This is the first episode of this season and the show is unveiling its trophy judge. The rehearsed frenzy of the audience collides with its spontaneous glee. In the cloud of cheer, the forgettable anchors are washed out of sight.

The dazzle of Madhuri Dixit's Mohini-Radha-Janki-Seeta-Gauri-Ganga-Pooja-Ketki-Chandramukhi smile eclipses all else. Even before she begins to dance, anticipatory tension makes your veins taut. The memory of her filmi splendour directs expectations as, in familiar Bollywood magic, her ornate Sabyasachi sari morphs into a fisherman's net and she squirms on the floor. She throws off the net to become one with 'Hum ko aaj kal hai intezaar', her oomphy dance number from *Sailaab* (1990). A traditional Maharashtrian nose-pin, the sari tied like a Koli fisherwoman's, an unabashed choli and flowing hair that defies the hairstylist's invasive rebuttal are arresting, but only till she breaks into her first dance move. After that, little matters. Costumes and colours fade in and out as she dances to a series of her hit numbers—'Dhak dhak karne laga' from *Beta* (1992), 'Choli ke peechhe kya hai' from *Khalnayak* (1993) and 'Maar dala' from *Devdas* (2002). She is in meditative bliss, revelling in her dance, becoming aware by losing herself. By now, you are thinking in clumps and a handful of worn-out clichés—'wow', 'my god', and 'isn't she great'— stumble out as expressions. The sets of *Jhalak Dikhla Jaa* have been redeemed in your mind's eye and you know why you have chosen their pink to the sapphire of the night sky.

That's how Subhash Ghai felt about Madhuri Shankar Dixit in the mid-1980s. Born and raised in a Maharashtrian Konkanastha Brahmin family in Bombay (now Mumbai), Madhuri was a first-year student of microbiology when Ghai first spotted her. She had debuted in *Abodh*, a 1984 film made by Rajshri Productions. That film, like two others—*Swati* (1986) and *Khatron Ke Khiladi* (1988)—which followed it, were quickly washed out from recall. But Madhuri lingered on in some minds. Propelled by his cinematic instinct and perhaps by the not-so-secret personal admiration for her, Ghai knew that Madhuri would usurp Sridevi as the consummate diva of Bollywood.

When N. Chandra's *Tezaab* released in 1988, Ghai's conviction didn't seem so facile. The film portrayed the righteous India of the '80s, a war between a scornful villain and a patriotic hero who had been turned into a singeing cynic played by Anil Kapoor. Madhuri was Mohini, a damsel in distress, feverish with love and longing, yet pulled by the call of duty. Her strength and sex appeal left audiences transfixed. The way she moved to the music in the kitschy dances would write a new chapter in the guidebook of Bollywood dancing. But it was her eyes that stoked a fiery yet comforting notion of womanhood. Not to be misread as quivering girlhood. Audiences counted 'Ek, do, teen' and Ghai counted the days before *Ram Lakhan* (1989) would release and prove his predictions correct.

Mohini, the name of the character which Madhuri played in *Tezaab*, means enchantress in Sanskrit. In Hindu mythology, Mohini is the name of the only female avatar of Lord Vishnu, a damsel who enthrals lovers, sometimes leading them to their doom. The earliest mention of Mohini was in the samudramanthan episode of the Mahabharata. Mohini stole the amrit (nectar) from the asuras, the villains, and gave it to the devas, the gods. This story is retold and recounted in numerous ways in different texts and puranas. Even in Bollywood.

Madhuri Dixit would become Hindi cinema's only Mohini. Madhubala was mesmerizing, Waheeda Rehman engrossingly attractive, Hema Malini the ultimate dream girl and Rekha sensational, but Madhuri—oh, she was something else. An incidental sum total of desirable parts of moh (allure) and maya (illusion).

In the post-liberalized India of the '80s and '90s, every big and small idea was in the churn of social transition. The story of the New Indian Woman, which would become a laborious cliché by 2000, had just begun to be written. On the one hand there was the clear emergence of the women's movement through strident anti-dowry protests. On the other, even before fashion became an industry, female models were interpreting women's liberation with their bold choices.

A bald Nafisa Ali, the lissome Lubna Adams, the stick-thin Mehr Jessia and the tall, dark Noyonika Chatterjee infused new ideals of commercial beauty into popular consciousness. The first Kamasutra condoms advertisement in 1991, shot by photographer Prabuddha Dasgupta and modelled by Pooja Bedi and Marc Robinson, wasn't just daring, it was erotic. Never before had a female model been seen in an audacious sexual embrace. It upset the moral police. As did another commercial also photographed by Prabuddha, which had model Madhu Sapre, another middle-class Maharashtrian girl, wearing nothing but a python around her navel and a pair of Tuff shoes as she posed with her boyfriend Milind Soman.

That was a multilayered time in popular culture. It provoked both shock and awe. Feminists like Madhu Kishwar and Nandana Deb Sen worked hard to liberate women from the confines of body and beauty, and models worked hard to enslave them.

Film heroines did neither. Hindi cinema had manufactured popular consent for the angry young man with Amitabh Bachchan's undisputed reign, but hadn't begun to script or record the women's movement in any way. Nor was the flagrant indulgence of the fashion industry reflected anywhere except in the costumes of cabaret dancers. Leading ladies were compassionate women, not fashion models or feminists. Zeenat Aman, the sexy Zeenie baby of the former decade, had seen success and popularity, even envy, but hadn't been able to recast the notion of womanhood in the minds of directors or audiences. Heroines still had to be Mohinis—beautiful, provocative, meaningful even, but nourishing and companionable, never wild or bizarre.

In 1989 both Yash Chopra's *Chandni* with the sultry Sridevi, a trained Bharatanatyam dancer, and Subhash Ghai's *Ram Lakhan* with Madhuri, a trained Kathak dancer, were released. *Chandni* left audiences awash in its romantic glow with the lovelorn twists of its story, but Madhuri in *Ram Lakhan* was the new moon. This was the kind of woman that India then was comfortable with—a noble enchantress; a flash of lightning between Madhu Kishwar and Madhu Sapre.

Madhuri was named Radha, not Mohini in *Ram Lakhan*. Same difference. Heartrending and evocative, she convinced audiences that seasons changed with her smile. Men lusted for her and women engaged with her at an emotional level. She had sexual shimmer, charisma, mystique and the nobility people searched for in the (ideal) New Woman. Comforting, but not numbingly conformist as a doff of the hat to modernity. Madhuri could beautifully depict all the nine emotions, the navrasas, of any filmi script with her dancing talent. *Dil*, her 1990 film with Aamir Khan, proved that when she expressed viraaha (separation) from her beloved, viewers felt something was wrong with the world. That was the popular and the critical perception as the role got Madhuri her first Filmfare Best Actress Award.

Most successful film stars have a web of creative people around them: writers, directors, dance directors, song writers and playback singers who work towards making them who they are. Sometimes they consciously create an aura or image around them; that's how the life script of an actor begins to be written. In Madhuri's case, directors and scriptwriters were dazed by her charisma initially but soon withdrew in relief. There was no need to change a film's script for Madhuri or especially write one for her. They could go back to worrying about the New Indian Hero's role. The heroine was taken care of by Madhuri's natural grace. All big banners wanted to work with her, because of her easy heroine-ness and her dancing glamour.

Madhuri was brought up in a middle-class home in Bombay, the youngest of four children. Her mother Snehlata Dixit, an artistic lady who also sang, could never complete her dance training because in that generation, girls of 'good' Maharashtrian families did not dance. 'You could be a Lata Mangeshkar, but you could not be a dancer,' Madhuri told an interviewer about her mother's unrealized dreams. To compensate, Snehlata Dixit sent all her three daughters to learn Kathak at a very young age.

The origins of Kathak, one of the eight classical Indian dances, are traced to the nomadic bards of ancient northern India, known as *kathaks*, or storytellers. Singing in village squares or at melas, the bards would recount mythological and moral tales from the scriptures through theatrical dancing set to the beats of instrumental and vocal music. Kathak was also strongly influenced by the Bhakti movement.

Dancing was bhakti (devotion) for Madhuri. She was a gifted dancer, graceful, focused and hard-working. For the eight years that she formally learnt Kathak, she gave it everything she had to chisel her art. That aura of devoting herself to her talent showed on her face, becoming a halo, setting her apart from other actors. Bollywood's foremost dancers—Vyjayanthimala Bali, Rekha, Hema Malini, Sridevi, Jaya Prada—were all south Indian girls. Classical dance was rooted in their tradition. Hema Malini who formally called dance her first love, and learnt and performed many classical forms, is like a dance institution. But Madhuri, as choreographer Saroj Khan would say, 'had everything'.

Khan, who first choreographed Madhuri in *Beta*, went on to be her 'masterji' for more than two dozen films. Some of Bollywood's biggest dancing hits—'Dhak dhak karne laga' from *Beta*, 'Choli ke peechhe kya hai' from *Khalnayak*, 'Akhiyan milau' from *Raja* (1995) and most dances from *Devdas*, to name a few—were the combined magic of these two talents. In 'Akhiyan milau', Madhuri expresses a part of the song only with her eyes. Saroj Khan would rightly remember many years later that no one else in Bollywood could have managed that.

Kathak guru Birju Maharaj, who mentored Madhuri for 'Maar dala', a Kathak-based dance in Sanjay Leela Bhansali's *Devdas*, too was moved by her oneness with her craft. Not once did she miss the rehearsals or come late. She touched the guru's feet every morning and for fourteen days learnt from him like an earnest student for whom nothing else mattered but his guidance and her art. If Madhuri once again found euphoric liberation in that song, the film found a self-aware Chandramukhi in her. *Devdas*, Bhansali's exercise of romantic excess could not clutter Madhuri's spontaneous elegance. Pitched against the rare beauty of Aishwarya Rai who played Paro with intelligence and vigour, Madhuri brought unimagined layers of meaning to the word 'chandramukhi' (as beautiful as the moon). Our Mohini was now Chandramukhi who looked like she had been raised on a diet of dazzling gemstones. Between the perfomances of Madhuri and

Aishwarya, the audiences also understood why self-awareness in acting and in beauty could be superior to self-consciousness.

Madhuri was born in 1967, and when the Barjatyas of Rajshri Productions first cast her in *Abodh* in 1984, she was barely out of her tenth class. She had just been voted as the best student in school for her participation in dance and cultural programmes. Rajshri Productions was looking for 'a young, innocent girl with long hair in plaits' and Madhuri's family went to meet the Barjatyas to see if the production house suited their middle-class notions. With no evil stories of the casting couch to worry them, they allowed their daughter to go ahead. After a long post-audition wait, growing her hair, then chopping it off in frustration, Madhuri started shooting.

Abodh, directed by Hiren Nag, propelled Madhuri to ask herself if acting was her calling. She accepted *Swati* and *Awaara Baap* (1985) to explore that thought alongside her studies as a microbiology student but boys in her Vile Parle college would whistle and tease her every day after her films released. College became burdensome while the film industry beckoned.

The whistles of boys that bothered Madhuri in college would become predictable expressions of fanhood amongst the millions of her male fans who thronged to watch her in cinema halls. As a heroine, Madhuri was neither the 'imported' Alpha Cat nor the Omega Kitty but a rare combination of 'Hindustani sexy'.

Not too much has been written about the heroine's cleavage in Hindi cinema but if it were, Madhuri's mention would be in the foreword. She had an anatomical kit bag, not a theatrical one. Acting prowess was seen as a subsidiary talent in Bollywood of the '90s, just as well for her. Anatomical correctness may sound crude while dissecting a star's appeal, but without its mention, Madhuri's Mohinihood would be only partially understood. Her smile was a perfect symphony as her eyes and mouth danced in tandem, darting between high and low emotional notes. This emotional notation of a smile distinguishes a real smile from a fake one, as California psychologist Prof. Paul Ekman noted in his outstanding study of the human face. First presented in the late '70s, the study evolved over the decades as Ekman continued mapping the geography of the human face. The psychologist listed seventeen kinds of smiles as a part of that research that was made public in 2003, the year *Devdas* released. In a rare comment, Madhuri's husband (she was by now married) said that he was stunned when he saw her smile in the film.

Madhuri didn't just have an engrossing smile; she was also busty and voluptuous. Those were not the days of size zero, and well, Madhuri was bigger on the bust than even a size twelve; but her cleavage contributed to the way in which she got interlocked in the consciousness of the audiences. Sexy, yet 'good'. In the Indian man's psychological battlefield where sexy women are not good and good women are either desexualized or must be made so by marrying them, Madhuri brought a peculiar resolution of conflict. She was a combination of compassion and sensuality; unobstrusively desirable. Never come-hither.

'Choli ke peechhe kya hai', her jaunty, sexy number in Subhash Ghai's *Khalnayak*, was fused out of this matrix—her smile and voluptuousness as well as the intense awareness she had of both these virtues. She played Ganga, a police officer—symbolically both holy and justice-seeking. But with the director's poetic licence, Ganga was once again turned into Mohini in that song, biting her lip, heaving her chest as Alka Yagnik's amorous playback voice and Neena Gupta's steamy side act added fuel to the fire.

Madhuri became a powerful actress only later. She was first an enchantress with a wholesome figure and a heart-stopping smile—blessings which could be easily exploited on celluloid and in art. It also explains why painter M.F. Hussain made her his muse. Later in 2000, he would make a film called *Gaja Gamini*, ostensibly a tribute to the actor's beauty but really a celebration of her femininity that combined the risqué and the conventional.

Her sex appeal wasn't incidentally noticed. The 1988 film *Dayavan*, directed by Feroz Khan, a remake of the Tamil *Nayagan*, had Madhuri playing Neelu, a prostitute who is married to an underworld don, Vinod Khanna, while in the Vidhu Vinod Chopra–directed *Parinda* (1989) she played Shirley and had stark and rapturous love-making scenes. Madhuri was the flickering hot candle and the moth found his release in his death in her fire. And yet, there was a distance that she could maintain. With her demeanour, she bridged two worlds of womanhood in cinema. Not every emotion that she depicted could be interpreted as sexual.

By the time *Beta* was released in 1992, she had learnt how to present a thoughtful blend of her acting abilities (still very much work-in-progress), her sex appeal, her dancing talent and her feminine niceness. The unforgettably unabashed 'Dhak dhak karne laga' was evidence of her growing self-awareness about what she brought to Hindi films. A star's persona takes time to evolve and in the early '90s Madhuri seemed to grapple with what she was blessed with, juxtaposed with the roles she got. *Beta* showed that she was evolving a personalized synthesis given the reality around her. Her not-so-subtle gestures towards her body and her promises of love in that seductive dance would etch the film in the minds of cine fans for many years. Directed by Indra Kumar, this was a remake of a 1969 Kannada movie *Mallamana Pavada* and it got Madhuri her second Filmfare Award.

By 1995, when Madhuri played Ketki in *Mrityudand*, fighting for gender and social justice, she had learnt how to recognize and capture unique moments of acting within herself and repeat them at will. She could get angry, weep and laugh and be mirthful and the actress in her could dominate the womanly vulnerability of her personality. She would turn this around to the audiences in a mirror-effect, reflecting a speck of their socio-political consciousness.

She was the potential number-one female actor even before the 1994 film *Hum Aapke Hain Koun*, made by Sooraj Barjatya of Rajshri Productions, unleashed a frenzy in India. Fourteen enjoyable songs stuffed into a family saga soaked with weddings, finery, truth, loyalty, love, longing and motherhood; our Mohini cavorting through the navrasas of a young woman's life as Pooja,

strung between love and viraaha; an unprecedented run at the
box office till then and the film wrote history. It brought home
another Filmfare Award for the leading lady.

The purple crepe sari that Madhuri wore with a backless
choli while dancing suggestively to 'Didi tera dewar deewana',
raising Salman's Khan smiling sexual distress in the film, must be
given its due. It became 'Indian fashion'. It lured desis and
NRIs in droves. Manish Market in Mumbai or Lajpat Nagar in
Delhi, designers or darzis, everybody was busy making clones
of that purple sari and its lehnga-esque cousins. Local sari
traders and garage boutiques realized that when embellished
with sequins, shimmer and gota patti, the original six yards
could become bestselling wedding bling. Shaadi fashion, the
most unoriginal idea that rules the retail market today, was born.
Madhuri saris are still around.

She wore tacky and badly fitted clothes in some films. In
fact, the so-called gown that looked like a deflated wine-coloured
balloon she wore in a dance sequence with Aamir Khan in *Dil*
would have made even Manish Malhotra—her designer-stylist
for many years—cringe. But these instances got sidelined because
of the way she carried her drapes. She was also lucky that there
was no real fashion critic around. If the sari is a potent amalgam
of revealing and covering, Madhuri worked its unstitchedness
completely to her advantage. She was a true exponent of the
Yash Chopra school of chiffon sarism. Even here she gave
gritty competition to Sridevi who had been the chiffon sari's
showstopper. Madhuri oozed oomph without Rekha's red lips and
smoky eyes and brought a moral seriousness to her sexiness. Plastic
phoniness or celluloid fashion, which can make distinction of
look such a losing battle, never challenged her. She never looked
fake. Her smile, that conspiratorial companion of hers made
it difficult for audiences to chide her, to ridicule her even, like
we do with Aishwarya Rai.

Some of it is explained by the way Madhuri acted. This is
evident in the way she handled her role in *Hum Aapke Hain Koun*,

which was, as the intelligentsia said, a slickly produced wedding video. She brought integrity and dignity to Love in the film. She was a self-sacrificing idealist who did not become idiotically selfless. You saw her wince and weep but there was no disillusionment in her. Not once did she slip into a manic depressive mode. It was difficult for even the harshest critic to lament her 'type'. She hovered on the cusp of reality and fantasy and we had to take our academic arguments back home. She was always the heroine in the way she lived up to the we-shall-overcome side of her story. She was Seeta, even Geeta, but never Shrupanakha. Desdemona, yes, never Lady Macbeth. She was Everywoman, only better.

The Family Happiness Inc., formally inaugurated by *Hum Aapke Hain Koun* as a school of cinematic exploration, didn't just influence directors like Aditya Chopra and Karan Johar. It became inspiration in the life of the Indian television soaps. Till today, TV serials are reworked subsets of *Hum Aapke Hain Koun*. Blingy saris and lehngas, kind uncles, bitchy aunts, men in kurtas with tassels hanging from their stoles, boondi laddoos, marigold flowers and rangolis, festivals celebrated with joy and ghee— that's still the sum and substance of fictional TV. All held together by the bahu as the glue, goodness incarnate. That is a Madhuri construct of the perfect woman, a noble, beautiful, daughter-in-law.

Unlike movies which have moved on to the 'glocal' street-smartness and come-hither womanhood of Priyanka Chopra, Bipasha Basu, Katrina Kaif and Kareena Kapoor, TV soaps are still playing house-house in Madhuri's memory.

Madhuri did sixty-five-odd films in the first innings of her career. But few remember the really tacky ones like *Paapi Devta* (1995), *Rajkumar* (1996), *Mahaanta* (1997) or *Wajood* (1998) amongst many others which disappeared. For *Wajood,* she even did some playback singing. Yet when she erred, it was all right, the audiences were willing to look the other way. The good girl label didn't come unstuck even when she broke off, as many felt, unceremoniously with Sanjay Dutt in 1993. She allegedly ditched him overnight when reports about his arrest for his alleged involvement in the Bombay riots and the TADA case trickled in. They had acted together in *Saajan* (1991) as well as in *Khalnayak* (1993) and had shared more than professional amorousness. But in the tormenting days when Dutt became the boy on the burning deck and the reel-turned-real khalnayak, Madhuri stood back as a mute spectator, refusing to accept or support him. Yet we forgave her, not once putting her in the dock for her lack of compassion while Sanju Baba kept going to court for the whole decade and more.

That was the effect of her filmi charm. *Anjaam* (1994), *Pukar* (2000), *Lajja* (2001) and *Dil To Pagal Hai* (1997) kept pushing her up the dizzying ladder of success. The last got her yet another Filmfare Award and by this time, many trophies had become hers. A few Star Screen Awards, a couple of Zee Cine Awards, even a Kalaabhinetri Award from the government of Andhra Pradesh in 1997. In 2001 Madhuri was listed by Forbes as one of the five most powerful Indian movie stars. Her role as Chandramukhi in *Devdas* got her a Filmfare for the Best Supporting Actor Female in 2003. The Padma Shri would come much later in 2008.

What she cherished most—and wrapped herself completely around—was the trophy of Mrs Nene. Even as *Devdas* was being shot, Madhuri Dixit married Dr Shriram Nene, a practising cardiovascular surgeon settled in Denver, USA, in a private ceremony in 1999. He had proposed to her after a brief courtship, initially strategized by her family. Dr Nene belonged to the same caste of Maharashtrian Brahmins as Madhuri and had little interest in Hindi films, least of all, quipped gossip magazines, in Hindustani apsaras. Soaked in the attention given to her back home by her million fans, Madhuri found Shriram's ignorance of her fame a big attraction. So impossibly Mills & Boon! They were drawn to each other instantly, we were told, and her heartbroken fans first saw Madhuri's husband in a few photographs reluctantly released by the family. Later in Mumbai, where the couple threw a reception for friends in Bollywood, Dr Nene became a *Hum Aapke Hain Koun* groom in a gold brocade sherwani. The bride wore her filmi persona accessorized by a Manish Malhotra lehnga. There was nothing exceptional in their wedding wear, not even in their chemistry perhaps, but her smile was a little more heady, if that was possible. She laughed a lot at her reception, say those who attended it. If happiness is an act of grace, as French intellectual Pascal Bruckner would say, Madhuri looked happy.

I met Madhuri Dixit Nene in November 2007 when she came to Mumbai to promote her film *Aaja Nachle*, directed by Anil Mehta. It was a Yash Raj film and Madhuri's publicist had asked *Marie Claire* India, which I edited then, whether we would be interested in a cover and interview with her. I said yes, without giving it another thought. After all, it was Madhuri— wasn't that reason enough? A few months after the cover story was published, I noticed that none of the other fashion magazines— *Elle* or *Vogue*—had put her on the cover. A captivating smile and luscious boobs render themselves meaningless in fashion. They can even be impediments in fashion's manic search for glamour as starved hauteur. Madhuri was never the fashion-magazine cover girl or the ramp showstopper. What would she wear? Not bikinis and hot pants, of course. Not even the androgynous clothing that fashion cyclically develops a fascination for. Dior couture? Nah, too busty for them, a tad short too. It was just as well that she left the industry before the fashion media got into everyone's pockets, judging every top female actor also by the number of magazine covers she does and the luxury gowns she borrows and wears for red-carpet appearances.

Madhuri Dixit isn't fashion, she is Indian womanhood, I reminded myself when I met her in her vanity van at Bandra's Mehboob Studios. She stood up to shake hands, a polite half-grin on her face. Calculatedly distant but impeccably well mannered. She had ordinary skin, regular, just-shampooed wavy hair that would need a lot of attention from the hairstylist, a body that wasn't a fashion model's at all and her age, then forty, showed in the way her diet and weight loss had left her, a little low on energy, I would think.

I was used to tantrum-throwing Bollywood actresses who we shot with every month for covers, not courteous celebs. Cover girls would throw back clothes at stylists, never mind if the fittings had been done the previous day, ask for a certain kind of grilled fish that wasn't available anywhere, insist on working with the one and only photographer they 'trusted', as well as the only make-up person who could make them look drop-dead gorgeous, demand instant cash payments for their drivers and mundus-at-large. Some would insist upon taking away designer clothes they had liked at the shoot without offering to pay for them.

Madhuri's diva-ness would have been easier to handle but I didn't know what to do with her good manners. She was polite, precise in her sentences, very amiable. She agreed to try on all the clothes for photographer Farrokh Chothia so that he could plan his lighting and quietly pointed out what she didn't like. I tried to convince her to wear a royal-blue embroidered Rohit Bal gown-dress from his recent Siyahi collection but she looked at me through the mirror and her eyes said no. I wanted to please her, she was so pleasing. Red and black were her preferred colours but she was really an unfussy star. No grilled fish, no sugar-free black coffee, no zero-calorie salad or nude stockings because she had forgotten her own or half-informed monologues on how and what to Photoshop.

When photographer Farrokh Chothia turned on the lights in the studio, and she stood against the white background in a red dress, she became someone else. No, she became herself, Madhuri Mohini Dixit. She flashed that terribly high-watt smile and my colleagues and I ran for cover.

After the shoot, I drove with Madhuri in her car to the Yash Raj studios. She had nothing much to say, no opinion on anything. If she had great ideas about cinema, she didn't do anything to express them. She replied with diplomatic correctness, never once becoming reflective, incisive, open, analytical or even subjective. She couldn't even pin down her most memorable cinema moment! I asked her about her sex appeal, her Mohininess as I had learnt to call it. Her response to that was the most insightful one in the interview. 'My appeal is not visual, it is not physical, it is not in my form. It's the reflection of a feeling, a thought that comes from deep within me. It has to be subtle,' she said. The only other subject that got her conversationally engaged was dance. Bhav (emotion), raag (melody), taal (rhythm)—she was enslaved by dance in mind and body.

At that time, Madhuri was clearly looking forward to the release of *Aaja Nachle*. She talked lovingly of her two sons, her yearning to practise Kathak again in Denver but was bashful about Dr Nene. 'Getting married and having kids is a transition from girlhood to womanhood but then everything revolves around others. I have done this film for myself,' she said. She asked me if I had seen the promos of the film. I had and told her that she deserved a more powerful comeback. Her face fell immediately and noticeably. She became momentarily quiet but didn't dismiss me. That's when I got my headline: Guess Who Wants To Be Madhuri Dixit?

She was back in the industry, with a Yash Raj film, a story scripted around her famed dancing prowess. The same formula again? It was safe but insipid, too tried-and-tested to make a comeback argument of it. Why would Madhuri Nene want to be Madhuri Dixit once again?

The 2003 film *Main Madhuri Dixit Banna Chahti Hoon*, directed by a nondescript director Chandan Arora, in which Antara Mali plays a small-town girl wanting to make it big, is a significant metaphor for why we were obsessed by Madhuri. Most of her roles were muscled with conventional fibre and except for Rahul Rawail's *Anjaam*, where she plays a doctor who kills for revenge, and *Mrityudand*, where she plays a disempowered wife from Bilaspur who fights for justice, she is never shown as a radical or revolutionary character. Credit goes to her for repeatedly churning out hits from the same blueprint of a sensuous but correct female character, one who would do anything for personal conviction. Madhuri was our most culturally compatible female star. Nothing was dismissive in her personality and she relied a lot on her personal sensitivity to repeat her act. As she herself admitted later, her films were barely properly scripted, but she depended on herself to essay the roles of a daughter, mother, daughter-in-law or lover.

Curiously, or maybe not, it was *Mrityudand* that she chose to first show to her husband Shriram Nene, to introduce her actor life to him. That was the one film where Madhuri did not play the conventional damsel in distress.

If she was the Best Actress many times over only because she was an engaging idea of Indian womanhood, it is an irony. The industry converted this into one of her biggest talents. Versatility, as fame analysts say, can startle stardom because it forces audiences to re-imagine their favourite star's identity in their minds. But Madhuri's roles seldom challenged her viewers. She was always Madhuri Dixit—nice, sexy, beautiful, dignified, caring— the one and same personality across personal and professional appearances. She started playing herself and it became her filmi character. Or maybe she started playing the role of this self-righteous beautiful woman who then became her. We do not know.

What we do know is that she became a megawatt star without any PR machinery that now helps stars strategize and sell an image. She wasn't caught in the market trap of stylists, trainers, power yoga gurus, hairstylists, make-up artists, fashion designers, promotion managers or the cult of youth that now defines Bollywood's body shop. During Madhuri's best years, the industry did not strive for technological, technical or organizational excellence as it does now. Then, if filmi fame was tough, individuality was tougher. Yet Madhuri had an individuality of look spiced with a dignity that all stars crave for. It was a very physical thing and did not emanate from her intelligence or from a political or social stand that she took, because she never took any. Given that she is remembered as the only female superstar of Hindi cinema, she was never ironically insightful like SRK, vulnerably sure in opinions like Amitabh Bachchan or strategic like Aamir Khan. We have no idea what she thought of Bollywood's dark relationship with the underworld or of Bal Thackeray's Marathi manoos politics. Did the good girl cast her votes every time there was an election? No idea.

Aaja Nachle repeated our fixation with Madhuri Dixit's good-girl act but the India of 2007 had stopped caring for that stereotype. The storyline was fragile; the direction of the film, uninspiring. Madhuri's dances were terrific but her metaphorical narrative needed to move on. It didn't, and the audiences rejected it.

She smilingly went back to Denver. Only to return in 2010 but this time to the Idiot Box that has valiantly hung on to a reconfiguration of the *Hum Aapke Hain Koun* box of emotions and styling. She is a celebrity judge on *Jhalak Dikhla Jaa*, a dance show, but see her closely and she is still that good bahu or beti in sequinned drapes. She has also become the lifestyle ambassador for chef Sanjeev Kapoor's new food channel called Food, Food.

It was during designer Varun Bahl's show at Delhi Couture Week in July 2011 when whispers that Madhuri would come back to Mumbai and settle down here with her husband and kids sneaked around. She was Bahl's front-row gem and although she was more than an hour late, the audience waited patiently for her to arrive. When she did, she flashed that smile and the lights went on.

Madhuri did come back to live in Mumbai indeed. She has been working on getting her make-up right and looks more chiselled than she did in the last decade of her vibrant motherhood. In contradiction to my former thesis about her not being the most sought-after cover girl for a fashion magazine, Vogue India did put her on the cover for its August 2011 edition. Madhuri wore a black gown and looked the part. Quite suitably, the edition was called The Age Issue. Most things Madhuri has chosen to do since seem to be in tandem with her mature looks; she endorses Olay skin regeneration cream, Neesa basmati rice and Comfort fabric conditioner among other brands that make sense of forty-plus women. Her smile still tugs at people's hearts but her coming back to Mumbai is not just a flash of benign beauty. Madhuri has brought a sharp edge to the competition among older girls like Karisma Kapoor, Juhi Chawla and Sridevi still vying for brand endorsements, film roles and media attention. But depending on how you do your math, Madhuri Dixit is now Mohini ma'am, the lovely celeb judge on TV, or even Mohini aunty if you really like basmati rice.

A natural progression in the Bollywood heroine's life as a cliché.

MY FIVE FAVOURITE MADHURI DIXIT FILMS

1. *Devdas* (2002). Directed by Sanjay Leela Bhansali. Co-stars: Shahrukh Khan and Aishwarya Rai. Based on Saratchandra Chattopadhyaya's novella of doomed love, this was the most expensive film of Bollywood till 2002, mounted for Rs 50 crores. With grand performances, opulent sets and chartbusting music by Ismail Durbar, the film won ten Filmfare Awards, was screened at Cannes and was India's official entry as Best Foreign Language Film to the Oscars in 2003.
2. *Khalnayak* (1993). Directed by Subhash Ghai. Co-stars: Sanjay Dutt, Jackie Shroff and Rakhee. A racy tale of love and danger in which a police inspector, Ram, and his love interest, Ganga, chase a hardened terrorist, Ballu. The terrorist falls in love with Ganga too. It was a blockbuster and the Ila Arun and Alka Yagnik song 'Choli ke peechhe kya hai' was like a thrown sparkler in Indian pop culture, raking in adulation and blazing controversy.
3. *Tezaab* (1988). Directed by N. Chandra. Co-stars: Anil Kapoor, Anupam Kher and Chunkey Pandey. The song 'Ek do teen' was a booming success. Madhuri Dixit's first real big hit, it was the story of an honest and patriotic young man

forced to become a flaming cynic, a bad guy. It ran straight for fifty weeks in theatres.

4. *Mrityudand* (1997). Directed by Prakash Jha. Co-stars: Shabana Azmi, Om Puri, Mohan Agashe and Ayub Khan. Set in Bilaspur, Bihar, of 1996, the film was a commentary on social injustice and visceral gender injustice. It reflected two genres—art and commercial cinema. Semi-classical music with lyrics written by Javed Akhtar and performances that churned righteous anger in the viewers. The film got numerous awards.

5. *Hum Aapke Hain Koun* (1994). Directed by Sooraj Barjatya. Co-stars: Salman Khan, Anupam Kher and Renuka Shahane. A remake of *Nadiya Ke Par*, a 1982 film also produced by Rajshri Productions, it revolved around the relationship between two families, two people, two sisters and its complexities when the older sister dies and the younger one is expected to marry her brother-in-law. A lavish interpretaion of life as a wedding procession. With superhit songs and a lilting soundtrack by Raamlaxman, it forever changed the meaning of the term 'box-office success' in Bollywood history.

AAMIR KHAN

POWER POINT

DEEPA GAHLOT

He was once nicknamed 'QS Cutie' by the film press. Today it is difficult to match the image this label evokes with the most powerful man in the Mumbai film industry—Aamir Khan.

So perfectly planned has this makeover been, like everything else he does, that the pre-*Lagaan* Aamir Khan has almost been wiped out of people's memories—short as they are. It is the post-*Lagaan* Aamir they know, the man who picked up a failed actor and director, Ashutosh Gowariker, produced his film, and took it right up to the Oscars.

A small flashback here: the year is 1984, a rambunctious group of young men has descended upon the Film and Television Institute of India in Pune. They are shooting for Ketan Mehta's *Holi*, the story of a youth rebellion set in a college campus and based on Mahesh Elkunchwar's play. The leading man is a tall, dark, lanky, curly-mopped Ashutosh Gowariker and one of the faces in the group of young rebels is a short, fair, nineteen-year-old Aamir Khan. Even though he is just 'one of the guys'—helping with props, eyes crinkling with laughter as boyish humour flies around—everybody around knows he is different, and they are slightly awed.

Because this young man belongs to a very famous film family. His father is Tahir Hussain, producer of films like *Caravan, Anamika, Zakhmee*; his uncle Nasir Hussain is a producer-director-actor who has made films like *Dil Deke Dekho, Teesri Manzil* and *Yaadon Ki Baraat* (in which Aamir appeared as a child actor). They have family links with Maulana Abul Kalam Azad.

Holi has two more actors whose lives are linked with Aamir's— Raj Zutshi, who married Aamir's cousin Nuzhat, and Amole Gupte, who unwittingly and unwillingly turned Aamir into a director with *Taare Zameen Par* (2007). In the film, Aamir played the boy who yanks off the towel Amole is wrapped in, and chases him down the hostel stairs in his undies (it would have been naked, but for censor rules). Of some innocuous moments are movie legends made.

Born on 14 March 1965, in Mumbai, Aamir grew up in what was then the centre of the film industry—Bandra. Stars and film-makers lived at and around Pali Hill; Mehboob Studio was the playground of many an industry kid. It was natural for him, his brother Faisal and his cousin Mansoor to harbour film ambitions. With the rudiments of video technology, Mansoor even made a film or two. Aamir also showed signs of wanting to be a film-maker. He dropped out of college, assisted uncle Nasir Hussain on the films *Manzil Manzil* and *Zabardast*. For a while Aamir, Mansoor, Aditya Bhattacharya and the Bandra gang even started a band. Aditya's film *Raakh* (1989) was the first Aamir signed after *Holi*, but it was released later. For a while, Aamir joined the late Mahendra Joshi's theatre group Avantar, and worked backstage. (His sister Nikhat married Joshi.)

Eventually, the two young cousins got serious and started their film careers together, with *Qayamat Se Qayamat Tak* (1988)— popularly dubbed *QSQT*—written (with inputs from Aamir) and produced by Nasir Hussain, with Mansoor as director and Aamir as leading man opposite 'beauty queen' Juhi Chawla.

When Aamir entered the industry, Amitabh Bachchan's superstardom was taking a bit of a battering. Younger stars were competing for the top slot, and it was the time when the 'son rise' was still on. A few years earlier, industry boys like Anil Kapoor, Sanjay Dutt, Sunny Deol and Kumar Gaurav had made their debuts, and the film industry had almost shut its doors to outsiders. But still, Aamir needed a leg up—he was not the son of a star, nor was he spectacularly good-looking. In fact he was short, with spotty skin and jug ears—not what one would associate with a leading man. But he had a great smile that flashed *joie de vivre*, and, in the days of Dutt–Deol muscle, a friendly, non-menacing appearance—the kind girls would find attractive. Rajesh Khanna and Rishi Kapoor had that attractive imperfection that had made them into stars.

But fates were being written by a quirky hand. While Aamir's star entry was being planned, a young man was attracting attention in his role as a soldier in a TV serial called *Fauji*, and yet another industry kid was taking his first faltering steps into showbiz with a now-forgotten film called *Biwi Ho To Aisi*. They all happened to share a last name and the year of their birth—1965. A few more years down the line Aamir, Shahrukh and Salman would form the unbeatable Khan triumvirate—one that would rule Hindi cinema in India and across the diaspora. Bitter rivals and nawabs of large fan bases. Interestingly, it was an Aamir-reject that had given Shahrukh his star-making hit *Darr* (1993). Aamir had reportedly turned it down because it was what the industry calls a 'negative' role and he did not fancy a thrashing from Sunny Deol. This created a prolonged rift between him and the mighty Yash Raj Films (YRF) empire that was healed only when he starred in *Fanaa* (2006). Now he is about to star as a villain in YRF's crime-caper franchise *Dhoom 3*—an intellectual villain, not a muscle-flexing one. Now he can state his terms (uncompromising) and his price (astronomical).

Back in 1988, in the midst of an action wave of films that had deadly titles like *Mardon Wali Baat, Paap Ko Jalakar Raakh*

Kar Doonga, Andha Yudh, Hatya, Bhai Ka Dushman Bhai, Khatron Ke Khiladi, came a sweet, romantic, Thakurland version of *Romeo and Juliet*, in which the hero, on the last day of college sang the prophetic song, 'Papa kehte hain', making Udit Narayan the voice of the new hero. The film had Raj and Rashmi belonging to two warring clans. They looked so innocent and vulnerable; and when they died at the end, copious tears were shed in auditoriums across the country.

But something else also happened that was gleefully picked up by the gossip press, and it took all of Aamir's charm to reduce the damage. It turned out that Aamir had hidden his marriage to Reena Dutta—two years earlier he had married her against the wishes of the two families, eloping like the characters in *QSQT*. The reason for keeping the marriage secret was that he did not want his stardom to be affected by it. There was a bit of sniggering in the industry and in the press because actresses' careers usually come to an end after marriage, while no leading man's popularity has waned because of marriage. Still, in retrospect, it seems Aamir always had that slightly calculating streak in him. Now every word uttered, every move made is so carefully controlled. He is such a major star now that he can play push-and-pull games with the media and they are willing puppets. But for a newbie to risk opprobrium was both foolhardy and admirable. Right at the start of his career, he was saying: I am what I am.

Also, quite against his 'cutie' image, he went and did a dark, arty, crime film, Aditya's Bhattacharya's *Raakh*. In this film he played an angry and anguished man who, with the help of a disillusioned cop, turns vigilante to avenge the rape of a female friend. *Raakh* failed at the box office, but turned out to be one of those much-admired movies that keep turning up at film-club circuits; it was also re-released briefly at the peak of Aamir stardom in 2010.

Knowing how meticulously Aamir plans his career moves now, the awful films he picked almost wiped out the *QSQT* gains: *Love Love Love* (1989), *Jawani Zindabad* (1990), *Deewana Mujh Sa*

Nahin (1990), *Awwal Number* (1990, this one by Dev Anand, whom nobody can refuse), *Tum Mere Ho* (1990, by his father) . . .

He has said in interviews that this was the lowest phase of his career. At that time Mahesh Bhatt, riding a high, offered him a film; and even then Aamir had the courage to turn it down because he did not like the script. Bhatt still offered him *Dil Hai Ke Manta Nahin* (1991), the Hindi version of *It Happened One Night*, in which he played hard-boiled journalist Raghu Jaitley on the trail of a runaway heiress (Pooja Bhatt). He offers to help in the hope of getting a scoop, but falls in love with her. The romantic comedy was just the hit he needed at that time, and with the success of Indra Kumar's *Dil* (1990), opposite Madhuri Dixit, his career got second wind.

It was during the making of *Dil Hai Ke Manta Nahin*, that stories of his 'perfectionism' started trickling out. Till the corporate culture came in and tried a clean-up operation (only partially successful), the Bollywood film industry had a *chalta hai* (anything goes) attitude to everything. It was acceptable for a star to throw unreasonable tantrums—that was expected; but when a star had long, logical discussions on why the checks on Raghu's shirt should be of a particular kind and why he has a 'Captain' cap as an accessory, he was dubbed eccentric.

Still, a hit is a hit, and Aamir's stock rose a bit, went down again with duds like *Afsana Pyar Ka* (1991), *Isi Ka Naam Zindagi* (1991), *Daulat Ki Jung* (1991), *Parampara* (1993), and rose once more with *Jo Jeeta Wohi Sikandar* (1992), the lifeline thrown again by cousin Mansoor.

Aamir was twenty-seven but played a schoolboy quite convincingly. He proved early on that if an actor is sure of what he is doing, and plays his part well, age does not matter. This confidence allowed him to play a teen when he was past forty, and get away with it.

The pleasing underdog-coming-out-trumps film set in a hill station told a classic tale of haves looking down on the have-nots, the rich winning everything as matter of right, the poor trying hard to belong, and a spoilt, ne'er-do-well brat finally fighting for the dignity of his family, and to win back his estranged friends, by beating the town bully in a cycle race. The film was a hit and also seemed to stand for what Aamir was doing—trying to get to the top and stay there.

His selection of films was getting better, his performances showing a remarkable mix of preparedness and spontaneity, quite evident in his next film with Mahesh Bhatt. *Hum Hain Rahi Pyar Ke* (1993)—ripped from the 1958 Cary Grant– Sophia Loren starrer, *Houseboat*—had him playing an uptight garment-factory owner forced to adopt the three mishievous kids of his dead sister as well as a girl (Juhi Chawla, who has done the maximum films with Aamir—seven—even though they were not on talking terms for many years) running away from an unsuitable match. He co-wrote the script and, if rumours are to be believed, even ghost-directed it, since Bhatt was busy with his many other projects.

If *Dil Hai Ke Manta Nahin* and *Hum Hain Rahi Pyar Ke* showed that the serious-looking, argumentative, perfectionist (a film magazine had given him the nickname *Pakav*, which is Mumbai slang for bore) Aamir had a mad streak for comedy, then *Andaz Apna Apna* (1994) sealed it. This Rajkumar Santoshi film was not too well received when it was released, but has turned out to be a cult comedy. In *Andaz Apna Apna*, Aamir played one half of a good-for-nothing duo that dreams of getting rich the easy way—by marrying rich girls. They get into an insane scenario involving duplicates, heists and kidnapping. It is also the only film in which Aamir and Salman appeared together. Later efforts to get them to star in the same film proved futile; Aamir and Shahrukh have never acted together.

His next, *Baazi* (1995), brought him together with *Holi* co-star Ashutosh Gowariker, making his second film as director after the first, *Pehla Nasha*, flopped. The film, a cop caper, is memorable only for the effort Aamir put into playing a woman. He was so keen on doing the drag act to perfection that he actually cracked a rib due to tight corsets.

Rangeela and *Akele Hum Akele Tum* were both released in 1995, the first by maverick director Ram Gopal Varma and the other by Mansoor Khan. In one he played a *tapori* (slang for loafer), Munna, a black marketeer of movie tickets; in the other, a *Kramer vs Kramer* remake, he played a single dad. The success of one and the critical appreciation of the other allowed *Aatank Hi Aatank* (1995) to go unnoticed.

By this time Aamir was moving towards creating a strong brand identity for himself. Soon after this, he not only chose to skip attending awards functions, he decided to devote himself solely to doing one film at a time, and be involved with it from script to promotion. Exclusivity ensured demand from producers and the curiosity of filmgoers. He would, in a decade's time, be acknowledged as the best marketing expert in showbiz.

He was beginning to broaden his horizons as an actor, creating unique characters who would be remembered by their names and personality traits, instead of being the generic 'hero' without surname or background.

The streetwise guys he played in *Rangeela*, *Raja Hindustani* (1996) and *Ghulam* (1998), for instance, were all distinguished by their names, varied appearances and personas. Munna of *Rangeela* was generous and guileless, the kind of man the heroine would pick over wealth and fame; Raja of *Raja Hindustani* was charming but with a provincial machismo; Siddharth Marathe of *Ghulam* (a rehash of *On the Waterfront*) grew from the romance of 'Aati Kya Khandala' (sung in Aamir's own voice) to killer rage. At the time, very few stars went for the physical transformation that Aamir attempted. Nobody could say Aamir is Aamir in all his movies. He became, to the extent possible, the character he was playing.

Ishq (1997), *Mann* (1999) and *Mela* (2000) were the last films he would do with conventional, old-style Bollywood, perhaps to pay his debts to Indra Kumar and Dharmesh Darshan who had supported his career with hits when he needed to stay in the race. During this phase he also sneaked in an international film, *1947: Earth* (1999), with Deepa Mehta, and

it was nteresting to watch him—till then a conventional 'hero'—
do something so different.

The end of the 1990s was approaching. Winds of change
were blowing in Bollywood. Younger film-makers were trying to
tell stories that were closer to reality as compared to commercial
films till then that seemed to exist in a parallel universe. The
family-run production houses were slowly being eased out to
make way for professional production companies running with a
corporate set-up. Increasingly, scripts were actually written and
bound, storyboards prepared and contracts signed. Slowly being
eased out was the old haphazard way of making films, unaccounted-
for funding from dubious sources, payments in 'black', lines
being written on the set and shootings being extended for years
on the star's whims.

The A-list star, too, could no longer exist in an ivory tower,
protected by secretaries and sycophants. Aamir was quick to grasp
this, and start working towards the next, more significant phase
of his career—which included film-making and opinion-building.

Aamir did *Sarfarosh* (1999), a powerful cops-and-terrorists thriller,
in which he played a grim and upright cop, Ajay Singh Rathod,
with debutant director John Mathew Matthan, ad film-maker and
outsider to Bollywood. In this film, for the first time, the audience
could feel the brain ticking behind the character; Aamir was in
complete control, but not to the extent of smothering everything
else about the film. Rumours of his ghost-directing surfaced again.

15 June 2001 marked the release of *Lagaan*, the film that
pushed Aamir firmly into Bollywood's power list. His friend,
director Ashutosh Gowariker, told Aamir a story that was
germinating in his mind about a cricket match in a period
setting. Aamir turned it down. Ashutosh wrote out the script
and took it back. It was rewritten till it was right. Then,
realizing that no conventional film producer would take on
this film, Aamir decided to produce it himself and Aamir
Khan Productions was born.

Shunning the lure of unimaginable fees and the label of

'superstar' (for which Shahrukh Khan and new face Hrithik Roshan were the other contenders), Aamir devoted the next few years of his life to making *Lagaan*, the most talked about Indian film on the international scene. The West, which had been looking upon Bollywood films as lightweight song-and-dance melodramas, started considering India as a film-making centre worthy of respect.

Set in 1893, in Champaner, the film had Aamir playing Bhuvan, a villager who challenges the might of the British Empire through a game of cricket. If the villagers won, the back-breaking tax (*lagaan*) in the drought-struck village would be waived. He creates a winning team out of a ragtag bunch of poor, barefoot, desperate men. Even though the film ran for three hours and forty minutes, and most of it was the cricket match, which audiences knew would be won by Bhuvan's men, it still went on to become a major hit and won countless awards. It was India's entry for the Oscars that year, Aamir Khan's hectic lobbying took it up to the final five, where it lost to Bosnia's *No Man's Land*. Since then, no other film has made it to the nominations for Best Foreign Language film.

When Bhuj was rocked by an earthquake in 2001, Aamir, the cast and crew of *Lagaan* contributed to relief efforts, the first indication of Aamir's social commitment that grew more visible over the years. His subsequent support to the Narmada Bachao Andolan resulted in *Fanaa* being banned in Gujarat till the courts intervened.

The other big hit of Aamir's career that year, *Dil Chahta Hai*, launched Farhan Akhtar (son of Javed Akhtar and Honey Irani) as a director. An exuberant buddy movie that captured the lifestyles and aspirations of urban youth, it had Aamir play a rich young man, Akash Malhotra, who thinks love is a waste of time. Word was that Aamir had not only been given a huge remuneration to star in the film, but also a share in the profits.

After a longish self-imposed break, came his next film, *Mangal Pandey: The Rising* (2005), in which he played the initiator of the 1857 revolt against the British Raj. But in the interim years, his fifteen-year-old marriage to Reena (they had two children—Junaid and Ira) ended in divorce. His personal life was speculated about, he was rumoured to be dating a famous TV journalist, as well as British film researcher Jessica Hines, who, according to reports unconfirmed by both, had a child by Aamir.

It soon became clear that he was in a committed relationship with Kiran Rao, who was an assistant on the unit of *Lagaan*. They made no secret of their romance, and married in 2005—a private wedding away from Mumbai which nevertheless resulted in a media tamasha. He already had problems with his father over his remarriage, as well as a painful episode when his brother Faisal's mental illness and family battles were splashed all over the media.

The TV and internet boom had by now changed the way films were promoted. It became essential to build up and sustain interest in the making of a film. Stars had to participate in promotion in a big way. For a while Aamir went on an anti-media phase, expressing in an interview the contempt he had for the frivolity of contemporary media. When *Rang De Basanti* (2006) was released, he refused to do any promotional interviews or appearances.

The Rakeysh Omprakash Mehra film about a group of young men, led by Aamir Khan (who was over forty in 2006, but still youthful enough to play a man in his twenties), taking on a corrupt establishment, was a success and, for a while, fuelled a sort of youth activism. In fact, a 2011 film, *No One Killed Jessica*, gave credit to *Rang De Basanti* for galvanizing public anger against the acquittal of the prime accused in the Jessica Lall murder case. The civil protests and media campaign that followed led to eventual sentencing of the accused by the Delhi High Court.

Then came Aamir's directorial debut, *Taare Zameen Par*. Initially, Aamir had decided to produce Amole Gupte's film about a dyslexic child (Darsheel Safary) whose problems are ably addressed by a sympathetic teacher, Ram Shankar Nikumbh, played by Aamir Khan. But during the making of the film, the star took over as director, causing a great deal of bitterness, while also steering the film to major success. It brought the issue of learning disability and inadequacies in the educational system into the spotlight.

His film, *3 Idiots* (2009), directed by Rajkumar Hirani, from Chetan Bhagat's bestselling novel, went hammer and tongs at the mode of education that ignores aptitude, discourages questioning and suppresses imagination. Aamir played Rancho, the rebellious genius who lampoons and bucks the system.

Aamir's choice of films, his marketing acumen and intellect have made him everybody's favourite star guest—be it a literary meet, a policy summit or meetings with heads of state, Aamir Khan is sure to be on the guest list. His films are used for management studies, his methods analysed by media courses. He is Bollywood's star representative at prestigious international film festivals.

So even when he does a pointless action film, *Ghajini* (2008), about a man suffering from short-term memory loss, trying to avenge the murder of his girlfriend, the media's entire focus is on his six-pack bodybuilding, his strange buzz cut and the novel methods he employs to promote his films, like giving *Ghajini* haircuts to fans, or having ushers sport that hairstyle in a cinema running rival Shahrukh Khan's movie. (He makes no bones of this rivalry, going so far as announcing that he has a dog called Shahrukh.)

What he makes sure of, however, is to keep everyone guessing as to what he will do next. His production house has supported Abbas Tyrewala's romantic comedy *Jaane Tu Ya Jaane Na* (2008), which introduced his nephew Imran Khan to the movies; Anusha Rizvi's *Peepli Live* (2010), a dark satire on farmer suicides; his wife's debut movie *Dhobi Ghat* (2010), a sharp and whimsical ode to Mumbai; and the quirky *Delhi Belly* (2011), directed by Abhinay Deo and starring Imran.

Not only does Aamir have an instinct for scripts, a certain ruthlessness in matters of picking films (he turned down subsequent films by Ashutosh Gowariker and John Mathew Matthan), a keen sense of how best to promote his movies and which markets are to be targeted, but he also handles each film with complete focus from pre-production to post-production and publicity. All his films have been successful in recent years; and right now Aamir Khan can do no wrong—star, master strategist, trend-setter, trend-breaker, the thinking person's movie idol, guru figure, Padma Bhushan.

Still, he lives a relatively simple life, moves around without an entourage and does not flaunt designer labels. He politely declined the offer of a wax replica at Madame Tussauds. In the age of ostentation, he is a freak. (Rumour has it that he is now shopping for a bungalow, which would go with his superstar status.)

When the whole industry would be willing to have him in their films at any price, he chooses to play a cop in Reema Kagti's film (she is wife Kiran's friend too) and the villain in Aditya Chopra's *Dhoom 3*. He will make sure Kagti's film succeeds, and there's no way *Dhoom 3* can fail.

Today Aamir Khan is unbeatable.

What next? Some believe a political career and if he does enter this arena, he won't rest till he is prime minister. But with Aamir Khan, nobody can tell what's next. At best they can guess, and will get the answer when he is good and ready—accompanied by that puckish smile that crinkles the corners of his eyes.

FIVE FAVOURITE AAMIR KHAN FILMS

1. *Sarfarosh* (1999). Directed by John Mathew Matthan. Co-stars: Naseeruddin Shah, Sonali Bendre, Mukesh Rishi. A well-researched, courageous film on cross-border terrorism, which pointed a finger at Pakistan.
2. *Lagaan* (2001). Directed by Ashutosh Gowariker. Co-stars: Gracy Singh, Rachel Shelley, Paul Blackthorne. Music by A.R. Rahman. The story of a barefoot village team challenging the British garrison to a game of make-or-break cricket made it to the Oscar shortlist.
3. *Jo Jeeta Wohi Sikandar* (1992). Directed by Mansoor Khan. Co-stars: Ayesha Jhulka, Mamik, Deepak Tijori, Pooja Bedi. One of the few sports films in Bollywood. Launched the

career of composers Jatin–Lalit; Farah Khan shot to fame as a choreographer with the song 'Pehla nasha'.

4. *Qayamat Se Qayamat Tak* (1988). Directed by Mansoor Khan. Co-stars: Juhi Chawla, Dalip Tahil, Goga Kapoor. Melodious music by Anand Milind. Story of star-crossed lovers in feudal Rajasthan, marked the beginning of the end of the age of this kind of tragic romantic movie.

5. *Taare Zameen Par* (2007). Directed by Aamir Khan. Co-stars: Darsheel Safary, Tisca Chopra. A sympathetic teacher gives hope to a dyslexic child. Important because it showed how mainstream cinema can tackle issues.

SHAHRUKH KHAN

YUPPIE PRINCE OF LIBERALIZED INDIA

NAMRATA JOSHI

It was a close encounter of the glitzy kind with Shahrukh Khan on the ultra kitschy set of his 2007 home production, *Om Shanti Om* (hereafter *OSO*). The cheesy anthem 'Dil mein mere hai darde disco' was being shot at Mumbai's Yash Raj Studios and a shirtless SRK in faux-leather pants was dancing alongside tall, lissom white girls with a huge eagle looming large as the backdrop. He was in a jolly good mood that day, hell-bent on showing off his newly acquired six pack abs. 'How do you think I look?' he'd ask everyone around rhetorically, and then without even waiting for a reply he'd smile, flashing his famous dimples: 'I have the abs; I don't need to act now.' Unsparingly mocking, he was sending up everything for a lark: the Yash-Raj-Films-inscribed cutlery with which he was eating his McDonald's burger, Rahul Rawail's new film *Buddha Mar Gaya*, and, most of all, yours truly for asking him 'Shabana Azmi–like' (read pretentious) questions. SRK was even sending up SRK that day, complaining to director Farah Khan about how he hated shooting with leggy models: 'They make me look and feel like a chaprasi (peon).'

But it wasn't just fun and games at the shoot that day. Seriousness surfaced as SRK began reading the scripts of the promos of *OSO*, red-stemmed glasses perched firmly on that unmistakable nose. The film was ready, the marketing and hype was about to unleash and you could see he was keen to get all the details of the launch right. The performer's job was done; the producer-businessman had taken over.

That up-close-and-personal meeting with him was enough to make one understand that the seemingly impulsive amusement and exuberance and the simultaneous attention to detail wasn't just to do with this specific film; over the years forty-six-year-old SRK, with seventy-odd films behind him, had built his mammoth star persona with similar canniness and care. Behind all the flamboyance and fun, the instant jokes, cheeky repartee and self-deprecatory humour that he is identified with, there has been a razor-sharp mind that has managed, built and promoted Brand SRK in a manner that has given it an unmatched recall for over two decades now.

However, no one would have expected this unbridled showmanship from an energetic, enthusiastic young Delhi lad when he started off gingerly in Bollywood in the early 1990s. He was a complete outsider with neither a father nor godfather within the industry to hold his hand and support him through his struggles. In fact, the boy who grew up in Delhi's Rajendra Nagar and Gautam Nagar, studied in St Columba's School and Hansraj College and was a dropout of the prestigious Mass Communications Research Centre, Jamia Millia Islamia, came to Bombay (now Mumbai) in 1991, to find himself and a life after his parents' (Meer Taj Mohammad and Fatima Lateef) early, untimely death. All he had behind him were a stint in Barry John's Theatre Action Group, the cult success of TV serials *Fauji* (he had girls swooning over his electric Commando Abhimanyu Rai) and *Circus*, and a small role in Pradip Krishen's TV film *In Which Annie Gives It Those Ones* (1989).

Nasreen Munni Kabir's intimate documentary, *The Inner World of Shah Rukh Khan*, provides us a rare peep into those early days, unveils the invisible past of SRK's ubiquitous present stardom, the less-than-perfect roots of this brassy, bouncing superstar's seemingly fairytale life. SRK lost his parents when he wasn't yet twenty-four. He talks in the film about his gregarious mother with whom he'd watch Dilip Kumar films on the VCR. 'She worked hard for us and I tried hard to impress her ... I wanted to be bigger than even 70mm and Cinemascope,' he says. He talks about his Peshawari father who came home one day and announced: '*Yaara doctor kah raha hai mujhe cancer hai.*' He talks about his chronically depressive elder sister Shahnaz Lala Rukh and faces up to his own fear of loss and death: 'I am hyper, scared to the extent of being silly.' For someone traumatized by a feeling of abandonment and separation, acting has been an escape from the unbearable sadness of being and from his innermost insecurities: 'The only way I could avoid getting depressed was by putting on make-up and becoming someone else,' he says in the film.

Early days in an alien city were not easy. In the initial phase of his struggle he used to be angry with Mumbai, with its small houses, cramped spaces and expensive things. He admits in the film of having shouted out into the sea that he'd own the city one day. 'It was foolish of me ... Ten years down the line the city owns me,' he says in the film. 'It's the greatest city in the world.' The city that finally gave him a home called Mannat.

What followed over the years in Mumbai has been a formidable reign as the Hindi film industry's top star, something SRK himself finds unbelievable. 'Such great things have happened to such a normal guy like me. I am a nobody who shouldn't have been able to do all this but I have done it,' he told us in an interview. No wonder he has been perennially trying to get used to stardom, seeing it as a role he is playing in some film. 'I tell everyone that there's this myth I work for; there is this myth called Shahrukh Khan and I am its employee. I have to live up to that myth, convince people. People expect me to speak well extempore; they can't see me read from my notes. So I'll do it, I am an actor. But I can't start believing in this myth,' he said.

SRK's stardom has truly been unique. It has been all about steady continuities as well as radical departures. He could well be the veritable bridge between Hindi cinema's old-world and new-age icons. Stardom is notorious for its impermanence but he has endured for decades. Like a classic Indian superstar he has consistently broken box-office records, won over people's hearts and has had an aura and appeal that has been of the moment as well as timeless.

But there have been ways in which he has also redefined stardom for contemporary times. His mystique and mythology aren't just confined to the multiplexes where his films are screened but come riding on an easy access and availability. He doesn't just star in films but in ads and TV shows (for instance, *Kaun Banega Crorepati* and *Kya Aap Paanchvi Pass Se Tez Hain*). He has been endorsing innumerable products (from Hyundai to Tag Heuer). In fact, till SRK came along Bollywood had always looked down on advertising. He did ads systematically and paved the way for them becoming the main source of income for stars other than films. He has run two production houses (Dreamz Unlimited[1] and Red Chillies[2]), he sings and dances in private marriage functions, he partly owns an India Premier League cricket team (Kolkata Knight Riders) and shops for its players. His Mumbai home, Mannat, is not an ivory tower because even though he may live in its privacy, SRK is also in our living rooms day in and day out.

Adman and columnist Santosh Desai regards SRK's stardom as that of the market. 'It's not about enigma. It's like a product–consumer relationship. So it's symbiotic unlike, say, a Rajesh Khanna who was aloof, on a pedestal, he was soaking it in from

[1] In partnership with Juhi Chawla and Aziz Mirza, under which he made *Phir Bhi Dil Hai Hindustani* (2000), *Asoka* (2001) and *Chalte Chalte* (2003).

[2] Under which he produced *Main Hoon Na* (2004), *Paheli* (2005), *Om Shanti Om* (2007), *Billu* (2009), *Always Kabhi Kabhi* (2011), *Ra. One* (2011).

the fans but not giving back. SRK has a reciprocal relationship with his fans,' he says. He gives as much as he gets.

Stars are often not just built on personal aura, they are also a product of their times. So SRK's stardom isn't just dependent on those poses, witticisms and mannerisms—the pout, arched brow, flared nostril, boyish charm and sarcastic half-smile. His image has fitted in perfectly with the times. It's as though SRK was waiting to happen. In the liberalized India of the '90s the Angry Young Man had to make way for the romantic family hero. Many see SRK embodying, through the Rajs and Rahuls he has played, the spirit of post-liberalization, feel-good, ambitious, assertive India—just as Big B's Angry Young Man represented the angst-ridden India of the '70s and the '80s.

However, this persona took a while to take shape. SRK started out in mainstream Bollywood on an unassuming note in 1991 with *Deewana*, in which he played a young man who falls in love with and marries a widow. His famous early roles were those of the anti-hero, like the avenger in the garb of lover in *Baazigar* (1993) where he shocked the audience by killing his own girlfriend (played by Shilpa Shetty) and delivered the iconic dialogue: '*Kabhi kabhi kuchh jeetne ke liye kuchh haarna padta hai aur haar ke jeetne wale ko baazigar kehte hain*.' It was followed by two films in which he played the obsessive, violent, psycho lover—*Darr* (1993), which made the stutter 'K-K-K . . . Kiran' the buzzword of the nation, and *Anjaam* (1994). In fact, his first credited film, Mani Kaul's *Idiot* (1991), based on the Fyodor Dostoevsky classic, has him playing the dark Raghujan (Rogozhin) who kills the woman he loves when he realizes he can't have her.

SRK eventually metamorphosed into the perfect yuppie loverboy and, in the process, also redefined on-screen love for a brand new India. The crucial film that led him to this avatar was *Dilwale Dulhania Le Jaayenge* (1995), arguably one of the biggest grossers ever in Bollywood. Popularly referred to simply as *DDLJ*, the film reinvented Bollywood romances so decisively that we can neatly divide them into two eras—before *DDLJ* and after *DDLJ*. Till then, love in Hindi films had been all about change and defiance. *DDLJ* upheld peaceful negotiations over belligerent rebellion, and in doing so, instantly connected with both the young and the old. It bridged the generation gap that love stories are meant to widen. So love here was no longer about confronting class and caste differences but about persistent reconciliations. Raj in *DDLJ* has a flamboyant yet matter-of-fact, conformist attitude that reflected the spirit of a country in the throes of economic reforms: grounded, steady and practical rather than dreamy and idealistic.

SRK's subsequent romantic films, be it *Dil To Pagal Hai* (1997), *Kuch Kuch Hota Hai* (1998) or *Mohabbatein* (2000), have built on the *DDLJ* foundation. Love in Hindi cinema these days doesn't seem to face external hindrances; it's all about conquering your inner demons. Love as we once knew it—pure passion—has morphed into something fun and cool, embodied in SRK's characteristic outstretched hands in song after song or those blameless kisses he placed on many a heroine's neck. Commenting on the irony of this, Anupama Chopra writes: 'Shahrukh became Bollywood's biggest romantic icon without ever locking lips with a co-star.'[3] This persona, however, wasn't just SRK's own creation. It was propped up by his favourite directors—Aditya Chopra and Karan Johar—who built their films around him, who intuitively understood the power of SRK and exploited that into successful narratives. 'I trust them. We're on the same page. We're very clear about our reasons for doing things,' he said of Aditya, Karan and Farah in a March 2007 interview in *Tehelka*.

In *Kuch Kuch Hota Hai*, Rahul (SRK) wears a chain spelling out 'COOL' but also visits a temple every week. He personifies the trendy–traditional, conservative–modern, global–local schisms of the new India, its urge to move ahead and yet hold on to

---

[3] See Anupama Chopra, *King of Bollywood: Shah Rukh Khan and the Seductive World of Indian Cinema* (New York: Warner Books, 2007).

the past. He also made labels like Tommy Hilfiger, Polo and Gap a must-have in any consumerist yuppie's expansive wardrobe. In that sense SRK single-handedly shifted the focus of Bollywood away from the amorphous masses in small towns and villages to the Shining India of the urban malls and the nostalgic NRI. In fact his *Dil Se* (1998), despite flopping at home, became the first Bollywood film to break into UK Top 10 charts. As film-maker-writer Paromita Vohra writes: 'There are few anxieties or conflicts in his later movies. Rather, there are lush evocations of consumption and visual excess. Significantly, this doesn't constitute fantasy anymore—the holiday in Switzerland and those designer tiles are the reality of upper middle class life. The fantasy on offer is the absence of people unlike us—the poor, basically—who might show up the rather unpleasant inequities our lives are based on.'[4] Says Desai: 'He embodies the market, makes consumption look good.'

It was for consumption then that Sanjay Leela Bhansali wrapped up Indian literature's biggest loser—Devdas—in toothpaste glam. Bhansali's *Devdas* (2002) turned an intimate tragedy into a glitzy spectacle, replaced the gravitas of Dilip Kumar by the flamboyance of SRK and threw in populist, cheesy lines like: '*Gaonwalon ne kaha gaon chhod do, Bauji ne kaha Paro chhod do, Paro ne kaha sharaab chhod do, Ma ne kaha ghar chhod do, Ek din Woh* [read God] *kahega duniya chhod do.*'

Karan Johar's visual bubblegum *Kabhi Khushi Kabhie Gham* (2001) is, perhaps, the acme of this cinema of excess and consumption. In this world of chiffon-n-pearls, Scottish castles and choppers, SRK played the estranged adopted son of a tycoon who heads for London and builds a bharatiya nest in Hampstead where youngsters dance at proms but also sing *Jana Gana Mana*.

SRK has defended this brand of escapism. 'I don't think anyone of us has taken a girl in beautiful clothes to Switzerland and said, "I love you." I don't think anyone of us has sat down in a beautiful Porsche and sung "Tujhe dekha to yeh

[4] See Paromita Vohra, 'Astronomical Figures', *Outlook*, 19 May 2008.

jaana sanam . . ." It's escapist; it's beautiful because our reality is very harsh. I like to escape to video games. I think giving vent to my aggression in video games is better than beating people.'

But these 'easy', 'escapist' loverboy roles also ensured SRK often got roundly dismissed as a non-actor who made it at the box office with loads of charm and good luck but little talent. SRK has argued otherwise: 'I do a lot of things in my films that I know I can't do in real life. I live a fantasy life and give escapism to a lot of people. But that doesn't mean I am not a good actor. The work I do, and the way I choose to act in those films makes some people say, "I am not gonna like him." He is pouting, doing love stories set in Switzerland. Think beyond it and you might find an expression of mine that was good.'

SRK's stardom has been about entertainment—squarely and relentlessly—and he has been least apologetic about it. 'The idea is to entertain in as many ways as possible in one lifetime as an actor. I don't think we should intellectualize entertainment. I think intellect and logic should be left at the doorstep of film-making. I strongly believe films are for entertainment; messages are for the post office,' he told us in an interview.

SRK's logic has been that it requires tremendous amount of intelligence to be able to entertain. 'To do silly things is the most intelligent work. That's why we love cartoons; they are so silly. The most intelligent guys are the stand-up comedians. George Carlin—he used to talk seriously about society and he was so funny. Raju Srivastava knows so much about life you'd be shocked. For the level of seriousness, the level of knowledge has to be huge, more than that of the most intelligent guys. You can be very aware, but by seriously talking about serious issues you don't become intelligent. I really believe I am intelligent. Intelligence has to be off the cuff, it has to be easygoing,' he said.

Indeed a closer look at his résumé reveals that he has also played around with a broad spectrum of roles in his own way. These roles and films have unfortunately and unfairly got ignored in a hysterical celebration of Raj and Rahul. His best, perhaps, has come out in films which weren't squarely romantic, comedies like the *Shree 420*-inspired *Raju Ban Gaya Gentleman* (1992), about a simple small-town boy's tryst with the big city and the corruption it breeds; *Kabhi Haan Kabhi Naa* (1993) where he played a fallible yet utterly loveable boy next door; *Yes Boss* (1996) where his character, who sucks up to his boss and cares little about morals, symbolized the upwardly mobile, middle-class urban Indians' craving for success and *Phir Bhi Dil Hai Hindustani* (2000) where he played a television journo competing with fellow hack Juhi Chawla over scoops, but eventually coming together for a good cause. It anticipated the media circus much before *Peepli Live* (2010).

Then there were the mad, balmy, hysterical laughathons like *Baadshah* (1999) and *Duplicate* (1997). Why, SRK also did his quota of action movies like *Karan Arjun* (1995), a reincarnation-revenge drama, and *Josh* (2000) on young love blooming amidst street gang wars.

He experimented with offbeat films like *Dil Se* (1998), a stylized take on obsessive love set against the backdrop of terrorism and separatism. *Paheli* (2005) was based on Vijay Dan Detha's original story, 'Duvidha', about a ghost who falls in love with a beautiful woman and takes the form of her husband while he is away on business. *Asoka* (2001) was an attempt to revisit a well-known historical figure using contemporary cinematic elements and martial art forms like kalari, shadow puppetry and Kathakali. And a few would also remember *Maya Memsaab* (1992) which generated controversy because of SRK's appearance in an 'explicit' sex scene with Deepa Sahi. But the failure of each of these experiments made him return to mainstream, romantic roles.

SRK is at an interesting juncture in his career. In the last few years there seems to have been an attempt, however ineffective, to try and move away from the permanent posturing he's identified with and be a more real hero. It hasn't been about a continuation of Raj and Rahul but a reinvention of some of his less popular avatars. Take *OSO*. It could well be a refined version of the balmy *Baadshah* with SRK at his riotous best as the junior artiste reborn as the star son. It was comic book, cheeky and irreverent with side-splitting gags like the popular 'ennada rascal' and the MGR-and-Rajnikant-inspired 'tame the tiger by its tail' cowboy act.

SRK upscaled the action of *Karan Arjun* and *Josh* in *Don* (2006) while also trying a hand at an Amitabh Bachchan favourite. SRK's 21st-century *Don* was stylish with a self-indulgently moody feel. *Rab Ne Bana Di Jodi*'s (2008) nice, boring man—Surinder aka Suri—was a throwback to SRK's common Joe days of *Kabhi Haan Kabhi Naa*. Right from the look—those sports shoes with baggy trousers—to the little gestures—seeing love in a yellow tiffin box, the indecision on whether to leave behind a rose for his love—the idea was to play the regular and the ordinary.

Of late there have also been films with an overt sense of conscience. Like *Swades* (2004), arguably his best, about an NRI's return to roots. For SRK it embodied new-age patriotism. It talked about gaining knowledge from all around the world but coming back to help your country. 'We can't demean the advancement the Western world has made. We can go there, imbibe the language of technology and bring it back. I think that's modern nationalism. It's not about "West sucks and look at our culture". Every age demands its own kind of patriotism. I think post-Independence we needed that kind of cinema,' he explained to us in an interview.

Veer–Zaara (2004) attempted to mitigate the on-screen animus against Pakistan, seen in films like *Gadar*, and made way for some soft-focus, mushy duets between Veer Pratap Singh (SRK, read India) and Zaara Hayaat Khan (Preity Zinta, Pakistan). The film lacked intellectual ambition. Built on an emotional excess and lachrymose sentimentality, it presented a new pacifist, peaceful face of Bollywood but was effective nonetheless.

However, for me the most interesting aspect about SRK has

been the assertion of his Muslim identity on screen. SRK was Amjad Ali Khan in *Hey Ram* (2000), then went on to play a cosmopolitan Muslim, like himself, as Kabir Khan, in *Chak De! India* (2007). The hockey player, who is blamed for selling a win to Pakistan, eventually redeems himself by training a women's hockey team to victory. 'He is not a typical, caricatured Muslim, but a modern man,' said SRK of what he liked about Kabir. In fact, the character even says SRK's own prayer in one of the scenes: '*Nasrun minal lahe wah fatahun kareeb* (God give me strength to win)'. SRK is said to have kept reciting this prayer when his mother Fatima Lateef was on her deathbed.

My Name Is Khan (2010) again blended reel and real roles for SRK. Rizwan Khan, afflicted with Aspergers Syndrome, pays a heavy personal price for his surname and hits the road to explain to the American President that his name is Khan and he is not a terrorist. Through this larger-than-life character, SRK seems to stand up for the Muslims of the world and for Islam, a religion under fire post 9/11. Rizwan says his prayers in public, wears his cap, derives his identity from his religion, but rises well above it. So has SRK. Something he may well have inherited from his free-thinking, freedom-fighter father.

SRK married his childhood sweetheart, a Hindu called Gauri Chibba. In the library in his house I have spotted both 'Om' and 'Allah' insignias. He has himself spoken of how his children, Aryan and Suhana, recite the Gayatri mantra and also say Bismillah with him but actually enjoy celebrating Christmas the most. 'I am a believer . . . I need to be clearly standing for the goodness of Islam . . . I think I truly am [an ambassador of Islam]. I follow the tenets of Islam—peace, goodness, kindness to mankind . . . I read namaz when I feel like. But I would not like to believe in four marriages even if my religion allows it . . . But that doesn't mean I'm questioning the Quran. I'd like people to know that Islam is not only about being a fanatic, or radically different, angered person, or one who only does jihad. I'd like people to know that the actual meaning of jihad is to overcome one's own violence and weakness,' he said in a March 2007 interview in *Tehelka*.

Nasreen Munni Kabir's *The Outer World of Shah Rukh Khan*, a sequel to *The Inner World of Shah Rukh Khan*, followed SRK on his Temptations 2004 show as it toured twelve American cities, before ending in Toronto, Canada. On a day when the fans seemed unrelenting, Munni Kabir remembers asking SRK whether he found their keenness overbearing. SRK replied with a half-smile: 'The only time I find people invasive is when I'm eating. When I'm eating, I just don't like people looking at me.' But he was clear that he loved stardom: 'I love people loving me. If I'm not going to be in that situation, I'll just be with myself. I will not be able to come out of the four walls of my house.'

That love from the audience doesn't seem as unconditional now. Despite his well-intentioned performances SRK is very obviously struggling with his stardom. Not that he hasn't faced adversity previously—the folding up of srkworld.com, the flop films of Dreamz Unlimited, the rise of Hrithik Roshan, the surgery for his prolapsed disc and the legal loopholes and taxation issues regarding his home Mannat. However, now the battle is different. The other rival Khans—Aamir and Salman—seem to have figured their niche but SRK seems to be losing out on his hold on the upper class youth market. He doesn't seem to be 'happening' any more. Moreover controversies have been dogging him—be it his statement on Pakistani players in IPL, the ban on *My Name Is Khan* by the Shiv Sena or *Ra.One* (2011) going overbudget. He has been hitting the headlines for the wrong reasons—for his clashes with Aamir, Salman and Amitabh Bachchan. There is also a visible desperation in making money by opting to do dreadful TV shows like *Zor Ka Jhatka*. His home productions like *Billu* (2007) or *Always Kabhi Kabhi* (2011) too have come a cropper.

'You can see traces of bitterness in him now. His throwaway jibes are becoming darker. He is brooding. Cracks of various kinds are appearing in the happy land that SRK once constructed,' says Desai.

Most alarming has been the appalling response, from viewers and critics alike, to his most recent biggie *Ra.One*. The most expensive Bollywood film had SRK betting it all—his money, stardom, reputation. He never hard-sold a film like this one before. However, it's a film where he doesn't come across as the effortless, charming entertainer that he has always been but an irresolute superstar who is anxious to hold on to his fickle fan base. The sharp, smart sense of humour gets compromised with puerile, low-brow jokes. The quintessential romance and emotions get replaced by mechanical stunts and SFX. It's an SRK who is more alienating than endearing. Also for a 'star of the market' who has always had brands clamouring to ride on his equity, it's a major comedown to find Rs 52 crore worth of brand tie-ups shoring up his film's earnings instead.

'Everything changes. Stardom might seem eternal but it is not. You should have the ability to accept and do something inventive,' says academician Shohini Ghosh. Social anthropologist Shiv Vishvanathan too feels his superstar cycle is over and he needs to reinvent himself. 'Things have come to boring level,' he says. 'A new epoch in his career has to begin now.' Perhaps the directors who understand him and his persona—Aditya, Karan, Farah—hold the key to that. Or the more adventurous like Shimit Amin and Farhan Akhtar may do the trick by taking him on an unusual course.

We are waiting. So, perhaps, is SRK.

MY FIVE FAVOURITE SHAHRUKH KHAN FILMS

1. *Kabhi Haan Kabhi Naa* (1993). Directed by Kundan Shah. Co-stars: Suchitra Krishnamoorthi and Deepak Tijori. One of SRK's personal favourites, *Kabhi Haan Kabhi Naa* has him playing Sunil, a middle-class boy-next-door, who loves music and his childhood friend Anna (Suchitra). He doesn't think twice about lying to get the girl's affections and forges his marksheet to keep his dad happily oblivious of his academic

failure. Eventually his innate goodness wins the day. Both the character and the film struck a huge chord with the young and SRK bagged the Filmfare Critics' Award for the performance. The film taught him the basics of performing for the camera and laid the foundation for him as an actor.

2. *Baadshah* (1999). Directed by Abbas–Mustan. Co-stars: Twinkle Khanna, Rakhee and Amrish Puri. Despite being a straight lift of a minor Hollywood film called *If Looks Could Kill*, *Baadshah* works in its own cheesy and sublimely silly way, provided you have an appetite for the ludicrous. I do. Each character is more demented than the other in this riotous mistaken-identity comedy with SRK leading the pack as Raj, aka detective Baadshah, who saves diamonds, a kidnapped child and the chief minister, and also merrily spoofs James Bond and his funky gadgetry. According to SRK, *Baadshah* (as well as *Duplicate*) best reflects his whacked-out sense of humour.

3. *Kal Ho Naa Ho* (2003). Directed by Nikhil Advani. Co-stars: Preity Zinta and Saif Ali Khan. SRK plays Aman, the quintessential angel, who sets things right for people around him, but can do little to help himself. The love triangle combined the heartaches and pains of the big, beautiful NRI romances SRK came to be identified with after *DDLJ* along with the high emotions of an *Anand* and smart humour of a *Dil Chahta Hai*. Result: SRK at his squarely starry, romantic, charming and endearing best. Those hands outstretched in his trademark gesture and dimples flashing, of course!

4. *Swades* (2004). Directed by Ashutosh Gowariker. Co-stars: Gayatri Joshi and Kishori Balal. In arguably his best role, SRK is Mohan Bhargava, a non-resident Indian scientist at USA's NASA, who returns to a little north Indian village in search of his nanny, Kaveriamma (Kishori Balal). Moved by the problems there, he decides to stay on to try and make a difference. In a village ridden with dogmas, he successfully bridges the caste divide, helps solve the power and water

problems and saves the local school from near extinction. He literally gets the villagers together to build up a local self-governance movement. With rare restraint and maturity SRK brought alive the inner, metaphorical voyage of Mohan and his rediscovery of a forgotten India.

5. *Chak De! India* (2007). Directed by Shimit Amin. Co-stars: Vidya Malwade and Chitrashi Rawat. This is not a typical SRK film. It has no heroine or villain, no romance and song 'n' dance. A simple, endearing tale about Kabir Khan, a disgraced hockey player who coaches a ragtag team of girls from all corners of India to win the World Cup, *Chak De!* touches upon many significant issues of the day like religion, regionalism, gender bias, patriotism. One of the most well-appreciated SRK roles and films, *Chak De!* has him play himself—a cosmopolitan, liberal, Indian Muslim.

KAJOL

LIVING LIFE ON HER OWN TERMS

NIRANJAN IYENGAR

For an actress who has attained such overwhelming fame so early in life, Kajol wears her success rather lightly and therein lies her charm. For people who hail from film families, celluloid usually means everything to them. Their lives are intertwined with films and filmdom in some form or the other. Somehow in this world Kajol always seems an uneasy participant. Despite having a deep-rooted film lineage through her actress mother, Tanuja, and film-maker father, Shomu Mukherjee, there has never been anything remotely filmi about Kajol. In fact, seldom has there been a film star who maintains such a healthy distance from her professional surrounding as her. She attends very few parties, is close to very few of her film-makers or co-stars and is almost never curious about the goings-on in the fraternity. Ironically, this unconventional attitude towards the glamour world has its roots in the conventional wisdom that she never forgets to quote, 'If you have your priorities right, everything falls into place!' And ever since I have known her—i.e., since 1992—Kajol has always had her priorities in place. There are only three things she is serious about—the people she loves, the roles she enacts and the self she's constantly trying to protect.

Everything else—the autographs, the parties, the photo shoots and the glory—are all clumped together like so much bad mascara!

When Kajol left St Joseph's Convent, Panchgani, at the age of sixteen and came to Bombay (now Mumbai), Tanuja roped in her two close friends, Gautam Rajadhjyaksha (ace lens man) and Mickey Contractor (well-known make-up maestro) to shoot and style her photographs. As the shoot ended, both Gautam and Mickey were confident that a star was born. However, the early 1990s belonged to Sridevi and Madhuri Dixit who were larger-than-life glamour queens with skilful dancing abilities. The yardstick for a successful heroine then was to have conventional beauty and the traditional jhatka-matkas. Kajol's urban boarding-school upbringing made sure she had neither. So Tanuja decided to direct a film to launch Kajol. The film started but was shelved after a few days of shooting. In the meanwhile, Gautam, who was scripting a film for director Rahul Rawail, felt Kajol would suit the lead role of their project. And thus Kajol bagged *Bekhudi* (1992) which bombed at the box office when it released. However, despite Kajol's unconventional, south Bombay demeanor, every single person in the fraternity vouched for the fact that the light-eyed, dynamite of a performer was here to stay.

One of the first film-makers to sign her on was the duo-in-white, Abbas–Mustan, for their film *Baazigar* (1993). The film is a landmark in many ways. Apart from giving the present superstar, Shahrukh Khan, his first taste of success in an unconventional negative role, *Baazigar* also marked the coming together of *the* star pair of the last two decades—Shahrukh and Kajol. 'She is absolutely my favorite co-star because I can laugh with her and at her . . . There are no invisible walls with her. What you see is what you get,' says Shahrukh. And 99 per cent of her directors and colleagues will vouch for that statement. Kajol's dealings with people are very consciously transparent. 'I dislike 90 per cent of the people I meet,' she had said in an interview in the mid-'90s. 'Of the remaining 10 per cent, I tolerate 8 . . . I only love 2 per cent!'

Even though in her early twenties at the time, Kajol had clarity of thought that very few from her generation did. Though she was volatile in her day-to-day interactions, her approach to her career was almost Zen-like. In the two decades I have known her she has never been shattered by the failure of her films just as I have never seen her being ecstatic about her success. When *Dilwale Dulhania Le Jayenge* (1995) released to packed houses and won Kajol more and more accolades with each passing day, Kajol kept wondering what the fuss was about. Even today when you discuss this longest-running film of her career with her, she just reminisces about the joyful moments she shared with close friends like Aditya Chopra, Karan Johar and Manish Malhotra more than her role or the film itself. But then Kajol rarely dwells on her accomplishments. Give her a compliment on her terrific performances and she smiles uncomfortably. And when you persist in your flattery, you realize that her modesty is more out of a factual analysis. 'I don't think I'm a great actor,' she explains patiently. 'A good actor is someone who can play a variety of roles without a trace of their own personality—Like Sridevi! When you see her films you are left wondering what she would be like as a person! But with me I am always Kajol first and then the role!'

Interestingly, the few detractors she does have use this very argument as a form of criticism. According to them she has always played safe with her choice of films. Any character or role which is out of the realm of her personality evokes an instant refusal from her. I remember when *Virasat* (1997) was being remade Kajol was offered the role of Revathi (eventually played brilliantly by Tabu). She dragged me to watch the original *Thevar Magan* in Filmalaya Studios so I could translate the film for her. Though she was very impressed with the film and its characters she declared in the intermission that she wasn't doing the film. No amount of convincing changed her mind. 'I love the role but I can't do it . . . I'm not capable!' she said vehemently. The only time she made an exception was when she agreed to play a negative role in *Gupt* (1996). It was a bold decision to play a murderer in the film especially after the stupendous success of *DDLJ*. But Kajol pulled it off and even won a Filmfare Award for her negative role. Her resistance to venture into unknown territories may have stopped her from experimenting, but it has also allowed her to consistently live up to audience expectations. Even in unsuccessful films like *Udhaar Ki Zindagi* (1994), *Bambai Ka Babu* (1996) or *Hameshaa* (1996) one can never fault her for her lack of conviction.

'Kajol can never perform a scene unless she is convinced,' says Karan Johar, who has directed her in blockbusters like *Kuch Kuch Hota Hai* (1998), *Kabhi Khushi Kabhie Gham* (2001) and *My Name Is Khan* (2010). 'She can drive you up the wall if you don't have the right answers to convince her. But once she is convinced, there's no one who gives a shot like her!' he laughs. Her rule while selecting a film is quite simple. 'I always hear a story and think, "Do I want to watch this film?"' Kajol explains. 'If the answer is yes then I agree . . .!' This conviction is evident in her off-screen career decisions as well. At a time when world tours and stage shows were mega events to test a star's popularity (apart from being major revenue streams), Kajol remains the only star from her generation to refuse them consistently (except once). 'I have a massive stage fright and find it very uncomfortable to perform for a live audience!' is her explanation. That Kajol needs comfort to excel is indisputable. Her choice of films and film-makers also reflects this attribute. 'I need to get the right vibe from a director,' she says. 'I need to know that he has done his homework. I hate it when I have to do his job and graph my character. It's his vision that I'm executing . . . I don't want to "see" for him! I absolutely demand that comfort as an actor!'

Another interesting aspect of Kajol's personality that is unique to her generation is her aversion to glamour in its conventional form. Like legendary actresses Nargis and Nutan, Kajol is not a conventional beauty; and, like Meena Kumari, Kajol too never really managed a super slim or fit body structure and yet her allure is unquestionable. As her long-time designer and close friend Manish Malhotra explains, 'She is the only actress I know who can show her midriff even when it is not in its best shape and get away with it. That's because she stands with such confidence that you don't find anything odd about her!' Clothes again with Kajol are all about comfort more than glamour. 'It was a rule on Karan's [Johar] sets that the day Kajol was dressed as a bride no one should go into her make-up room!' laughs Malhotra. 'She is always in her worst mood on days when there were elaborate costumes or jewellery to be worn!' But then vanity has never been Kajol's strength as her close friend and ex-journalist Ryan Stephen explains. 'In the early '90s when all the actors revelled in various theme-based photo-sessions for film glossies, she was a nightmare!' he laughs. 'It used to be a three-month runaround to get her to pose for a still camera and she usually agreed only when she was emotionally blackmailed!'

While Kajol's personality has been consistently fierce and emotional in the last two decades, her marriage to Ajay Devgn in 1999 and her subsequent motherhood has reigned in her volatility to a great extent. During their courtship, one could already see the beginnings of this transformation. Even in the middle of a screaming match with her friends, his phone call would suddenly change her decibel level, causing her friends to coin the phrase 'Dolby becomes Mono' for her. When she decided to marry Ajay Devgn on 24 February 1999, there was a lot of speculation vis-à-vis her career. No one was sure how an audience would accept a married leading lady. Kajol, of course, was unperturbed and continued to work. Her *Dil Kya Kare* (1999) with Ajay Devgn bombed but *Hum Aapke Dil Mein Rehte Hain* (1999) with Anil Kapoor was successful. She teamed again with her husband in *Raju Chacha* (2000) which failed, thereby fuelling the myth that her on-screen chemistry with Devgn was weak. Just when things seemed bleak Kajol had *Kabhi Khushi Kabhie Gham* (2001), which was the largest overseas blockbuster for over five years and also brought back the Shahrukh–Kajol magic to the audiences. The stupendous success of the film put Kajol back on the map as a reigning queen when she won her third Filmfare Best Actress Award that year. Every film-maker worth his salt made a beeline for her with a script but once again Kajol's priority took precedence and she decided to take a sabbatical. She wanted to plunge into motherhood and no temptation could waver her from her goal. Nysa, her daughter, was born in 2003 and a new chapter began in Kajol's life.

The first year after Nysa's birth was like being on a roller coaster for Kajol, but it was a ride that she enjoyed thoroughly. Though she was new to motherhood, it almost seemed like she was born for it. During this period there were a lot of films that were offered to her. However she was clear that she wasn't even reading a script till Nysa was two. True to her promise she started hearing narrations in 2005. The period coincided with the scripting of Karan Johar's *Kabhi Alvida Naa Kehna* (2006). And, like Johar says, 'Every scene I write, I visualize Kajol enacting it! I wish she could be in every movie that is made!' So it wasn't surprising that the film was offered to her. She would have starred in the film had it not been for the ninety-day shooting schedule in New York. Kajol did not want to leave Nysa alone for that long and taking her daughter to New York for such a long period was not an option for her. 'I take my profession as seriously as I take motherhood,' she says. 'It would be very difficult to balance the two in the same space!' And so the film went to her cousin Rani Mukherji. However in the interim period Aamir Khan (who had never been paired with her before) read the script of *Fanaa* (2006) and felt the movie should only be made if Kajol agreed to play the lead. She did and thus she came back to movies after a six-year hiatus. The film went on to be a big blockbuster, and despite the early rumours of Aamir and Kajol's dislike for each other, they ended up having great camaraderie. Kajol bagged yet another Filmfare Award for the film.

While Kajol's strong and opinionated disposition remained unchanged to a large extent, there was a marked composure about her when she started work again. 'Motherhood builds a great deal of patience in you,' she quipped on the sets of *Fanaa*. 'And people are mistaking my patience for acceptance!' Though she laughed off the observation, there was no denying that the new Kajol was a little less brash and a little more receptive to a conflicting viewpoint. She was also rid of her earlier aversion to commercials and plunged into the world of advertising with zeal. She was the face of many brands that needed a credible ambassador. 'There's a tremendous respect that Kajol commands from the women audiences,' says Karan Johar. 'Which translates directly into buyers when she endorses a product!' Her scandal-free image and the dignity with which she conducts her life and career makes sure that the audiences take what she says seriously. According to the advertising industry, she is the first choice for any commercial that needs to communicate to a modern housewife!

Around 2007, Ajay Devgn found a script that inspired him to wield the megaphone and *U, Me and Hum* (2008) was conceived. The film released to a lukewarm response but Kajol's portrayal as an Alzheimer's patient was vastly appreciated and she bagged her tenth nomination as Best Actor at the Filmfare Awards. In the meanwhile Karan Johar wrote his ambitious *My Name Is Khan* and there was no way he was going to let anyone else play Mandira opposite Shahrukh Khan. This time round the outdoor schedules in Los Angeles and San Francisco were planned in two parts to accommodate Kajol. The film released amidst furore and controversy and went on to be an international blockbuster. There were a lot of pre-release screenings in Los Angeles owing to the fact that the film was a joint venture with Fox Searchlight and each screening had the Hollywood studio heads asking only one question, 'Who is this fantastic actress? And where has she been?' When there were suggestions that she hire an agent abroad as she could get a lot of international work, she brushed them off nonchalantly. 'I'm not interested in pitching myself for work anywhere!' she declared even as she prepared to have another baby. But before that she signed *We Are Family* (2010) for which she shot non-stop and even did a rock 'n' roll song in an advanced state of pregnancy. The film was not received well even though, as always, Kajol's performance as a dying mother was largely appreciated. Kajol gave birth to a son, Yug Devgn, on 26 September 2010 and Kajol plunged herself once again into full-time motherhood.

In February 2011, Kajol bagged her fifth Filmfare Best Actress Award for *My Name Is Khan* and equalled her aunt Nutan's record for the maximum Filmfare Awards. As soon as she got off the podium after receiving her trophy she received a message saying her son was crying and Kajol flew past everyone to her car and was home in ten minutes. 'Nothing gives me more happiness than motherhood,' she confesses. 'If I had my way I would have a child every year. After all what can be more creative than creating a life?'

My Five Favourite Kajol Films

1. *Udhaar Ki Zindagi* (1994). Directed by K.V. Raju. Co-stars: Jeetendra and Moushumi Chatterjee. Kajol wasn't even twenty when she played the role of Sita, the granddaughter who cannot bring herself to tell her grandparents about the death of their son. The intensity with which she played out her confrontation scenes got her great critical acclaim.
2. *Dilwale Dulhania Le Jayenge* (1995). Directed by Aditya Chopra. Co-star: Shahrukh Khan. One of the most successful films in the history of Indian cinema, the film cemented strongly the legendary nature of Kajol's pairing with Shahrukh Khan apart from making the names Raj and Simran synonymous with love. Kajol's multifaceted role as a lover, daughter and friend remains a favourite with virtually every youngster even today.
3. *Gupt* (1996). Directed by Rajiv Rai. Co-stars: Bobby Deol and Manisha Koirala. At the peak of her success, Kajol risked playing a negative role in this film and gave a stupendous performance for which she won a Filmfare Award.
4. *Kuch Kuch Hota Hai* (1998). Directed by Karan Johar. Co-stars: Shahrukh Khan and Rani Mukherji. Kajol's Anjali, who converts herself from a tomboy to a damsel after a bout

of heartbreak, remains a favourite story for millions, about friendship and love. Once again the brilliant chemistry between SRK and Kajol makes the film timeless.

5. *Kabhi Khushi Kabhie Gham* (2001). Directed by Karan Johar. Co-stars: Shahrukh Khan, Amitabh Bachchan, Jaya Bachchan, Hrithik Roshan, Kareena Kapoor and Rani Mukherji
From playing a verbose Punjabi girl to a sensitive wife to a dutiful daughter-in-law, Kajol enacted her part to perfection, making it a landmark role in her career.

KAREENA KAPOOR

POWERHOUSE PRINCESS

UDITA JHUNJHUNWALA

*Sometimes you are just born a movie star. Even when
destiny gave up on Kareena, her DNA didn't.*

—Karan Johar

I t's not always easy to recollect a first meeting; it's even rarer
to recall the first time you saw someone. Yet I vividly
remember seeing Kareena Kapoor for the first time. It was
a warm afternoon in Mumbai when a teenager dressed in a
pastel pink salwaar kameez breezed into Subhash Ghai's studio.
'That's Karisma Kapoor's sister and she's going to be the next
big star,' someone whispered to me.

Over a decade later, with more than forty films to her credit,
having weathered hits and flops and consciously reinvented herself
time after time, and having won every popular Indian film award
there is, not only has the granddaughter of Raj Kapoor established
herself as a star, but also as an actress worthy of her lineage.

Before making her foray into acting at the age of twenty,
Kareena made a half-hearted attempt at studying micro-
computers and law, but with acting in her genes (not only was

her father Randhir Kapoor an actor, her mother Babita, herself an actress, was the daughter of character-actor Hari Shivdasani and niece of 1960s' heroine Sadhana) a life in the movies was destined. 'Mom insisted on college so I tried my hand at law but ran away after six months,' says Kareena. 'This is what I always wanted to do. There is nothing else in my life that I have ever wanted to do, ever.'

When she was just a child, Kareena would dance to Sridevi's and Madhuri Dixit's songs in front of the mirror, wrapping her mother Babita's sari around her, clumsily applying her mother's lipstick, trying to imitate the expressions of those actresses. With older sister Karisma for company, Kareena would make the most of Babita being away at work, dancing around the house to Hindi film songs. This pretend-starry behaviour might not have been acceptable in the Kapoor household, but by then Babita and Randhir had separated and the Kapoors' attitude towards working women had been left behind. Then in 1991, when she was just seventeen, older sister Karisma made her debut in *Prem Qaidi*, defying Kapoor tradition and paving the way for her younger sister. Nine years later, the second Kapoor daughter made her entry into Hindi cinema. But Kareena chose an unconventional debut film and took a gamble with J.P. Dutta's epic love story *Refugee* (2000).

Having established that she was not just a pretty face with the right surname, Kareena ventured into conventional commercial cinema with *Mujhe Kuch Kehna Hai* (2001), *Yaadein* (2001) and *Ajnabee* (2001). She balanced these with Santosh Sivan's period epic *Asoka* (2001) in which she played Kaurwaki, a character that, like Kareena, was a blend of strong and vulnerable. A review in *Variety* said, 'Kapoor plays ornately tattooed Kaurwaki as a lively mix of flirtatious coquette and feisty warrior woman, kind of like J.Lo meets Michelle Yeoh.'

In the eleven years since, Kareena, who counts Nargis, Meena Kumari, Sharmila Tagore, Karisma Kapoor and Kajol as her influences, has worked with the best and most successful names in the Hindi film industry. Directors like Subhash Ghai,

Santosh Sivan, Abbas–Mustan, Karan Johar, Sudhir Mishra, Govind Nihalani, Rajkumar Hirani, Vishal Bhardwaj and Imtiaz Ali have given her some of her most memorable roles. She has also played opposite top Hindi film stars like Amitabh Bachchan, Shahrukh Khan, Aamir Khan, Salman Khan, Saif Ali Khan, Hrithik Roshan, Abhishek Bachchan, Ajay Devgn, Shahid Kapoor and Akshay Kumar.

Her contemporaries concur that she is an instinctive and spontaneous actor who enjoys a unique space in the Hindi film industry. Film-maker Karan Johar, who cast her in *Kabhi Khushi Kabhie Gham* (2001) says, 'She has a vulnerability which comes across in her roles. An actor's soul reflects on celluloid, and innocence and vulnerability come out in all her performances. She is one of the best actresses in our country today, revered and loved by directors.' As evidence he cites the last season of his talk show, *Koffee with Karan*, where out of approximately forty-five guests, almost thirty-seven rated her as the best. 'Even though she has not given many hits, yet she is a movie star.'

Co-star Imran Khan agrees. 'In her eleven years in the industry she's done some edgy work and some bad films, but she has tremendous inherent talent, a spark which is either there or it's not. She's really something. I cannot tell you how many times I have been caught off guard by what she is doing in her take. She's a star; a heroine with a capital H. She's stunning,' he says.

Interestingly, her career graph challenges notions of her status as the biggest and highest paid female star of Bollywood. She is in the select club of those actors whose star standing and popularity seem to be delinked from the fate of their films. Hits have usually been followed by a spate of flops; a slump has usually been the precursor to a reinvention; an unexpected role and some risk-taking have turned the tide making her the darling of audiences and critics alike. After her uber-glamorous role as Pooja or Poo in Johar's family drama *Kabhi Khushi Kabhie Gham*, Kareena found herself being cast time and again as the young, fashionable urban girl. 'Poo required a comic timing which she inherently has. A large section of the audience loved her, but a large section didn't get her humour either,' says Johar who concurs that after his film, 'she got into a Poo rut.'

Forgettable films like *Mujhse Dosti Karoge!* (2002), *Jeena Sirf Merre Liye* (2002), *Talaash: The Hunt Begins* (2003), *Khushi* (2003) and *Main Prem Ki Diwani Hoon* (2003) made her step back. In an interview we did in 2009, recalling that phase Kareena said, 'That period made me work harder and change things. I will never forget that period. But then look at Aamir, Hrithik, Akshay, Saif—they all went through flops on the route to stardom. I look at that phase as a good thing that happened on the route to superstardom. You become an achiever when you rise above your flops.' No one could have predicted her next move. In Sudhir Mishra's *Chameli* (2004), Kareena stepped out of her comfort zone to play a commercial sex worker. On watching the film today, her portrayal of Chameli comes across as a caricature—literal and without layers. She admits that given another chance, she would interpret her character very differently. '*Chameli* was a conscious effort to do something totally out of the box. I had to make that move happen,' she says.

The rest of the year saw Kareena in her most experimental phase. She took on the part of the simple yet smart student Meera in Mani Ratnam's *Yuva* (2004); she played the compassionate and brave Aaliyah in Govind Nihalani's *Dev* (2004), set within the Hindu–Muslim riots in Gujarat, with maturity; she played her first negative part as Neha in Ken Ghosh's *Fida* (2004). As critical acclaim was heaped on her, she oscillated back towards potential commercial success, opting for roles like that of Anjali in the regressive drama *Bewafaa* (2005). This marked the start of her next phase of box-office letdowns. But after *Kyon Ki* (2005), *Dosti: Friends Forever* (2005), *36 China Town* (2006) and *Chup Chup Ke* (2006), Kareena paused for breath. Even as the media began to write her off she took on a role that set a new benchmark in her repertoire and added an overwhelming respectability to her filmography.

Vishal Bhardwaj wrote a stunning character that fit Kareena like a glove. *Othello*'s Desdemona became *Omkara*'s Dolly. On the making of *Omkara* (2006), Bhardwaj says, 'In the play, Desdemona's breathtaking beauty forms the basis of Othello's jealousy and eventual breakdown . . . I was on the look out for a pure face who could play my Dolly . . . someone who's completely besotted with Omi and completely unaware of the workings of his jealous mind. In Kareena, I found that perfect balance of innocence and sensuality and she's quietly taken centre stage with her sensitive performance.'

With Dolly, Kareena's talent had achieved new heights. In a list of eighty iconic performances published in *Filmfare* in June 2010, Kareena's Dolly ranks at no. 30. According to the magazine: 'Her vulnerability is palpable, her expression of love endearing. It ties little knots in your stomach as you are aware of her impending fate. Kareena internalizes her character with stupefying intelligence and throws up a performance that leaves you overwhelmed. And she makes it look so effortless.'

Though the film was critically applauded, the box-office response was lukewarm. It took Imtiaz Ali's romantic comedy *Jab We Met* (2007) to give Kareena the critical and popular acceptance she had been craving. In the brilliantly written part of the impulsive, talkative, lovable Geet, Kareena displayed confidence as an actor, blending spontaneity with sincerity and bringing inflexion and modulation to her dialogue delivery—a facet missing from much of her earlier work. Ali, speaking on the making of the film on the DVD, said that Kareena is 'an impulsive actor who goes with the flow, a quality also in Geet . . . She has a high emotional quotient that was the basic motivation for me to want her in this film.'

Indeed her celebrated roles have been intense, emotional characters, parts which Kareena herself confesses to favouring. She finds crying on screen easy and considers comedy to be more difficult. However, the toughest scene she has done till date is, surprisingly, the drunken scene in 2009's blockbuster hit, *3 Idiots*. As a teetotaler, Kareena finds drunken scenes the most challenging.

A previous effort in *Main Aur Mrs Khanna* was rather silly, but Kareena seemed to enjoy the dhokla-fafda sequence with Aamir Khan in Rajkumar Hirani's film. 'That is the toughest scene I have done so far. It's difficult to pretend to be drunk and be convincing about it,' says Kareena who found the confidence to give such a scene another shot in Shakun Batra's romantic comedy *Ek Main Aur Ek Tu* (2012) produced by Karan Johar. 'Being drunk means coming out of your skin, and when you are drunk you lose yourself. It's so difficult to imagine what it would be like to be drunk.' She explains the challenge further in the book, *3 Idiots: The Original Screenplay*: 'Drunken scenes are not easy to do. It is very tough to get the consistency of drunkenness and the slurs have to be the same.'

It took the actress, who prides herself on delivering a shot in one or two takes, between fifteen–twenty takes to get that scene right. In the *3 Idiots* book Kareena admits that Hirani said he would 'manage something in the edit'. She added, 'I was feeling terrible thinking maybe I could not deliver as per expectations. But then the film released and people went wild about the dhokla-fafda scene.' Audiences were once again ready to forget the debacle of *Tashan* (2008) and the vacuous *Kambakkht Ishq* (2009) with the former almost only publicized on Kareena's newly acquired size-zero figure. Size zero became a rage, dominating headlines and airwaves. The phenomenon extended to bestselling books describing how it could be achieved and electronics giant Sony developing a size-zero laptop with Kareena as the brand ambassador.

If her figure makes national news, so does her relationship status. Much like the generation she belongs to and represents, Kareena has been disarmingly honest about her romantic life. It is this same candour which comes through in her movies and makes the audience root for her character. 'My films and the way I have conducted myself speaks for that generation which is career-oriented and gives time to relationships, while coming from a family that is proud of its traditions and culture,' says Kareena.

Perhaps that is why audiences reject her overtly glamorous

roles, like those in *Tashan* and *Kambakkht Ishq*, but embraced Daboo of *Golmaal 3* (2010). The vulnerability and honesty in the characters she plays seem to connect with the audience. The pride and dignity with which she carries her family name and the unabashed devotion and gratitude to her mother and sister endear her further. She said in that interview in 2009 that her mother is 'the most important person in my life, my living god. Personally and professionally, everything Lolo [Karisma] or I are is because of our mother. My sister is 50 per cent responsible for my career because when she was a top actress everyone knew me as her baby sister. She is my confidante and best friend.' Today she says her father is a friend and encouraging of her profession. In November 2008, she told *People* magazine, 'I have been brought up to be very strong. Our strength is the reason why we have faced with dignity all that life had to throw at us. We are proud to be an all-woman household.'

In the latest phase of her career, Kareena is concentrating on cementing her position at the top. In the last year she has acted with the industry's biggest stars including the Khan triumvirate of Aamir, Salman and Shahrukh. When it comes to competition, you cannot help but feel Kareena is running her own race. It brings to mind the dialogue from *Jab We Met* when Aditya (Shahid Kapoor) asks, '*Tum apne aap ko bahut pasand ho, nahin?*' (You like yourself very much, don't you?) and Geet replies, '*Bahut . . . Main apni favourite hoon.*' (Yes, I am my favourite person.)

Unlike many actors who immerse themselves in 'method', 'characterization', 'nuances', etc., Kareena's USP is her spontaneity and directors realize that rehearsing her too much can be detrimental to her performance. Imran Khan has seen this up close on the sets of their rom-com *Ek Main Aur Ek Tu*. 'Kareena does not work half as hard as anyone else I have worked with, but she can just turn on a switch and she's magnetic. You cannot take your eyes off her. I have worked with actors who will sit on the character, dialogue, inflexion, subtleties. She does none of that.'

It is this spontaneity which affects the quality of her performance, vacillating from brilliant in some films to predictable and jaded in others. 'I feel the more effort I put into things, it just becomes boring, bland and filmy. By then I have lost interest, which is part of my nature. I lose interest very quickly,' says Kareena. Her performances do not hinge on craft but simply on instinct. And she has often described herself as a director's actor. In an interview to Rediff.com in May 2008, she said, 'I'm a puppet in the directors' hands. I'm not a thinking actor or an actor to get involved. I do what my director asks me to do.'

Director Rohan Sippy puts the role of the director–actor team in perspective. 'The media puts so much on an actor's plate that you forget how much of a role the director plays. If a director does not know his job, it's easy to palm it off on what you see on screen. Finally, as the director, I have to say OK to a take that I like, and if I say OK to a take that is not up to the standard that does not mean the actor cannot deliver. You can take the shot again and again till you get it right, especially from someone who is not a newcomer and knows her job. With good directors at the helm, Kareena's films have been very likeable. In a bad film, everyone looks bad.'

In the last few years, there has been a palpable adjustment in her performance technique. One notices a greater restraint in her body language and expressions, a quiet understanding. Johar believes that Kareena 'has finally realized that understanding the part is integral to her portrayal. But, like Kajol, she will deliver what she feels at the time. She can blend into any character and demographic, be it the rural elegance of Dolly in *Omkara*, the spitfire Geet of *Jab We Met* or an over-the-top rich girl. As an actor, she doesn't care for the scene before and after. She has no interest in layers and subtext. All she wants to know is if she is looking good.'

In the chapter on 'Stereotypes and Clichés' in the *Encyclopaedia of Hindi Cinema* (2003), Kareena Kapoor has been singled out as being among those new millennium actresses who 'have built their careers principally on their sex appeal and their ability to play the seduction game without a semblance of diffidence.' Things have changed in the eight years since the book was published. Kareena's youthful energy, spirited but measured lifestyle, style-icon status and calculated professional choices suggest that the diffidence has been replaced by a confidence, a command of the space and a quiet but steady journey on a planned path. The path touches on marriage, parenthood and continuing to act.

'I come from a family of stars and I enjoy being successful. After you have tasted success who would not want to be on that high? That high may not last all the time, but the attempt is to get that high. What's the point of drinking for the sake of it,' says the actress who, as the great granddaughter of Prithviraj Kapoor, has been a fitting ambassador for the fourth generation of Kapoors. She has set her own standards and corrected herself whenever she has not risen to them. In an interview to IndiaFM.com in February 2005, when asked what he thought was Kareena's USP, director Dharmesh Darshan said, 'Kareena's unique selling point is that she is a Kapoor! And she knows it.' It would be more accurate to say Kareena's USP is the very fact that she is Kareena Kapoor.

MY FAVOURITE FIVE KAREENA KAPOOR FILMS

1. *Jab We Met* (2007). Directed by Imtiaz Ali. Co-stars: Shahid Kapoor, Tarun Arora and Pavan Malhotra. Her performance as the chatty, lovable, infuriating, impulsive Geet won Kareena her first best actress award (she won five that year). The change in her character, as she mellows through suffering, shows her growth as an actor and makes Geet one of her best roles to date.
2. *Omkara* (2006). Directed by Vishal Bhardwaj. Co-stars: Ajay Devgn, Vivek Oberoi, Saif Ali Khan and Konkona Sen Sharma. Vishal Bhardwaj's interpretation of *Othello* saw Kareena cast in the rural Indian version of Desdemona.

The role set a new benchmark in her career and silenced her critics. Bhardwaj used her stillness to enhance her innocence and vulnerability.

3. *3 Idiots* (2009). Directed by Rajkumar Hirani. Co-stars: Aamir Khan, Sharman Joshi, R. Madhavan and Boman Irani. By playing a small but significant role as medical student Pia, which finally saw her working with Aamir Khan, Kareena became part of a film that broke all records on its release. In the hands of master director Rajkumar Hirani, Kareena made an overall impact as every-girl Pia. The teetotaler also delivered the toughest scene of her career till date (the drunk 'dhokla-fafda' scene).

4. *Yuva* (2003). Directed by Mani Ratnam. Co-stars: Ajay Devgn, Vivek Oberoi, Abhishek Bachchan and Rani Mukherji. Meera is one of the most real characters Kareena has played. She used her body language to convey the awkwardness of a small-town college girl and her fresh youthfulness radiated on screen in Mani Ratnam's episodic drama.

5. *Refugee* (2000). Directed by J.P. Dutta. Co-stars: Abhishek Bachchan, Sunil Shetty, Kulbhushan Kharbanda and Reena Roy. As Nazneen, the teenager who is separated from her love by a vast desert and a heartless border, Kareena established herself as an actor with her very first film. It was a far cry from the glamorous, designer launch vehicles associated with star kids. It was a gamble and though the war drama was not well received, Kareena was.

NOTES ON CONTRIBUTORS

Rauf Ahmed is a distinguished journalist and film critic who has been active for over three decades in both the print and the television media. He switched from mainstream reporting to film journalism in the late 1970s and launched *Super* (1997) and *Movie* (1982) as founder-editor. He later edited *Filmfare, Screen* and *Zee Premiere*. He was chief of bureau, *The Asian Age*, Mumbai, from 1994–96. In 2011 he took over as head of programming for Zee Cinema and Zee Music channels. He is the author of *Mehboob Khan: The Romance of History*. He also served on the Central Board of Film Certification from 2005–09.

S. Theodore Baskaran, a nature writer, writes in Tamil and English. He is the author of *The Dance of the Sarus* and has edited the wildlife anthology *Sprint of the Blackbuck*. He was honorary wildlife warden in Chennai and is a trustee of WWF-India. He retired as chief postmaster-general, Tamil Nadu.

Sidharth Bhatia is a journalist and columnist who has written for publications both in India and abroad. He was a Press Fellow at Wolfson College, Cambridge University. He is a regular commentator on current affairs in print and on television. His book *Cinema Modern: The Navketan Story* was published in 2011. He lives in Mumbai.

Meghnad Desai was born in Baroda in 1940 and studied at both the University of Bombay and the University of Pennsylvania. An active member of the British Labour Party since 1971, he was made Lord Desai of St Clement Danes in 1991, and was awarded the Bharatiya Pravasi Puraskar in 2004 and the Padma Bhushan in 2008. A scholar and writer with several books and articles to his credit, he has also been a fan of the films of the 1940s and 1950s. Having written *Nehru's Hero: Dilip Kumar in the Life of India* in 2004, he has a forthcoming book on *Pakeezah*.

Deepa Gahlot is a journalist, critic, columnist, editor and author. She has won the National Award for Best Film Criticism, and edited several cinema journals. Her work has appeared in anthologies on women's studies and cinema. Her books include *The Prithviwallahs* (co-authored with Shashi Kapoor) and biographies of Shahrukh Khan and Shammi Kapoor. She heads the theatre and film department of the National Centre for the Performing Arts, Mumbai.

Avijit Ghosh is a senior editor with the *Times of India*, New Delhi. Born in Agartala, he grew up in different small towns of Bihar and Jharkhand. He is addicted to films, music, cricket and football. He has written two books: *Bandicoots in the Moonlight*, a novel, and *Cinema Bhojpuri*, a National Award-winning book on films. He is currently working on his next book.

Niranjan Iyengar is a screenwriter and lyricist. He has worked extensively with movie maverick Karan Johar on films like *Kal Ho Naa Ho*, *Kabhi Alvida Naa Kehna* and *My Name Is Khan*.

Madhu Jain worked with *India Today* magazine from 1986 to 2000, writing on cinema, art, society and books. She has also written for *Sunday*, the *Statesman* and the French newspaper *La Croix*. She is the author of *The Kapoors: The First Family of Indian Cinema*.

Udita Jhunjhunwala is a writer, film critic and author. She has served as entertainment editor at leading publications like *Mid-Day* and *Hindustan Times* and also contributed to *Vanity Fair, GQ, The Observer* (London), *Time Out, Vogue, Screen International, L'Officiel, Man's World, Men's Health, Mint, New Indian Express, DNA, Bazaar India, People, CNNGo.com* and *Hi Blitz*, among others. She is one of the featured authors in the series *Women in Indian Film*.

Namrata Joshi is associate editor and film critic with *Outlook*. She is the winner of India's National Award for Best Film Critic for 2004. A member of FIPRESCI, the international federation of film critics based in Munich, she has been on the panel of the FIPRESCI critics' juries at several international film festivals. She has also been on the selection committee for the Indian panorama section at the International Film Festival of India, Goa, 2008. In addition to regular columns for *Outlook*, her published work includes monographs on actresses like Nutan and Mumtaz for *Women in Indian Film* as well as several essays.

Nasreen Munni Kabir is a London-based documentary film-maker and author of eleven books on Hindi cinema, including *Guru Dutt: A Life in Cinema, Talking Films* with Javed Akhtar, *Lata Mangeshkar . . . In Her Own Voice* and four books featuring the dialogue of *Mughal-e-Azam, Awara, Mother India* and *Pyaasa*. Her most recent publication is *A.R. Rahman: The Spirit of Music*. Her many documentaries, produced for Channel 4 TV (UK), include *Follow that Star* (a profile of Amitabh Bachchan), the forty-nine-part series *Movie Mahal* and *The Inner/Outer World of Shah Rukh Khan*.

Urmila Lanba hails from an Army background and has studied in various schools all over the country. She graduated from Indraprastha College, Delhi. At the age of forty-five, she decided to study law and joined the bar association in the Delhi High Court in 1993. A practising advocate, and now a mediator with the Delhi High Court, Lanba has been passionate about Hindi cinema from a very young age, an interest that culminated in her writing a biography of her favourite actor, the legendry Dilip Kumar, in 2003.

Pran Nevile was born in Lahore. After a distinguished career in the Indian Foreign Service and the United Nations, he became a freelance writer specializing in the study of the social and cultural history of India. His particular fascination with the performing arts inspired him to spend many years researching libraries and museums in the UK and USA. His most recent work is *K.L. Saigal: The Definitive Biography*.

Bhaichand Patel saw his first film sitting on his mother's lap in Fiji Islands and fell in love with Maria Montez and Madhubala before the onslaught of puberty. He has seen films on every continent and sat on a number of juries including one at the venerable Venice Film Festival. While he was posted with the United Nations, he studied film-making at New York University. He writes regularly on cinema and is the author of *Happy Hours: The Penguin Book of Cocktails*.

Jerry Pinto is a writer, poet and journalist based in Mumbai. His published books include *Helen: The Life and Times of a Bollywood H-Bomb*, which won the National Award for the Best Book on Cinema, and the recently published film anthology *The Greatest Show on Earth: Writings on Bollywood*, which he edited.

Vikram Sampath is the Bangalore-based author of two widely acclaimed books: *Splendours of Royal Mysore: The Untold Story of the Wodeyars* and *My Name Is Gauhar Jaan!: The Life and Times of a Musician*. He has also contributed regularly to leading Indian dailies and magazines like the *Hindu*, the *Deccan Herald* and *Bangalore Mirror* on a wide array of topics.

Cary Rajinder Sawhney is a film-maker, writer and film festival programmer. He is also director of the London Indian Film

Festival. Cary has formerly worked at senior management level at the British Film Institute, Institute of International Visual Arts (INIVA), while also being active in curatorial roles at the National Media Museum (UK) and Birmingham Museum & Art Gallery. For the last fifteen years Cary has been South Asian programmer for the BFI London Film Festival. He is a fellow of the Royal Society of Arts & Manufacturing and a member of the British film academy BAFTA.

Bhawana Somaaya has been a film critic for thirty years and has contributed columns to publications like the *Hindu*, *Hindustan Times*, *Pioneer* and the *Sunday Observer*. She is the former editor of *Screen* and has authored nine books on cinema that include well-received biographies of Hema Malini and Amitabh Bachchan. *Lexicon* is her tenth book and third on Bachchan after *The Legend* and *Bachchanalia*. She is the editor of Ticketplease.com, the film expert with 92.7 Big FM and also serves on the advisory panel of the Central Board of Film Certification. Somaaya is currently writing her first work of fiction.

Pavan K. Varma is a writer and diplomat. A member of the Indian Foreign Service since 1976, he has served in Moscow, New York, London and Cyprus. He is at present India's Ambassador in Bhutan. His books include *Ghalib: The Man, The Times*; *Krishna: The Playful Divine*; *The Great Indian Middle Class*; *Being Indian: Why the 21st Century Will Be India's* and *Becoming Indian: The Unfinished Revolution of Culture and Identity*, all published by Penguin.

Shefalee Vasudev is a journalist who writes on popular culture, social trends and fashion. She is currently an associate editor with the *Indian Express*. She was the first editor of *Marie Claire* (India), and before that had worked with *India Today* as assistant editor. She also anchored and scripted a Hindi TV programme for DD News.

INDEX